BRITISH COLUMBIA AND YUKON

GOLD HUNTERS

A HISTORY IN PHOTOGRAPHS

BRITISH COLUMBIA AND YUKON

GOLD HUNTERS

A HISTORY IN PHOTOGRAPHS

DONALD E. WAITE

Foreword by Iona Campagnolo

VICTORIA • VANCOUVER • CALGARY

Heritage House Publishing Company Ltd.
heritagehouse.ca

CATALOGUING INFORMATION AVAILABLE FROM LIBRARY AND ARCHIVES CANADA

978-1-77203-077-8 (pbk)

Edited by Helmi Braches and Karla Decker
Proofread by Lara Kordic
Cover and book design by Johannes Schut and Jacqui Thomas
Cover photos: *The Keith and Wilson Mine on French Hill, Yukon Territory*, University of Washington Digital Collection #HEG495, photographed by Eric A. Hegg, 1898 (*front*) and *A View up Williams Creek to Barkerville*, A-03748, Royal BC Museum and Archives, photographed by Frederick Dally, 1868 (*back*)
The following chapters were written by, and used with permission of, their respective authors: "The Legend of the Spanish Mound," pages 164–65 (Stan Copp); "Granite Creek" sidebar, pages 166–67 (Gino Del-Ciotto); "The Bralorne Gold Discovery," pages 169–72 (Arthur Raymond Ryckman); "The Hedley Gold Mine at Nickel Plate," pages 172–80 (Marilyn L. Morris); "A Fly in the Ointment," pages 181–84 (David Gregory and Jennifer Douglass); and "Chief Isaac," pages 246–47 (Allison Krissie Anderson).
The author has made every attempt to locate and accurately credit the copyright holders of the images contained in this book. Please contact the publisher with notification of any errors or omissions.

This book was produced using FSC®-certified, acid-free papers, processed chlorine free, and printed with soya-based inks.

Heritage House acknowledges the financial support for its publishing program from the Government of Canada through the Canada Book Fund (CBF), Canada Council for the Arts, and the Province of British Columbia through the British Columbia Arts Council and the Book Publishing Tax Credit.

Nous reconnaissons l'aide financière du gouvernement du Canada par l'entremise du Fonds du livre du Canada et le Conseil des arts du Canada, et de la province de la Colombie-Britannique par le Conseil des arts de la Colombie-Britannique et le Crédit d'impôt pour l'édition de livres.

19 18 17 16   2 3 4 5

Printed in China

CONTENTS

Foreword, 7

Introduction, 8

Part One—**BRITISH COLUMBIA**

The 1851 Queen Charlottes Gold Rush, *10*

Gold along the Fraser, *18*

The Peter Dunlevey Party, *19*

James Douglas and the Mule Trails, *24*

Breaking Trails and Creeks of Gold, *38*

Richfield, *66*

Barkerville, *74*

Cariboo Cameron's Story, *77*

The Overlanders, *87*

Captain Evans and His Company of Welsh Adventurers, *94*

The Burning of Barkerville, *100*

The Cariboo Wagon Road, *112*

The Golden City of Rossland, *152*

The Legend of the Spanish Mound, *164*

The Bralorne Gold Discovery, *169*

The Hedley Gold Mine at Nickel Plate, *172*

A Fly in the Ointment, *181*

Part Two—**YUKON**

The Original Yukon Gold Hunters, *186*

The Yukon Gold Diggers, *200*

Grand Forks, *205*

The Yukon Order of Pioneers, *224*

Yukon Legends Klondike Joe and "Swiftwater Bill" Gates, *230*

The Lion of the North, *244*

Chief Isaac, *246*

Klondike Kate, *250*

Acknowledgements, 255

Bibliography and Further Reading, 257

Index, 258

FOREWORD

There are strange things done 'neath the midnight sun
By the men who moil for gold . . .

So begins the iconic Robert Service poem "The Cremation of Sam McGee." They are words that might have been written by Don Waite for this comprehensive look at the passionate pursuit and harvest of gold in British Columbia and Yukon over the past one and a half centuries.

This is a story that takes you from the very early gold hunters and their followers through gold rushes, both real and imagined. In these pages you will find golden "bonanzas" that brought some men riches beyond their dreams and others to utter despair.

The story begins in 1851 in Haida Gwaii (then called the Queen Charlotte Islands), from where you make your way to Rock Creek. You hear of the irrepressible Billy Barker, who struck it rich in 1862. Quickly won and almost as quickly lost, Billy Barker's golden treasure was consumed by bad loans and equally bad investments. Barker's legacy can be experienced today in the splendidly restored and accessible village that bears his name, Barkerville, where visitors can experience the authentic lure of gold.

You will meet the celebrated "Cariboo" Cameron and learn of the vital building of the Cariboo Wagon Road. You will experience the arrival of the Overlanders, then head north again to join in the struggle up the Chilkoot Trail with the original discoverers of gold in Yukon. Dawson City, at the confluence of the Klondike and Yukon Rivers, was an instant town that saw vast fortunes won and lost. The romance of the Trail of '98 endures more than a century later, as visitors to Dawson marvel at the Northern Lights or the Midnight Sun. You can still walk with ghosts in the Yukon Order of Pioneers (Y.O.O.P.) cemetery. Larger-than-life characters come alive the in pages devoted to "Swiftwater Bill" Gates and adventurer "Klondike Joe" Boyle, who was rumoured to be Queen Marie of Romania's confidant. Sam Steele was a prototypical officer of the North-West Mounted Police who personified the contrast between the law as practised in Yukon and in nearby Skagway, Alaska. And you will learn about two contrasting Klondike Kates: one was a shrewd, opportunistic dance-hall star, while the other was an early feminist named Kate Ryan.

Most of the gold ever found is today snug and safe in gold bars behind vaulted walls. If it could speak, the gold would tell the stories of those whose search for the precious metal unfolds in these pages.

—Iona Campagnolo, COMOX, BC, FEBRUARY 2015

The Honourable Iona Campagnolo, OC, OBC, was lieutenant-governor of British Columbia from 2001 to 2007 and is the Honorary Patron of Barkerville.

OIL PAINTING BY DAVID GOATLEY. GOVERNMENT HOUSE COLLECTION, DAVIDGOATLEY.COM

QUEEN VICTORIA (1819-1901)

Queen Victoria's reign began in 1837 and ended with her death in 1901. British Columbia's capital, Victoria, was named in her honour. She was also responsible for the naming of New Westminster, known as the Royal City.

OIL PAINTING BY FRANZ XAVIER WINTERHALTER. ROYAL COLLECTION: QUEEN VICTORIA WOA 3154

INTRODUCTION

In the 1960s, while working in Maple Ridge as a policeman, I was intrigued by legends of lost gold in the Pitt Lake area of BC's Lower Mainland. Although the stories have never been proven or disproven (see Mary Trainer, Brian Antonson, and Rick Antonson's entertaining book *Slumach's Gold*), I decided I wanted to find out more about the discovery of gold in BC. In the early '70s, I travelled through the Fraser Canyon to Barkerville and later wrote books on those areas. This book contains what I consider the main events of those early gold-rush days in these and other areas of BC and Yukon.

While researching the story of gold in these regions, I saw many historical photographs in several archival collections. These well-preserved original glass-plate negatives and prints were of incredible high quality, considering the conditions under which they were obtained and stored for more than a hundred years. The striking images of miners working with primitive means, braving the elements and incredibly harsh conditions, really told a remarkable story.

In particular, the images captured by early British Columbia photographer Frederick Dally and Yukon photographer Eric Hegg stand out. They not only paint a picture of the times, but, with their masterful composition, are also works of art on their own. I would like to have been there in those days, taking photos, which is why I am giving photography such a prominent place in this book. Cleaning up the damage inflicted by time on these archival prints and retouching them has been a very satisfying project for me.

NUGGETS FROM LOWHEE, CREEK, CARIBOO
CANADIAN MUSEUM OF NATURE, 53131

A 4.9-CENTIMETRE-WIDE NUGGET FROM PIONEER MINE IN BRALORNE
CANADIAN MUSEUM OF NATURE, 56706

BOULDER CREEK, SURPRISE LAKE, CASSIAR
GEOGRAPHICAL SOCIETY OF CANADA, 10418

I have tried to collect the most memorable facts and stories on this topic, which combined with the photos will give readers a true feeling of what it was like to hunt and mine for gold in those days.

The stories in this book show to what extent the interiors of British Columbia and Yukon were developed because of the rushes for gold. Gold was the impetus that made BC into a Canadian province. The first "roads" were tracks to the goldfields, and the first communities were posts that carried supplies for the miners. Some of these early settlements are now ghost towns, but many have evolved into modern towns.

The activity in my book stops a hundred years ago, but that doesn't mean the desire for gold has stopped. Throughout the remainder of the twentieth century, gold was still being mined on a large scale. And the quest continues, not only for gold but also for other precious metals, minerals, and coal.

—*Donald E. Waite*, MAPLE RIDGE, BC, MAY 2015

THE TURNAGAIN NUGGET, DEASE LAKE AND STIKINE RIVER

ROYAL BC MUSEUM AND ARCHIVES

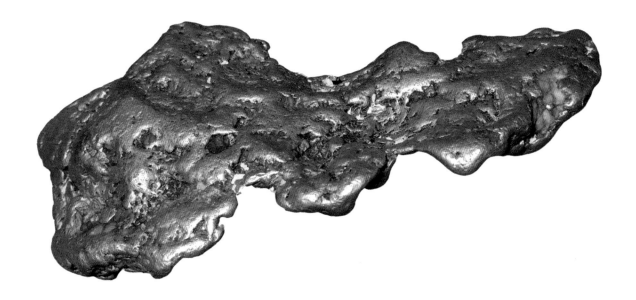

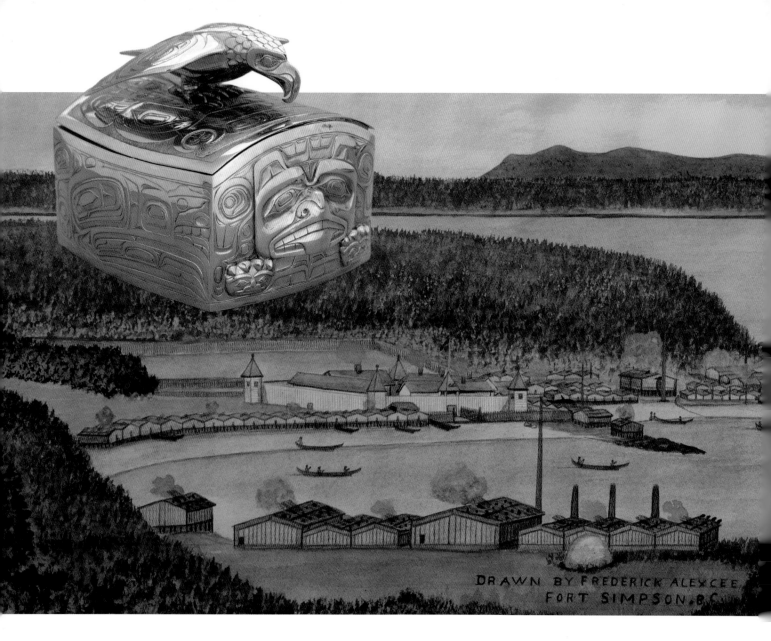

DRAWN BY FREDERICK ALEXCEE
FORT SIMPSON.B.C

THE 1851 QUEEN CHARLOTTES GOLD RUSH

The era of British Columbia gold rushes started in 1851 with the discovery of gold in the Queen Charlotte Islands (now Haida Gwaii) after a Haida man traded a twenty-seven-ounce nugget in Fort Victoria for fifteen hundred Hudson's Bay Company (HBC) blankets. Governor Richard Blanshard wrote Earl Grey, the British Secretary of State for War and the Colonies, on March 29, 1851:

> I have heard that fresh specimens of gold have been obtained from the Queen Charlotte Islanders. I have not seen them myself, but they are reported to be very rich. The Hudson's Bay Company's servants intend to send an expedition in the course of the summer to make proper investigations. The brigantine Huron was dispatched accordingly, ostensibly to

Part One

BRITISH COLUMBIA

trade, but really to search for gold. Failing in which, the men broke up part of a quartz ledge, and carrying pieces on board their vessel, returned in triumph to Victoria.

John Work, the Hudson's Bay Company's chief factor at Fort Simpson (now Port Simpson), showed visiting Haida chief Albert Edward Edenshaw some gold specimens, promising huge rewards if he could direct him to the newly reported gold discoveries on the Queen Charlottes. After Edenshaw returned home, an old woman guided him, his wife, and their four-year-old son, Cowhoe, to an outcropping of gold. Leaving the boy in the canoe, the three adults started chipping the rich gold ore from a quartz vein and placing it in a basket. When the basket was full, Edenshaw's wife walked back to the canoe, emptied the gold samples into it, and then returned to help her husband collect more gold. At dusk the three gold pickers

OPPOSITE, TOP

A gold box created by Haida artist Bill Reid.

UBC MUSEUM OF ANTHROPOLOGY OBJECT #NB1.717A-B

ABOVE

Watercolour landscape painting of Fort Simpson, or Lax Kw'alaams, surrounded by Dené homes.

UBC RARE BOOKS AND SPECIAL COLLECTIONS
RBSC-FRAMED-LANDSCAPE-017. FREDERICK ALEXCEE

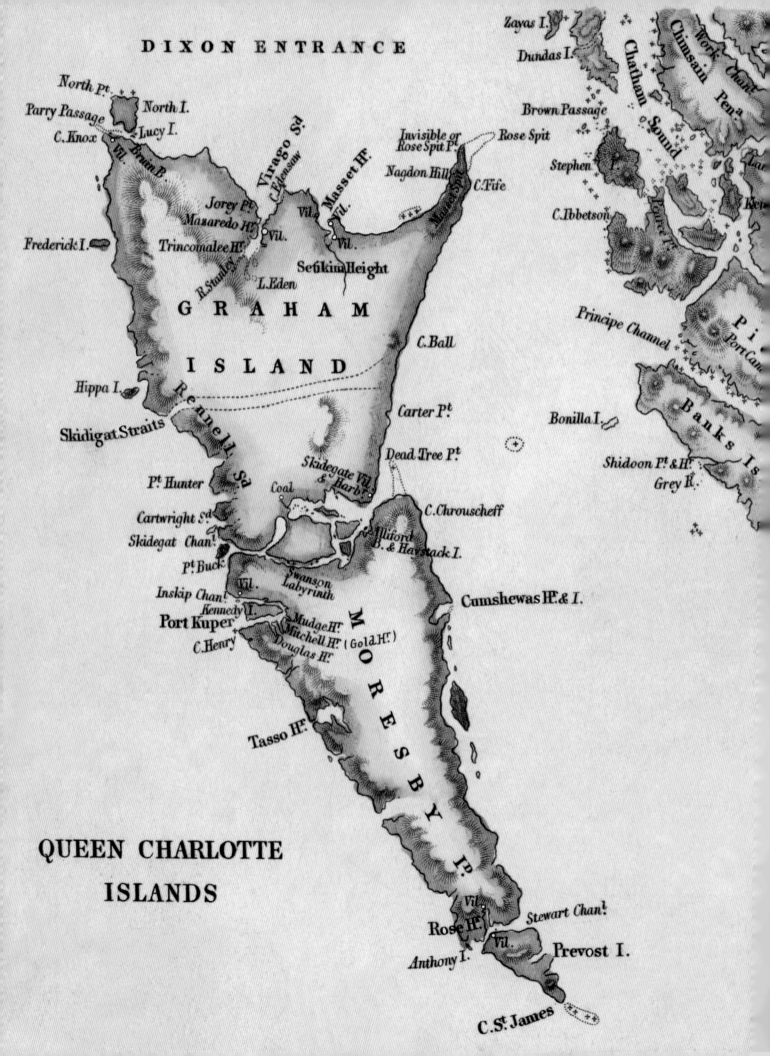

returned to the canoe, only to discover that young Cowhoe had thrown all the gold samples into the ocean. As a result, the number of gold samples collected on this outing and later shown to Work was relatively insignificant.

On May 13, 1851, Work travelled by canoe from Fort Simpson to the Charlottes to investigate the gold discoveries for himself. He made his way toward Masset, over 120 kilometres (75 miles), in a flotilla of 10 cedar canoes—each 14 metres (48 feet) long, 1.5 metres (5 feet) wide, and 76 centimetres (2.5 feet) deep. The canoes were equipped with sails and manned by a crew of local Haida. On May 20, Work's canoe was almost swamped in ocean waters. He wrote in his diary about a couple of smaller craft: "We are afraid the Indians before us are lost."

Work continued south three days later and reached the west coast of Moresby Island at what was later named Gold Harbour. His men immediately commenced blasting the rock some thirty-six centimetres (fourteen inches) deep but found only a few fragments containing quartz with gold. The following day was no more encouraging. Work wrote:

What gold the Indians found was all a distance of 16 yards along the shore and about 6 yards from above the high water mark to low water mark among the loose stones and in the cracks or seams of a clayey slate rock that dips to the southeast. All the larger pieces were found among the loose stones and a little at the end of the seam of quartz.

It is my opinion that all the gold found is travelled or has been brought there and that where it came from plenty more may be found. The Indians are dissatisfied and disappointed that we have found no gold by blasting as it dampens their hopes of having a fort. We can blast no more as our borers are so broken in the head that they are too short. This I regret as I intended to have bored deep.

On his return route, Work visited Skidegate, where he managed to trade for a few ounces of gold in small lumps and grains. He declined purchasing one nearly pure lump weighing close to 0.5 kilograms (about 1 pound), and a

OPPOSITE

The Queen Charlotte Islands (now Haida Gwaii) are detailed in this portion of a larger map of the colonies of British Columbia and Vancouver Island. Compiled from original documents by John Arrowsmith, 1864.

UBC RARE BOOKS AND SPECIAL COLLECTIONS, MAP G-3510-1864-A7-QUEEN CHARLOTTE ISLANDS

BELOW—JOHN WORK (1792-1861)

The Hudson's Bay Company chief factor in charge of Fort Simpson, Work made a 240-kilometre (150-mile) return journey by canoe to the Queen Charlotte Islands to check on reports of gold discoveries.

HISTORICAL PHOTO A-01823, ROYAL BC MUSEUM AND ARCHIVES

second of about 170 grams (6 ounces), because the Haida placed too great a value on them. Work returned to Fort Simpson with little to show for his two-week excursion.

The HBC vessel *Una*, captained by William Mitchell out of Victoria, was the first to carry a crew to mine in the same area. They documented a vein 16.5 centimetres (6.5 inches) wide and some 24 metres (80 feet) long, with an estimated 25 percent gold content. The mining attempts proved difficult, because after each dynamite blast, the Haida, who were watching and who had by then fully grasped the value the Europeans placed on the gold, would rush to any exposed gold and attempt to gather it up before the *Una's* crew could get to it. According to the ship's logbook, they also grabbed the sailors by the legs to prevent them from harvesting the gold. Fearing bloodshed, and with at least one injured crewman, Captain Mitchell pulled up anchor and departed for Victoria. His ship was blown off course and wrecked off Neah Bay on the Olympic Peninsula, and the small amount of gold that had been recovered was lost. The officers and crew were rescued by the crew of another British ship, *Susan Sturgis*.

One of Mitchell's crew, William Henry Emptage, had been severely injured in a blasting mishap on this gold-hunting expedition and was most anxious to get medical aid at Fort Victoria. Born in Margate, Kent, England, the son of a Strait of Dover lifeboat captain, Emptage had joined the East India Company as an able-bodied seaman on ships plying trade routes between India and England. Then fate placed him aboard an HBC vessel bound for the North Pacific. After a long sea voyage, he reached Victoria just as it was being reported that gold had been discovered on the Queen Charlotte Islands. It was while the *Una's* crew was at Gold Harbour that a premature blast injured Emptage's left hand. In Victoria, Dr. John Helmcken gave his patient a healthy shot of whisky, placed a rock in his mouth to clamp down on to endure the pain, and then proceeded to amputate above the wrist. Then the doctor peeled the skin back from the bone and cut the bone a second time, an inch shorter. After his recovery, Emptage was sent to Fort Langley to work on the HBC dairy farm, where he was often seen carrying a milk pail in the crook of his arm.

Several American ships visited the Queen Charlotte Islands during this period. The first, the *Georgiana*, was wrecked on the east coast of the Charlottes and her crew taken captive by Haida warriors before they set the ship ablaze. The crew's freedom was

WILLIAM HENRY EMPTAGE (1837–1904)
Emptage, an HBC employee, was collecting gold specimens on the Queen Charlotte Islands when a premature dynamite blast caused him to lose his hand.

FORT LANGLEY NATIONAL HISTORIC SITE

paid for with HBC blankets by the next American ship to pull into what they now called Mitchell Harbour, in honour of the captain of the *Una* (and later the *Recovery*).

Word of the gold discovery spread quickly, and in the fall of 1851 ten American ships visited the Queen Charlottes in search of gold, but some unwelcoming members of the Haida Nation curtailed any actual mining. Then Captain Matthew Rooney of the *Susan Sturgis* befriended Chief Edenshaw and enlisted the chief and other warriors to join the ship's crew and act as guides and interpreters in other settlements. But when the ship pulled into Masset Inlet to trade, she was swarmed by the local Haida who rejected Edenshaw and his men. The American ship was destroyed, and Rooney and his men were taken captive. When Chief Factor Work heard of the event ten days later, he again had to travel from Fort Simpson, this time to negotiate their release and pay a substantial ransom.

When Governor James Douglas learned that the crew of another American ship had cut down numerous trees growing in the Haida territory to craft new spars for their ships, he became suspicious that the Americans were planning to annex the islands to the United States. After alarming the high command in London, Douglas was appointed lieutenant-governor in 1853 of a new colony: the Queen Charlotte Islands. Later that same year, Douglas issued a proclamation of the British Crown's ownership of all precious metals on the Queen Charlotte Islands, and thereafter all miners were required to pay a monthly fee to mine.

The next five years proved uneventful, but in his March 25, 1859, report to London, Governor Douglas expressed renewed interest in the land of the Haida when he wrote,

> *Great excitement has been recently produced in Victoria by the exhibition of a nugget of pure gold weighing 14¼ ounces, procured by the Agents of the Hudson's Bay Company from the Indians of Queen Charlotte's Island. There is a generally prevalent impression founded on the discovery of Gold in that Island in the year 1851, that it will yet become a productive gold field.*

Douglas recalled the first quest and the original discovery:

> *The gold collected at that period, with the exception of some waterborne pieces of small size, and a lump weighing 27 ounces found on the beach at the mouth of a fresh water rivulet, was procured by blasting from a vein of white quartz running*

A miniature tin gold pan holds placer gold and black sand taken from the Pend d'Oreille River.

The Gold Pan

A gold pan was generally made of sheet iron in the shape of a circular dish with flared but straight sides and a flat bottom. The most common pan, known as the "Australian," was 38 centimetres (15 inches) in diameter at the top to about 18 centimetres (7 inches) at the bottom, and 8 centimetres (3 inches) deep. The sides are generally angled at 30 to 45 degrees. The "American" pan is similar but had a straight lip at its top.

Panning was the simplest and most inexpensive of all the methods used to recover placer gold. In his book *The Guide to Gold Panning in British Columbia*, N.L. (Bill) Barlee wrote:

> *Although the origin of the gold pan, the device used in panning, is obscure, some authorities believe that it came into common usage among the placer miners of Transylvania, in the central part of Europe, no later than the 15th century, and possibly some time before then. In the alluvial gold-fields of North America, Australia, and other parts of the world, it was and is the prospector's inseparable companion, being ideally suited to test any gravels that were indicative of carrying placer gold.*

A miner would partially fill the pan with dirt containing placer, put it in water, and with a swirling motion, create a whirlpool that separated the stones and gravel from the gold due to specific gravity, the gold being twenty times heavier than water and five times heavier than the gravel.

The time required to wash a pan of gravel took ten to fifteen minutes, and it was considered a good day's work to wash fifty pans. Gold panning was used only to test gravel.

Pans today are manufactured in both metal and high-impact plastic for lightness, although Russian pans of heavy-gauge iron are still traditional. Steel pans are heavier than plastic pans; some are made of lightweight alloys for structural stability. Plastic gold pans resist rust, acid, and corrosion, and most are designed with moulded riffles along one side of the pan. Of the plastic gold pans, green and red ones are usually preferred among prospectors, as both the gold and the black sand stand out in the bottom of the pan.

parallel with the Coast, some of the masses of which were so largely impregnated with gold as to yield a return of 25 percent on the gross weight.

By this time, Douglas had resigned from the HBC to become governor of the single consolidated colony of British Columbia, which included the mainland and all coastal islands. In light of the new discovery, he dispatched a schooner to "Queen Charlotte's Island" with a party of professional gold hunters, including a Douglas appointee, "a respectable Scotchman named Downie, one of the most successful Miners in California, and known all over that State as Major Downie, the founder of the Town of Downieville."

The miners spent several months searching for gold after examining the site where the original quantities of gold had been taken out. William Downie wrote in his book *Hunting for Gold*:

The general nature of the gold was trap and hornblend [sic], and, at the head of Douglas Inlet, we found granite, as well as slate, talcose rock and coal, but not gold; and I concluded that the large amount of this metal, which had been found previously in those parts with so little difficulty, existed merely in what the miners call an off-shoot or blow-out, which can only be explained as one of those freaks of nature, so often found in mining country.

The men did not have the necessary tools to do any serious quartz-mining operations, yet they did manage to bring back about half a ton of specimens. In the great scheme of things, it was an insignificant "rush" that didn't produce much gold.

Far more predictive was the last paragraph of the Governor Douglas's missive to London in early April 1858, in which he speculated on future discoveries along the Thompson and Fraser Rivers: "In addition to the diggings before known on Thompson's River and its tributary streams, a valuable deposit has been recently found by the natives on a bank of Fraser's River." Douglas went on to add that while the "about eight hundred ounces . . . found in the possession of the natives" might have been considered small, this could have been due to the lack of proper tools and the "want of skill." He wrote, "On the contrary, the vein rocks and its other geological features as described by an experienced gold miner encourage the belief that the country is highly auriferous."

The Fraser River gold hunt would soon be on.

GOLD ALONG THE FRASER

DONALD MCLEAN (1805-64)

The chief trader in charge of the Hudson's Bay Company's Fort Kamloops, McLean made the first reports to his superior, James Douglas, that gold had been discovered in the Thompson River. McLean became one of the casualties of the Chilcotin War in 1864.

HISTORICAL PHOTO A-01454, ROYAL BC MUSEUM AND ARCHIVES

It is fair to say that the famous Fraser River gold rush of 1858 actually started on the Thompson River. One story is that in the spring of 1857, a Scottish man named James Houston sought shelter at Fort Kamloops after being robbed and later found, lost and desperate, by a prospector. He began panning the creeks around the fort for gold, and claimed to have found it in Tranquille Creek. He used the gold to pay for his board at the fort.

The person responsible for bringing the discovery of gold in the area to the attention of the government, however, was the Hudson's Bay Company's chief trader, Donald McLean. Shortly after his arrival at Fort Kamloops in 1855, McLean traded for gold with a Shuswap man and reported the transaction to Chief Factor James Douglas, his superior in Victoria. McLean was instructed to keep the information quiet since both men knew a gold rush would damage the fur trade. Douglas wrote in his diary:

Gold was first found on Thompson River by an Indian a quarter of a mile below Nicomin. He is since dead. The Indian was taking a drink out of the river; having no vessel he was quaffing from the stream when he perceived a shining pebble which he picked up, and it proved to be gold. The whole tribe forthwith began to collect the glittering metal.

After exchanging letters with Hudson's Bay Company officials in England, Douglas encouraged McLean to buy gold from the Natives. McLean requested that spoons be shipped to him at Fort Kamloops for trade with the Shuswap people so that they could be used in the extracting of nuggets from the crevices of the bedrock. After McLean reported to Douglas that he had filled a couple of pickle jars with gold and sent his booty to Victoria, Douglas reported, "The reputed wealth of the Couteau mines [the local name of the Thompson–Fraser River area] is causing much excitement among the population of the United States of Washington and Oregon, and I have no doubt that a great number of people from those territories will be attracted thither in the spring."

In February 1858, Douglas sent the eight hundred ounces of gold south on the steamship *Otter* for minting at San Francisco. The mint superintendent, also a member of the local fire department, soon announced to his workmates that the next gold excitement would be on the Fraser River. Just weeks later, the first vanguard of miners, many who had travelled north by land, began to arrive on the Fraser River. A few kilometres above Hope, they discovered the first rich pay on a bar they named Hill's, after the man who had washed the first gold there. As both the HBC chief factor and the colonial governor, and highly motivated to ensure British jurisprudence, James Douglas hired gold commissioners to intercept American gold hunters at the border and make them buy miners' licences, stake claims, and record their findings.

JAMES HOUSTON (1823-1902)
This charcoal portrait of Houston is displayed at the Langley Centennial Museum. Houston is often credited with being the first European to discover gold on the mainland of British Columbia.

LANGLEY CENTENNIAL MUSEUM

THE PETER DUNLEVEY PARTY

In addition to those prospectors who had scurried north through the Oregon Territory, the spring of 1858 saw shiploads of miners from San Francisco make their way up the coast to participate in the Fraser River gold rush. The first paddlewheel steamer, the *Commodore*, docked at the wharf at Fort Victoria on April 25, 1858. Official steamship records show that from San Francisco alone, 455 miners left for Victoria in April, 1,262 in May, 7,149 in June, and 6,278 in July. In reality, each vessel carried passengers far beyond its capacity, and the ship owners did not dare to publish the true figures. Officially, the *Sierra Nevada* carried 900 passengers, but at Fort Victoria she unloaded 1,900. An estimated 23,000 people left San Francisco by sea in May, June, and July, while another 8,000 made their way overland to the new diggings. Those gold seekers who arrived at Fort Victoria soon learned that they were still over six hundred kilometres (four hundred miles) from Fort Kamloops.

Vancouver Island's Fort Victoria, with a population of only four hundred souls, was totally unprepared for the sudden invasions of thousands of miners and became a tent town almost overnight. Initially the miners' presence was a real boon to the economy, and saleable items went for incredible prices, but once these goods were

PETER CURRAN DUNLEVEY (1833-1905)
One of the earliest gold discoverers on the Fraser River, Dunlevey later owned a stopping house at Soda Creek, where he grew grain crops for the horses and oxen. He later owned a large property in fledgling Vancouver.

HISTORICAL PHOTO C-08624, ROYAL BC MUSEUM AND ARCHIVES

gone, many residents were anxious to see the miners on their way. Need being the mother of invention, the more aggressive miners built their own boats and made the thirty-two-kilometre (twenty-mile) crossing from the Island to the mainland without waiting for the riverboat steamers. It was estimated that three hundred skiffs, each containing an average of five passengers, passed up the Fraser River to Fort Yale during the low-water season. Just below the fort, the miners began panning four to five ounces of gold per man per day. Many lingered at these gold-bearing river bars, but a few of the more determined professional miners began hiking upriver in search of the motherlode.

In this vanguard were five Americans led by Peter Curran Dunlevey of Pittsburgh, Pennsylvania. The party consisted of James Sellars from Texas; Ira Crow, an ex-California miner; Thomas Moffat from Williamsport, Indiana; and Thomas Manifee. They immediately joined the hordes staking claims above Fort Yale. All summer, miners moved upriver to the confluence with the Thompson River and beyond. By May 1859, Dunlevey and his men were busy sluicing for gold opposite the confluence of the Chilcotin and Fraser Rivers when they met Tomaah, the son of Chief Lolo St. Paul. He asked the miners what they were doing and was shown the flakes and small nuggets of gold before being invited by Dunlevey to share their meal. The young man scarcely touched the bean-and-bannock mixture after the initial taste, but a cup of well-sugared tea was an instant success, and he gulped it down only to hold out his empty cup for more. It was after he'd drunk the second cup that Tomaah told the miners that he could show them a river where gold lay like beans in a pan. He explained that he worked for the Hudson's Bay Company at Fort Alexandria and that he would not be available to take them to the location until after a jamboree. He told them that all the First Nations from the New Caledonia District would be gathering at Lac la Hache in sixteen days for summer games before continuing on to Fort Kamloops to trade their winter and spring harvests of furs. He suggested to the miners that they return to Lillooet and then go by way of Marble Canyon to Fort Kamloops to purchase fresh supplies and to take a message to his father. From Fort Kamloops, they could travel to Lac la Hache, where he would meet them before the beginning of the jamboree and that after the games, he would guide them to this "River of Gold."

The next morning the miners awoke to find Tomaah gone. They wasted no time and were soon headed downriver toward Lillooet.

Here they traded a canoe for two horses before heading toward Fort Kamloops. They spent the first night in an old fur-trading encampment that dominated the Native village of Fountain. The miners were on their way at daybreak the following morning and soon reached the village of Pavilion. From here they pushed on and reached the Fort Kamloops trading post, where they met several discouraged Thompson River prospectors who were happy to sell their miners' tools to Dunlevey for a fraction of their value.

Dunlevey, after grooming himself and before visiting the HBC post for supplies, called on Chief Lolo. The old Iroquois man had retired from the company in 1843 to begin developing a horsebreeding empire and had amassed a sizeable fortune by hiring out pack animals to his former employees for the transportation of furs to the coast. His two daughters had recently converted the original rundown HBC post into a stopping house.

Chief Trader McLean was suspicious of the immaculately dressed Dunlevey and at first refused to fill his order because he had been instructed by the company not to become involved with the miners. Gradually, the trader warmed to the mannerly Dunlevey, and the next morning the miners were able to leave the fort with twelve of Lolo's pack horses loaded with over a ton of provisions. John Moore and John McLean joined the Dunlevey party as axe men.

On the evening of the fifteenth day since they had seen Tomaah, the group camped a few kilometres from Lac la Hache. Just as they were crawling into their blankets, Tomaah and another Native man named Baptiste appeared out of the darkness. The next morning the seven white men and two Natives continued to Lac la Hache. Shortly after their arrival, the miners sat with Tomaah and Baptiste as the Native chiefs from the New Caledonia districts (the north-central parts of present-day BC) addressed the great throng of athletes and spectators gathered in a semicircle. As the chiefs talked, Baptiste translated their words to the attentive miners. Because the orations concerned the welfare of all the miners coming into the country, they were indelibly etched into the memory of Dunlevey, who

in later years was able to recite them almost word for word to his biographer.

Old Chief Dehtus Anaheim of the Chilcotin was the first to speak:

It makes warm my heart to come to this old time meeting place of the Shuswap, to visit with our brothers the Dené and the Yubatan. These games are the chief attraction, for they keep us brave and strong, eager and fleet, not only for the hunt but to scare away our enemies. It is mainly for this last point that Anaheim of the Chilcotin has come to talk with the brother chiefs at this meeting.

For some time our scouts have been bringing us news of white men coming up our rivers. We have tolerated these men thinking them to be weak-minded and therefore entitled to the reverent regard that all Indians have for these weak ones as dictated by the Great Spirit. However, we have found out that these men are really not crazy and are washing out little pieces of yellow stone that they call gold and which they use as money such as we use fur skins to trade for other goods. The Indians of Lillooet have already been corrupted. It is said that they have learned the white man's skill and are also finding little pieces of yellow gold.

The priests have told us to shun the firewater as we would the devil that they have told us of but how can we keep clear of their firewater if we allow them to come among us and ruin our women with their diseases? Will we not be ruined as other tribes far to the east that the priests have told us about?

Another thing, this money really belongs to us and the white men are taking it without asking our permission. The priests tell us that this is stealing. If we steal the priests tell us that their God will punish us. Will their God punish them for this bad act or have they made a convenient arrangement with this God? Has He one law for the Indian and another one for the white man?

We must keep these white men out! We tribes must act together. If we do not act immediately we will only have to drive them out later. This will result in much bloodshed for them and also for our own people. We must act now or we are lost!

This is not my country or my camp. If it were I would say to the white men to go back to the country you came from and induce your white brothers to do likewise. You are not wanted here. If you still choose to come and disregard my warning then with sorrow I say that your blood be upon your heads and hands and not on ours.

A feeling of fear passed through the Dunlevey party, for the speaker's arguments were all too true. Unchallenged, his words could easily result in the amalgamation of the Shuswap, the Yubatan–Dené, and the Chilcotin for the purpose of warring against the sudden influx of miners. When Chief Anaheim finished his oration, he stepped back from the centre of the circle and nodded for Chief Shuswap Williams of the Williams Lake Nation for a rebuttal. Chief Williams, instead of addressing the crowd, shifted the onus of responsibility for a decisive vote for or against bloodshed by inviting Chief Lolo, because of his age and wisdom, to be the first to reply to the chief of the Chilcotin. Fortunately for the Dunlevey party, Tomaah's father was apparently a more forceful orator than his former enemy, Chief Anaheim. Dunlevey quoted him as saying:

It is just as useless for our three tribes to resist these white men as it is for one of us to try and resist. We know that our resistance would only result in needless bloodshed and possible annihilation.

The Indians can never win against the white man because of his numbers, his guns, his learning, and his craftiness.

Chief Lolo's comments certainly received more plaudits than those of the previous speaker. He went on to talk about the years of his early manhood spent near Fort Alexandria. He told them of the time the Chilcotin had tried to attack Fort Alexandria, which resulted in the killing of their war hero by a Yubatan who shot an arrow from across the river through the champion's heart.

Chief Williams was the last leader to speak, and he sided with Chief Lolo and encouraged the First Nations to live in harmony with the white men. He concluded his speech by telling the athletes to enjoy the games.

One of the main events at the games was a wrestling match between Baptiste, representing the Yubatan-Dené, and Red Bear, representing the Chilcotin. It was a well-matched fight involving much betting between the tribes. Sellars got into the spirit and bet on Baptiste. It was a long, drawn-out match, but the Yubatan eventually came out victorious and Sellars ended up winning an Indian pony that he immediately gave to a beautiful maiden named Agat, a cousin of Baptiste. She in turn gave the spirited animal to her sister At-t'uss, Tomaah's girlfriend, because she had the necessary skill to ride the wild bronco.

At the conclusion of the games, Tomaah asked Baptiste to take the miners to the "River of Gold" so he could spend time with his girlfriend before returning to Fort Alexandria.

After several days' travel, Baptiste brought the men to a creek, soon to be named the Little Horsefly because of the annoying insects. Here, Ira Crow panned the first coarse free gold to be taken from an area soon to be known as the Cariboo. Only twelve hours after the Dunlevey party reached the river, another group of miners arrived and joined their forces. These men were Hans Lars Helgesen (a Norwegian), Joseph Devlin, Frederick George Black, Duncan McMartin, and Edward Campbell.

Some of the original miners faded into oblivion. Of the others, Peter Baker, who had come to the area around the same time as James Houston and was one of the first to find gold, mined for a few years around Quesnel Mouth, a small community at the confluence of the Quesnel and Fraser Rivers. He later settled down to married life at Albion, a small settlement across the Fraser River from Fort Langley, now in the municipality of Maple Ridge. James Houston accompanied Baker out of the Cariboo and homesteaded upon the ruins of the original Fort Langley of 1827. Baker lived until 1897, and Houston until 1902.

Peter C. Dunlevey left mining temporarily in 1861 to open a stopping house and fur-trading post at Beaver Pass, and James Sellars married Agat and became Dunlevey's assistant. A few years later, John McLean settled at Quesnel Mouth, where he operated the Occidental Hotel for the next thirty years until his retirement in 1902. In 1862, Hans Lars Helgesen married Lillian Colquhoun, an Irish woman he had met in San Francisco, and settled down to family life at Metchosin on Vancouver Island. Legend claims that one of his partners had shot a caribou near Quesnel Forks, a predominantly Chinese community near the junctions of the Cariboo and Quesnel Rivers, and Helgesen suggested that the district be called the Cariboo. Duncan McMartin, one of the men feasting on the steak, seconded the suggestion, and the remaining miners unanimously agreed.

Duncan McMartin and Edward Campbell both had creeks in the Cariboo named in their honour. McMartin died in New Westminster. Campbell died in the town of Horsefly, which lay on the banks of the river from which he had panned his gold.

Following their rich strike of gold on Little Horsefly Creek, Peter Curran Dunlevey and his partners invested their wealth in roadhouses and freighting outfits along the Cariboo Wagon Road. When the news broke that James Reid was building a sternwheel ship on the Upper Fraser in 1862 to ply between Soda Creek and Quesnel, Dunlevey took up good farmland just to the north of Soda Creek and quickly developed many acres of grain fields and gardens, as well as a roadhouse to cater to the needs of the miners and freighters. Dunlevey, in association with John F. Hawkes, in later years invested his wealth to purchase shares in the City of Vancouver's Coal Harbour Land Syndicate, which owned half of the Saltwater City (an early Chinese nickname for Vancouver).

When news of the building of a sternwheel steamship on the upper Fraser reached New Westminster in 1861, it caused great excitement among the business population of the Lower Mainland, who looked upon it as a great opportunity for the future. Wasting no time, Robert McLeese and his partner Jospeh Triffle Senay set out for Soda Creek, where they secured a building lot close to the steamboat landing and proceeded to build a two-storey log structure that they called the Colonel Hotel. Like Dunlevey and his partners, they wanted to capitalize on the tiny community of Soda Creek, knowing that it would soon become a beehive of activity.

JAMES DOUGLAS AND THE MULE TRAILS

This woodcut appeared in the October 9, 1858, issue of New York's *Harper's Weekly* with the caption "Fort Yale and the Gold Hunters' Camp, Fraser's River." COURTESY WERNER KASCHEL

FOLLOWING PAGE SPREAD

James Douglas taking the oath as first governor of British Columbia at Fort Langley, November 19, 1858.

NATIVE SONS OF BRITISH COLUMBIA POST NO. 2

The first miners to the Fort Kamloops area either trudged over the Hudson's Bay Company brigade trail through the Columbia and Okanagan Valleys or chose the more treacherous First Nations' trails along the Fraser River. Those who travelled up the river found they would have to wait out the spring flood before they could proceed along the canyon. During their wait, many of these anxious miners panned the river below Fort Yale with relative success.

James Douglas, the HBC's chief factor for the area north of the Columbia River and acting governor for the Crown Colony of Vancouver Island, was aware of the deplorable travelling conditions on the mainland. After visiting Fort Yale in July, primarily to establish the best means to control the flow of gold and collection of taxes, he informed London, "Another important object I have in view is the improvement of the internal communications of the country, which at present are, for all practical purposes, nearly inaccessible, beyond Fort Yale." At great risk to his position, he set about organizing the construction of an improved route from the coast to New Caledonia, with the explanation that such a route would secure the area north of the forty-ninth parallel as British territory.

Dispatches to London normally took about forty-five days to arrive, so three months passed before the acting governor received a response to his request for both money and engineering aid. Douglas called a meeting and told the miners that his government would provide transportation, equipment, and food in exchange for labour in the building of a 1.2-metre-wide mule trail through the mountains as far as Lillooet. As a precaution against desertion and to put some money in the government coffers, Douglas required each miner to put up a $25 deposit to be refunded in goods at Lillooet, providing his conduct and work on the road proved satisfactory. If all worked out according to plan, Douglas realized this gamble could mean a great personal success as well as a British one.

Douglas had worked hard and spent much of his life influencing the right people to achieve his dual role in the British colonies. Born in 1803 in Lanarkshire, Scotland, to a Scottish father and Creole mother, he went at an early age to live in British Guiana, where his father had a large sugar plantation. Both parents died when James was very young. At sixteen, James accompanied an older brother to Canada to begin his apprenticeship in the North-West Company in Montreal. At Fort William on Lake Superior his intelligence and good working habits came to the attention of Chief Factor Dr. John McLoughlin. Shortly before the North-West Company was merged with the HBC in 1821, McLoughlin sent Douglas to Fort Chipewyan to supervise the fisheries of the district—an important responsibility, since it was the fish that the forts relied upon as a principal article of food. In 1825, Douglas was posted to Fort St. James on Stuart Lake in the District of New Caledonia, under Chief Factor William Connolly. The following year he accompanied his superior on the annual journey with packs of furs from New Caledonia to the headquarters of the Columbia Department to Fort Vancouver.

In 1827, Douglas married Connolly's eldest daughter, Amelia, and was placed in temporary charge of Fort St. James while his father-in-law went on the annual trip to Fort Vancouver. Consequently, it was Douglas who arranged the welcoming committee for the arrival of Sir George Simpson, governor of the Northern Department of the HBC.

Three years later, Governor Simpson transferred Douglas to Fort Vancouver to act as Chief Factor McLoughlin's chief accountant for the next fifteen years. In 1843, McLoughlin sent Douglas, now a chief factor, to construct Fort Victoria on the southern tip of Vancouver Island. The HBC, upon leasing the whole of Vancouver Island from the British government, moved their headquarters from the Columbia River to Fort Victoria in 1849.

For the proposed mule trail, Douglas chose the route explored by Alexander Caulfield Anderson in 1847 via the lakes and portages west of the Fraser River from Fort Langley to Lillooet. He appointed Anderson to take charge of the project.

Douglas moved quickly, and soon the *Umatilla*, the first steamship to reach the upper end of Harrison Lake, deposited on shore an eager force of newly recruited roadbuilders. That evening before supper, the men held a meeting and named their camp Port Douglas after the governor, then barked out three hearty cheers to honour him.

Anderson quickly organized the men into parties of twenty-five, each with its own captain, and by mid-August five hundred pick-and-shovel labourers were spread out along what came to be known as the Douglas Trail.

Douglas informed London of his progress, noting that miners following the route employed Native people with nine-metre dugout canoes to carry them across Anderson, Harrison, and Seton Lakes (named by Anderson for himself, an HBC shareholder, and an uncle in the British army), while mule trains skirted the lakes by following Native trails. The road-builders quickly widened the Native paths to facilitate the movement of pack animals. By mid-September, the trail had reached

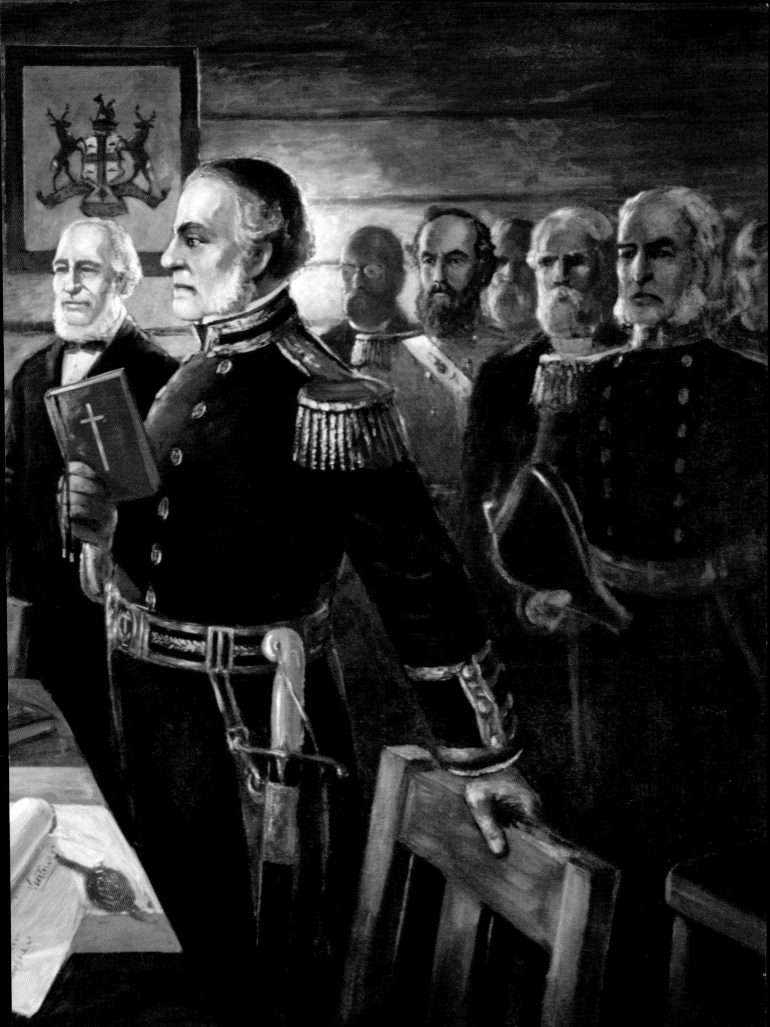

Lillooet Lake, and by mid-October Douglas was able to report to London that the road was finished.

Ironically, in late July, when Douglas was making his plea for military aid, Colonial Secretary Edward Bulwer-Lytton wrote in his own dispatch, "Her Majesty's Government propose sending to British Columbia by the earliest possible opportunity an Officer of Royal Engineers and a Company of Sappers and Miners made up to 150 non-Commissioned Officers and men."

This contingent, under the command of Colonel Richard Clement Moody, arrived and were accompanied by Judge Matthew Baillie Begbie. In one of his first official duties, Begbie, who would serve in both the colonial and provincial supreme courts until his death in 1894, held a ceremony at Fort Langley. On November 19, he swore in James Douglas as the Governor of the Crown Colony of British Columbia. Douglas's first act as governor of the mainland was the swearing in of Begbie as Chief Justice.

Two of the first tasks facing the Royal Engineers, known as sappers, were to deepen the channel at the south end of Harrison Lake, facilitating boat traffic to Port Douglas, and to conduct a survey for a second narrow mule trail through the Fraser Canyon from Fort Yale to Lytton.

On December 18, 1858, the *Victoria Gazette* announced: "Good boats are running on all the lakes, while numerous houses for public entertainment are opening up all along the line." Three small paddlewheel steamers, the Melanie on Lillooet Lake, the *Lady of the Lake* on Anderson Lake, and the *Champion* on Seton Lake, replaced the Native canoes.

Other examples of ingenuity were close at hand. Roadbuilder and entrepreneur Gustavus Blin Wright and partners Adam Heffley and Henry Ingram financed William Laumeister with $7,000 to purchase twenty-three camels from the United States army. The syndicate hoped to clear $60,000 the first season, believing that camels could easily carry twice the load and travel twice the distance covered by mules or horses.

Storekeepers at Port Douglas stared in disbelief when the sternwheeler *Flying Dutchman* towed a barge wharfside and a couple of men began unloading the humpbacked beasts of burden. Laumeister's troubles began when the first camel down the gangplank bit and then kicked a prospector's mule into oblivion. He soon learned that the camels' hooves, adapted for travel in sand, could not stand up to the rocky terrain, and many went lame. Laumeister fitted them with rawhide boots to solved that problem, only to find that the camels' potent odours caused any horse and mule trains encountered along the trail to stampede. The mule and horse owners sued for damages and signed a petition to have the "Dromedary Express" removed from the road. Several of the animals were later used, for a short time at least, on the Cariboo Road, until the rocky terrain proved too much for their soft, padded feet. Before two years were out, Laumeister was forced to admit that the entire venture had been a big mistake and an expensive learning experience. A few of the camels were sold cheaply to US circuses, while the rest were turned loose to fend for themselves in the Cariboo.

Miner John Morris, passing by Quesnel Forks, saw what he took to be a large grizzly bear and immediately blasted at it with his rifle. When he saw the animal topple over, he and his companions rushed to the spot only to discover one of Laumeister's camels, with a big gaping hole in its side. Henceforth he became known as "Grizzly" Morris, and the very rich mine he later discovered on Williams Creek came to be known as "The Grizzly" in memory of the incident.

The camels earned a perpetual place in gold-rush lore, and the last one died near Grand Prairie (now Westwold) in 1905.

Across the Fraser River from Lillooet an enterprising individual named Otis Parsons built a stopping house on the foundations of the HBC's abandoned Fort Berens. Parsons had worked on the building of the Douglas Trail until it reached Lillooet, where he decided to rig up a barge affixed to a ferry cable to transport pack animals and miners across the Fraser. His stopping house soon

CONTINUED ON PAGE 36

1858 Rock Creek Gold Rush

The Rock Creek gold rush took place in an area dubbed the Boundary Country, since it was just to the north of the forty-ninth parallel. The rush touched off when some Native people chased two American soldiers across the border. The soldiers escaped, and five kilometres (three miles) inside Canadian territory, chanced to find gold on the Kettle River where it was met by Rock Creek. Adam Beam filed the first claim.

The rush that followed mostly involved Americans and some Chinese people. All had come north from Fort Colville, just south of the border; some came all the way from the California gold rush. At its peak, this new rush brought an estimated five thousand men to the area. A new town, Rock Creek, sprang into being, with a population of about three hundred. Governor Douglas sent Gold Commissioner Peter O'Reilly to the area to collect duties on items coming across the border as well as to collect fees for mining licences. Unfortunately, just as O'Reilly arrived at Rock Creek, trouble broke out when Caucasian and Chinese miners drove the inexperienced gold commissioner out in a hail of stones, in what came to be known as the Rock Creek War. O'Reilly's recourse was to flee to Victoria to report the incident to Governor Douglas.

A short time later, Douglas, accompanied by William George Cox, who was to become the new gold commissioner, and Arthur Bushby, best known as Judge Matthew Begbie's clerk and companion, proceeded to Rock Creek. Douglas proved to be his ever-commanding self. He laid down the law to the American miners and told them that if they didn't behave themselves on British soil, he would return with five hundred marines. He further explained that the Chinese miners had the same rights to the gold workings as they had, and that any molestation by them would not be tolerated. As the men left the large tent, Douglas insisted on shaking each one's hand, looking them in the eye—and ingraining his personal expectations of each of them. The Rock Creek War was over.

James Douglas

SIR JAMES DOUGLAS (1803-77)
A fur trader with the Hudson's Bay Company, Douglas rose through the ranks to become chief factor. From 1851 until 1864, he was governor of the Colony of Vancouver Island. In 1858 he also became governor of mainland British Columbia. After his retirement in 1864, he travelled to England, where he was knighted by Queen Victoria and made a Knight Commander of the Bath. He has often been called the "Father of British Columbia."

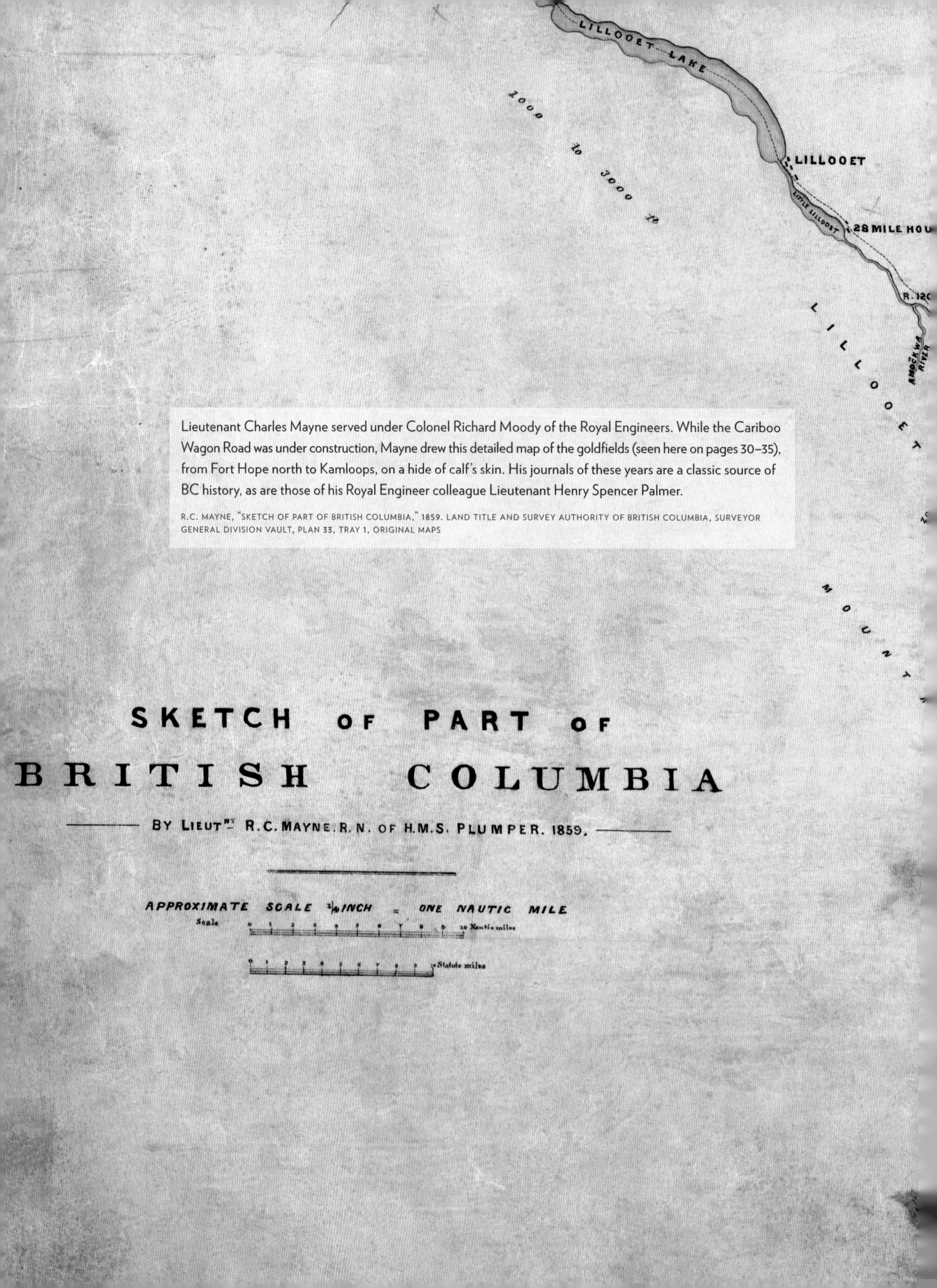

LILLOOET LAKE

1000 to 3000 ft

LILLOOET

LITTLE LILLOOET

28 MILE HOU

R. 12C

LILLOOET

AMOCKWA RIVER

MOUNTA

Lieutenant Charles Mayne served under Colonel Richard Moody of the Royal Engineers. While the Cariboo Wagon Road was under construction, Mayne drew this detailed map of the goldfields (seen here on pages 30–35), from Fort Hope north to Kamloops, on a hide of calf's skin. His journals of these years are a classic source of BC history, as are those of his Royal Engineer colleague Lieutenant Henry Spencer Palmer.

SKETCH OF PART OF
BRITISH COLUMBIA

BY LIEUTᴺᵀ R.C. MAYNE. R.N. OF H.M.S. PLUMPER. 1859.

APPROXIMATE SCALE ¼ INCH = ONE NAUTIC MILE

Scale   0 1 2 3 4 5 6 7 8 9   10 Nautic miles

0 1 2 3 4 5 6 7 8 9   10 Statute miles

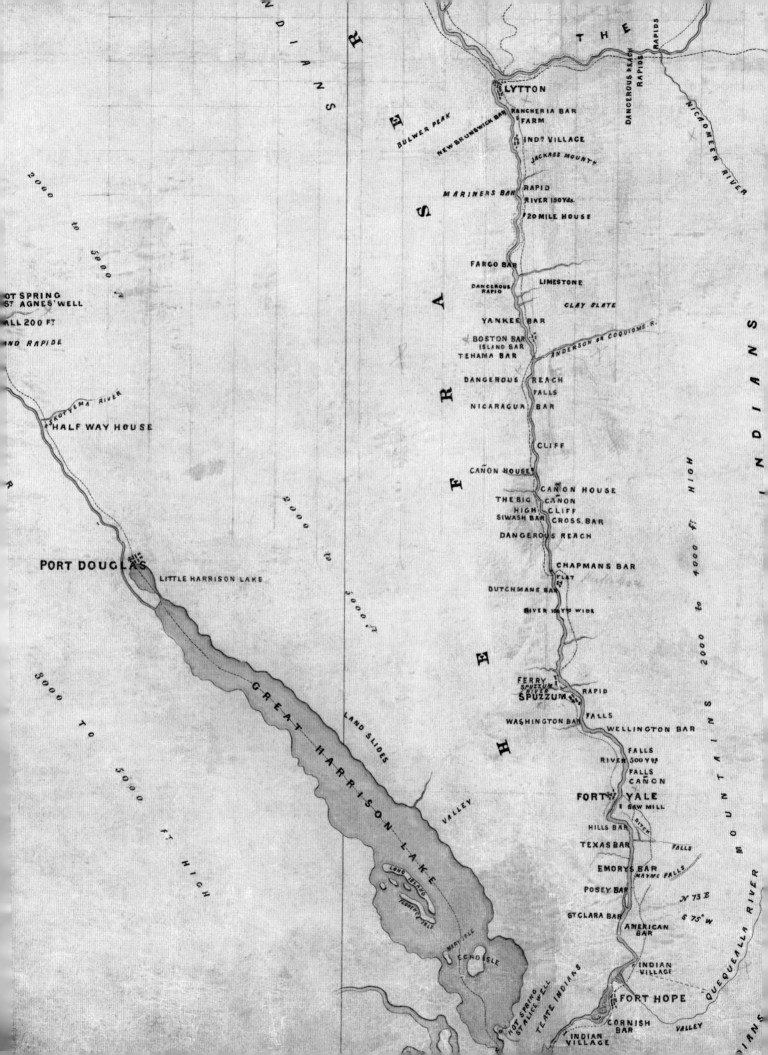

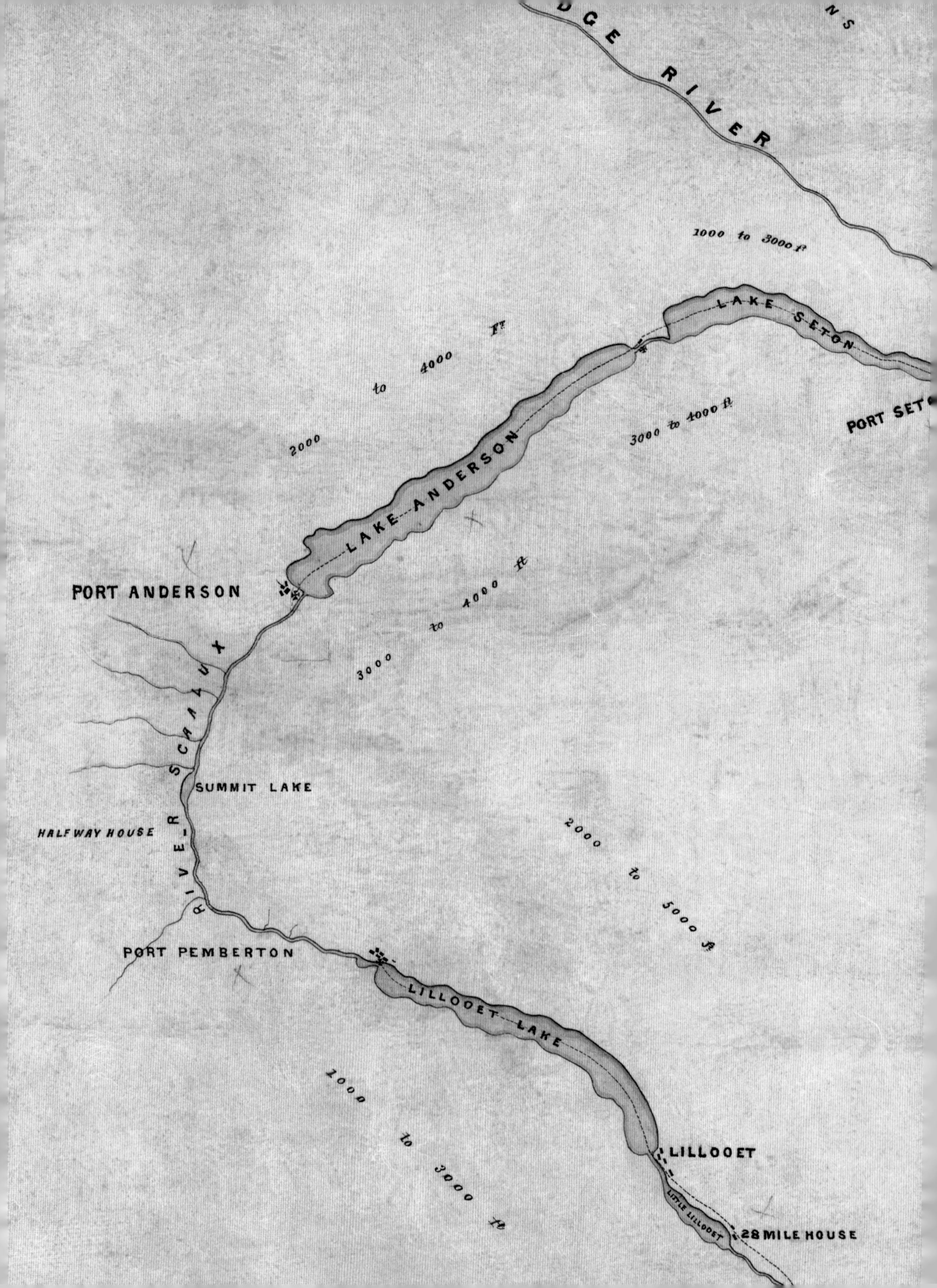

DGE RIVER
NS
1000 to 3000 ft
LAKE SETON
2000 to 4000 Ft
PORT SETO
3000 to 4000 ft
LAKE ANDERSON
PORT ANDERSON
3000 to 4000 ft
RIVER SCAAUX
SUMMIT LAKE
HALFWAY HOUSE
2000 to 5000 ft
PORT PEMBERTON
LILLOOET LAKE
1000 to 3000 ft
LILLOOET
LITTLE LILLOOET
28 MILE HOUSE

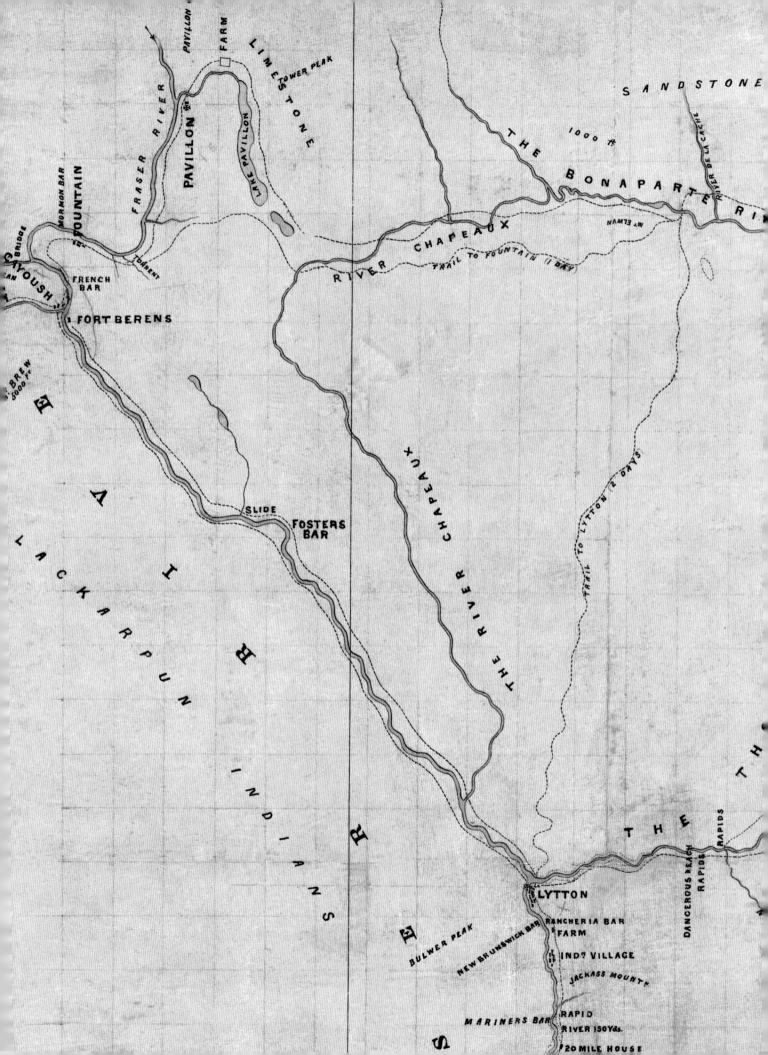

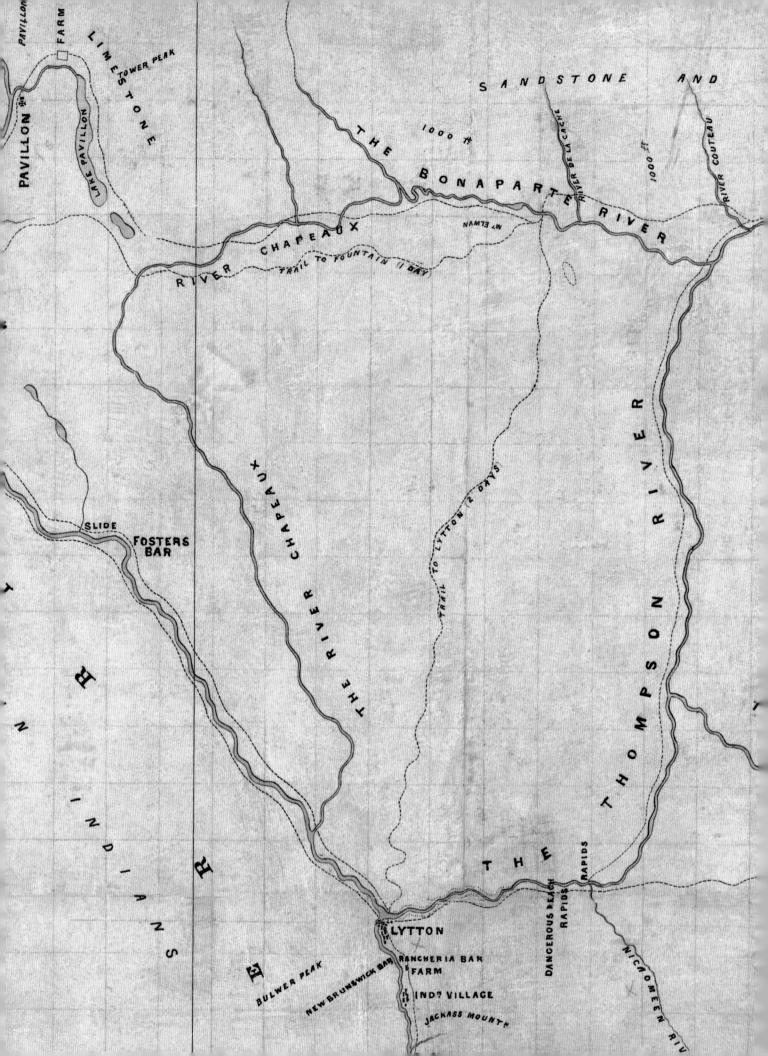

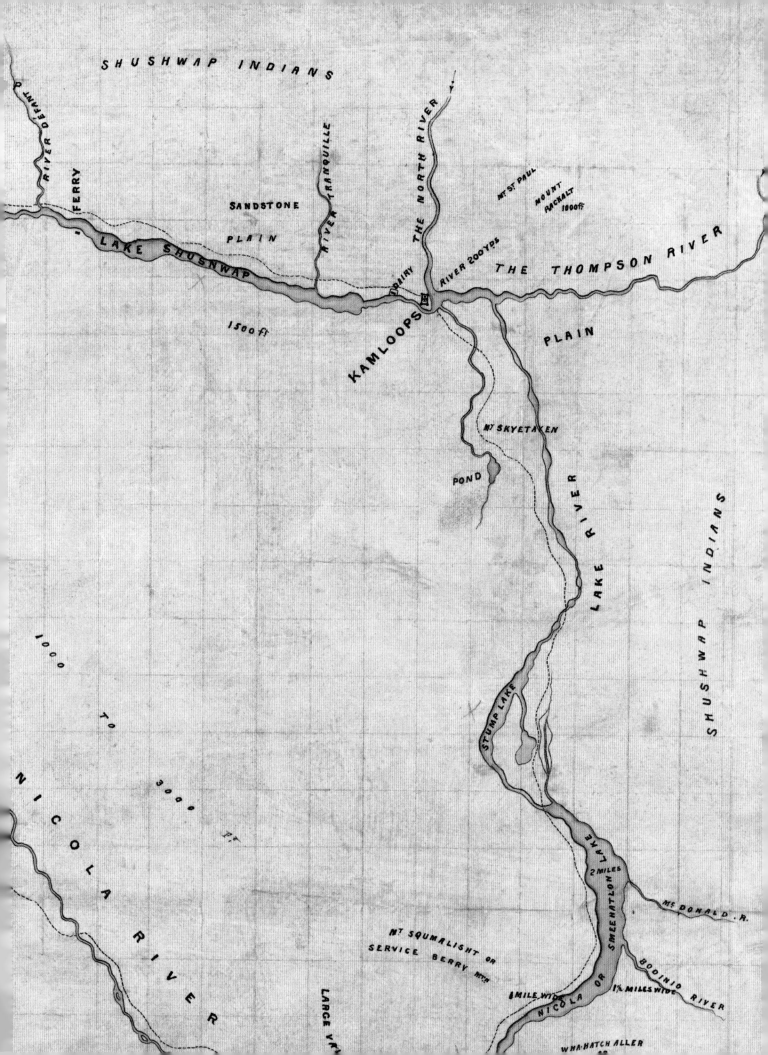

provided homegrown produce to feed the continuous stream of men heading to the goldfields.

By June 1860, with the Royal Engineer's Fraser Canyon survey complete, Governor Douglas granted a $22,000 contract to Franklin Way and Josiah Crosby Beedy to construct a mule trail that tamed or bypassed the treacherous rocky terrain along the Fraser River from nineteen kilometres (twelve miles) out of Yale to the Native village of Spuzzum. Here, Way built a stopping house and erected a cable ferry across the Fraser River to connect with a long-used path on the opposite shore. That fall Douglas let out a second contract to Hugh McRoberts and William Powers to begin extending the trail upriver from Spuzzum toward Lytton. From Lytton miners would follow the south shore of the Thompson River until arriving at Mortimer Cook's ferry crossing, the place at which Spence's Bridge was later built. Once on the north side of the Thompson River, the miners could follow an HBC trail that skirted the Bonaparte River to Robert Watson's roadhouse, located at the junction of the two competing trails to the Cariboo.

In the first years, the Fraser River route had its problems. Those who mastered the first section were finding their supply route cut off because of the dynamiting of the rock walls farther ahead. Aware of the great danger and long delays, packers became hesitant to use the route and turned instead to the Douglas Trail.

Anxious to restore traffic flow through their community, Yale merchants undertook an advertising campaign. Instead of discussing their new trail's merits, they chose to ridicule the competitive route via Harrison Lake. Of the Douglas Trail the ad stated, "Elegant and high-toned. Meals one dollar. Beds fifty cents. Crawlers thrown in gratis. Sit on an open deck in the cold; stick your nose in the cook's galley to warm it for free. Take your own snowshoes."

The advertising was effective; many travellers heading to the Cariboo were inexperienced men who had never lived outside a city. Regardless of their chosen route, these poor souls tramped the entire journey with just the clothes on their back and a small pack of provisions that sometimes only included a blanket. Stories about bears and inhospitable Native people terrified many of the novices into packing revolvers. One greenhorn wrote, "Accidents with firearms are of a frequent occurrence in this country, through the inexperience of their possessors. Furthermore, revolvers are of little or no use here, the same weight of good worsted stockings would be much more serviceable." One frightened lad went to sleep with a cocked revolver in his bedroll and, as he got up in the morning and began to roll up his blanket, the weapon's trigger caught on its fold. It discharged and killed him instantly, much to the astonishment and grief of his companions.

Once the canyon route was finished, Port Douglas storekeepers Joseph Lorenzo Smith and Thomas Marshall realized in 1861 that the newer trail was a much faster way to the goldfields than the Douglas Trail. They loaded all their worldly possessions onto their backs and headed for the new junction of the two routes with the intention of reaping wealth from the weary travellers by setting up a stopping house. Upon their arrival, they discovered that Robert Watson was already set up at the junction and doing great business catering to the needs of the miners; in fact, he was building a larger structure. Not to be thwarted, Smith and Marshall bought him out. When Smith died in 1871, his wife married Marshall, and by the time he passed away in 1877, one of Smith's sons was old enough to join his mother in the business, whose location is present-day Clinton.

From this stopping house, the miners followed an HBC trail to Alexandria (formerly Fort Alexandria). From here they worked their way northward, following trails to Lac la Hache and on to Chief Williams's village (later Williams Lake). Past Chief Williams's village, foot trails led the miners to Quesnelle Forks, where William Prosper Barry and Samuel Adler had constructed a sixty-metre (two hundred foot) toll bridge across the Quesnel River. These two industrious men made their money collecting tolls from travellers using the bridge; with the Cariboo gold rush in the offing, those tolls would continue to grow.

The Engineers' Road

ENGINEERS' ROAD

A Wagon Road Across B.C.—This was the ambitious scheme of the Royal Engineers in the 1860's as miners clamoured for better access to the Southern Interior. Sent from England, these military engineers replaced the first 25 miles of the Dewdney Trail with a wagon road. Their work halted when attention shifted to the gold-rich Cariboo.

DEPARTMENT OF RECREATION & CONSERVATION

The creation of an east-to-west wagon road across the southern portion of BC by Britain's Royal Engineers was an attempt to keep any gold found north of the Canadian–US border from making its way into the US. The militaristic Royal Engineers built the first few kilometres of road from Rock Creek toward Hope, but were then seconded away for the building of the Cariboo Wagon Road through the Fraser Canyon to the Cariboo goldfields. Civil engineer Edgar Dewdney built the first section of the Dewdney Trail from Hope to Rock Creek in 1861. Afterward he took the contract to build the section from Wild Horse to Rock Creek in 1864. Eventually, the road was built to Hope.

ABOVE

The Engineers' Road, or Dewdney Trail, runs parallel to Highway 3 near the western exit from Manning Park.

INSET—EDGAR DEWDNEY (1835–1916)

Civil engineer and surveyor Edgar Dewdney worked on the Dewdney Trail from Hope to Rock Creek. The trail was completed in 1864. Dewdney went on to become the lieutenant-governor of the Northwest Territories before becoming the fifth lieutenant-governor of British Columbia.

HISTORICAL PHOTO A-04735, ROYAL BC MUSEUM AND ARCHIVES. PHOTO BY WILLIAM NOTMAN, CIRCA 1865

BREAKING TRAILS AND CREEKS OF GOLD

Seasoned miners who had already proven their ability to find gold strikes made the first major gold strikes in the Cariboo. The best of them could simply look at a creek and know if it contained gold. George W. Weaver, William Ross Keithley, and John A. Rose were three such men. Weaver even had a California gold-rush town, Weaverville, named in his honour, while Rose's Bar, just below Yale, had more recently named for John Rose.

In the summer of 1860, Weaver, Keithley, and Rose persuaded the highly regarded Ranald MacDonald to lead them on an expedition along the north shore of Cariboo Lake. MacDonald had acquired valuable life experiences long before reaching the goldfields of the Cariboo. He was born Fort Astoria, in what was then the Columbia District, or Oregon Country. His parents were Archibald MacDonald, a Scottish HBC fur trader, and Princess Raven, daughter of Chief Comcomly, a leader of the Chinook tribe. After his mother died, the infant Ranald was raised by a maternal aunt until after his father was transferred to Fort Kamloops. From then until he was ten, he was raised by his father and stepmother at Fort Kamloops, Fort Langley, and Fort Colville before being sent east with the fall fur brigade to Red River for schooling. In 1839, at the age of fifteen, he apprenticed in a bank. MacDonald hated the indoor occupation, and within a year he had run away, much to the despair of his father.

By 1848, MacDonald was working on a whaling ship, and while sailing along the coast of Japan had requested a sailboat to put off for shore to explore this strange land. By first simulating a shipwreck and afterward ingratiating himself with those in authority by teaching English to fourteen Japanese interpreters, he escaped execution but still suffered almost a year in prison, since white men were banished from Japan at this time. American newspapers reported that he had drowned in the South Seas.

Once released, he was safely deported from Japan on an American ship bound for Australia and par-ticipated in the gold strikes near Melbourne. A short time after his father died, the prodigal son returned to St. Andrews, Ontario, to see his family, and it was there that he heard of the Fraser River gold rush. He persuaded his two half-brothers, Allan and Benjamin, to join him and participate in this new adventure. The trio sailed for Panama, and en route up the Pacific Coast, disembarked at Fort Vancouver, where Ranald made inquiries about his maternal grandfather. He was saddened to learn that Chief Comcomly had fallen victim to the smallpox plague in the 1830s. Upon reaching Fort Victoria, the trio paid a visit to their father's old friend, Governor Douglas.

Ranald or "Black" MacDonald, as he was later known in the Cariboo, was on the Lower Fraser by the fall of 1859. The following spring, he volunteered to guide Rose, Weaver, and Keithley into the hinterland. MacDonald's half-brother Benjamin, though only fifteen when he arrived in BC, was among the first to stake claims along the better gold-producing creeks in the Cariboo. He later became a shareholder in the Cariboo Cameron claim.

The four trailblazers eventually came across a gold-bearing creek that they named Keithley. Weaver and Keithley worked this creek with mediocre success but soon gave up to join Rose and MacDonald, who had gone deeper into the hinterland. Although the creek was not a rich source of gold, less experienced miners, who tended to follow experienced parties such as theirs, began staking claims along the stream, and by that fall, the settlement of Keithley Town sprang up as a supply centre. When winter struck, the reluctant miners built crude, igloo-like shelters in the deep snow to live in while protecting their staked ground from claim jumpers.

Weaver and Keithley followed Keithley Creek for several kilometres before heading off along one of the feeder streams. When this small creek petered out, the men crossed a high plateau and descended into a valley by following a stream so littered with deer antlers that they then and there named it Antler Creek. Continuing on, they met up with Rose and MacDonald, who were bursting with good news about this creek, which they had been working. They showed the amazed newcomers places where the rusty-coloured gold nuggets were in plain view in pockets of sun-exposed bedrock and announced that they had been able to take four to five ounces of gold to the pan.

Bedding down for the night, the four men excitedly planned their strategy. Because they were the discoverers of the creek, the four were each entitled to one thirty-by-thirty-metre (one-hundred-by-one-hundred-foot) claim as well as their regular claim of the same size. It was decided that they would search the creek for the richest spots on which to stake their eight claims and then pan the remaining areas until their food supplies ran low. During the night, however, the camp was covered with thirty centimetres of freshly fallen snow. Despite the change in weather, the men prospected feverishly up and down the creek and succeeded in staking out the choice areas. By this time supplies had run low, and they agreed that Keithley and Weaver would return to Keithley Town for winter supplies. Everything was planned carefully in order to keep the creek secret. They would use the Keithley Creek gold to purchase the supplies, since the store owner might notice the colour difference of the Antler Creek gold and suspect a new find. More importantly, Weaver and Keithley would have to make sure that their actions did not arouse any suspicions.

The two set off, and about a kilometre from Discovery Rock, the spot on Antler Creek where they first found gold, they located an easier route up to the plateau and then down again in practically a straight line southward in the direction of Keithley. They waited until supper hour to enter the town, knowing that the miners would be occupied with their meals. Entering the store, they made great effort to appear casual, even to the point of engaging in small talk while purchasing their supplies. Lingering so as not to appear hurried, they felt safe to leave by dark, but upon passing through the mining community they found that hordes of men were packed and wearing snowshoes, ready to follow the pair back to wherever they had come from. Their prospecting fame had defeated any measures they had taken to prevent interest in their actions and, like the Pied Piper, they led the merry horde to the gold.

Thus some dozens of parties set out for Antler Creek in two metres of snow. Many crossed the plateau on showshoes—hence the name Snowshoe Plateau—and before long, claims were being staked over already staked ground, giving rise to many disputes. Upon returning to their claims, Weaver and Keithley helped Rose and MacDonald build a small cabin from spruce and balsam logs as a shelter against the harsh winter. The other miners chose to live in tents or holes in the snow. Soon Antler Creek became so solidly staked that new arrivals began to look elsewhere, resulting in several rich creeks being discovered almost simultaneously. Four of these—Williams, Lightning, Lowhee, and Grouse—would soon become the chief source of gold in the rush that followed the discovery of Antler. Almost immediately, a depot called Antlertown was set up on Antler Creek to provide supplies for the area.

Williams Creek was discovered in February 1861. Born on the slopes of Bald Mountain, it flows in a northwesterly direction for about fourteen kilometres (nine miles) before emptying into the Willow River. At the midway point, the creek flows through a canyon or gulch before meandering through a broad valley.

In the winter of 1860–61, in the Antler Creek area, six prospectors were sharing a camp. They were Murtz J. Collins, Michael Costin Brown, John "Kansas" Metz, Wilhelm Dietz (a Prussian ex-sailor), James Costello, and Michael Burns. One evening Dietz, Costello, and Burns stumbled into their camp in a half-starved state, claiming they had found gold in a nearby unnamed creek. The next morning Brown joined Dietz and Costello in their exploration while Burns, Collins, and Metz decided to remain in camp. The trio moved around Discovery Rock and continued upstream until a wide creek (later named Racetrack) blocked their passage. Heading into the hills, they climbed up a mountainous slope, finally reaching a broad plateau that they named Bald Mountain because it was barren of any timber. Brown left the following account:

We crossed the divide, eventually making the headwaters of the creek and after some time we travelled to a place near a little gulch or canyon, where we camped for the night, building a little shelter.

On the following morning we separated to prospect the stream, agreeing to meet again at night to report progress. The story of that day's prospecting, which we recalled over the campfire, has become a matter of mining history in British Columbia. "Dutch Bill" made the best prospect, striking pay dirt at $1.25 a pan. Costello and I had done pretty well, finding dirt worth a dollar or so a pan. You can well imagine we were well pleased with the day's exertions, and each man in his heart felt that we had discovered very rich ground. I shall not forget the discussion that took place as to the name to be given to the creek. Dutch Bill was for having it called "Billy Creek" because he had found the best prospects of the three. I was quite agreeable, but I stipulated that Mr. William [sic] Dietz should buy the first basket of champagne that reached the creek. This appealed to Costello, and so the creek was then and there named—not Billy Creek but "Williams Creek."

The six men returned to camp and worked out certain plans: Costello would remain on the creek and guard their claims; Dietz, Burns, Collins, and Metz would return to Antler for supplies; and Brown would travel as quickly as possible the ninety-six kilometres (sixty miles) to Williams Lake to register their discovery with Philip Henry Nind Jr., the Cariboo's only gold commissioner.

Things began to go awry when news of their strike leaked out at Antler. They decided that Dietz should return to the claims the following morning. On snowshoes, he retraced his footsteps in a record three hours, but his strenuous exertions were of no avail, for the entire population of wintering miners at Antler followed his trail in the snow and within hours were staking claims up and down both sides of the creek.

Ironically, the discoverers staked claims that proved to be among the poorest on a creek that became among the richest in the world. After working like slaves for three months, most of the original discoverers sold their claims for modest prices and became involved with more productive sites. Brown ended up selling his shares to William Wallace Cunningham for $2,500.

An Irishman by birth, Brown had managed a hotel in San Francisco at the height of the California rush before catching the sternwheeler *Brother Jonathan* to join the flood of humanity heading north to the Cariboo. This experience prompted him to purchase a pack train to supply provisions to the growing hordes of miners. On one trip alone he took 3,630 kilograms (8,000 pounds) of provisions into the gold camps. He sold flour for $1.25 for half a kilogram (per pound); beans, bacon, and dried apples for $1.50; and tobacco for $2. He packed all summer, but that fall was caught in a snowstorm and lost forty-two horses. In the spring of 1863, he had carpenters build him a store on Williams Creek from whipsawed lumber at a cost of $4,500. He sold the store in 1864 to open the Adelphi Hotel in Victoria. Over the next forty years, he took part in the gold rushes to the Big Bend, Cassiar, Dease River, and eventually the Klondike. In 1904 he left Yukon for good and returned to Victoria, where he passed away ten years later.

Richard Willoughby came to the Cariboo from the US, where he had sold a mine for $35,000 in Arizona before leading a force of three hundred soldier-miners through hostile Indian Territory en route to the California diggings. Willoughby, Hanson Tilton, and brothers Asa H. and Thomas P. Patterson went around the canyon on Williams Creek and descended through a narrow valley before coming upon a lovely lake that was later called Jack of Clubs Lake. On their right a small stream flowed from the lake—later proven to be the source of the Willow River—while on their left a small creek disgorged itself through a narrow ravine between two mountains. The party found gold immediately, and Willoughby christened the creek "Lowhee" and their claim "The Great Lowhee," after a secret miner's society at Yale of which he was a member.

The men took their time and were careful to stake what appeared to be the most productive ground. In July the four partners returned with the necessary equipment to work their claims. Other eager miners followed them, and when Willoughby reached the diggings he turned to these men and announced, "Boys, this is it!" Lowhee Creek was fabulously rich and easy to work, for nowhere was the silt and gravel more than a metre deep to bedrock on which the gold nuggets rested. During five weeks of mining, Willoughby and his three partners took out four thousand ounces of nuggets from a 60-by-150-metre (200-by-500-foot) rectangle of ten claims. Upon leaving the Cariboo, Willoughby tried farming in Chilliwack in the Fraser Valley, but that occupation did not suit his reckless nature, and in 1869 he headed for the gold strikes in the Cassiar and Omineca country. The rest of his life was spent in northern BC and Alaska. He died in Nome, Alaska, in 1904 with a large fortune.

George Downey was one of a group of prospectors who followed Antler Creek to its source. From here, the men crossed an alpine pass to the headwaters of another stream that they named Grouse Creek. This waterway also proved to be a generous source of gold.

By the summer's end, twelve hundred men were working on the gold-bearing creeks around Keithley and Antler, and soon small companies of two and three men were busy taking out as much as twenty-four ounces of gold per man per day. The gold the miners were finding on Williams Creek was in hard blue clay two to three metres (eight to ten feet) below the surface, in what was believed to be an old creek bed.

As early as August, the Abbott and Jordan Company was reported to have amassed over 6,400 ounces of gold after expenses.

Not all of Antler Creek proved rich, as this account in the *Cariboo Sentinel* by disenchanted miner William Mark proves:

> *There has been a great deal said about the richness of this creek [Antler Creek] and the quantity of gold taken out from time to time; but not a word was said on the other side of the question, and there had been several companies ruined at this creek. One company, a party of eight Cornishmen . . . were on ground adjoining this rich claim. The day we left Antler they abandoned the place, and left it ruined men. This was the case with every other creek; some struck it rich, and this is blazed in every paper. Many lost all they had, and were completely beggared. This was never named but hushed down.*

George W. Weaver and William R. Keithley had to put in a six-kilometre- (four-mile-) long flume to carry water to their diggings.

RANALD MACDONALD (1824–94)
This gold hunter was one of the most interesting of all the gold discoverers to venture into the Cariboo. Seen here a few years before his death, MacDonald, the son of a Hudson's Bay Company chief factor, had participated in the Australian gold rush before coming to British Columbia. He was also a major player in the discovery of gold on Leech River at Sooke on Vancouver Island in 1864.
VANCOUVER PUBLIC LIBRARY. AUTHOR PHOTO

Although lumber for and construction of the flume were extremely expensive, the claim's gold output easily covered the overhead, and the two men accumulated a tidy fortune.

Ranald MacDonald mined a fortune before selling his claim to John A. Rose for a 320-ounce bag of gold. Thereafter, MacDonald engaged in packing supplies from his ranch on the Bonaparte River into the gold camps. After packing for several years, he retired to Colville, Washington (formerly Fort Colville), to write his autobiography. Several publishers refused his manuscript, fearing his story was too fantastic to possibly be true. There are monuments honouring MacDonald in both Rishiri and Nagasaki, Japan. He died a poor man in Washington State in 1894, and his last words to a niece were reportedly "Sayonara, my dear, sayonara."

John Rose, nicknamed the "Man of Destiny," was last seen rafting down the Willow River with an unknown companion in the fall of 1862. The bodies of the two men were later found buried under the ashes of their last campfire. Speculation had it that they had either swamped their raft, losing their provisions and consequently dying of starvation and hypothermia, later to be buried by passersby, or that they had been ambushed by Native people who sought to conceal their dastardly deed by burying them.

George Weaver later went to the Kootenays, where he met his death while working alone in a ground-sluicing claim on Weaver's Gulch. He had been buried up to his neck in cold mud for two days before being found. He almost survived the ordeal. He was buried not far from where the accident took place.

OPPOSITE

John Innes's 1.8-by-2.7-metre (6-by-9-foot) painting of the discovery of gold in 1861 by a party led by Wilhelm "Dutch Bill" Dietz. His companions agreed to name the creek in his honour provided he pay for the first case of champagne that arrived at the diggings.

NATIVE SONS OF BRITISH COLUMBIA POST NO. 1

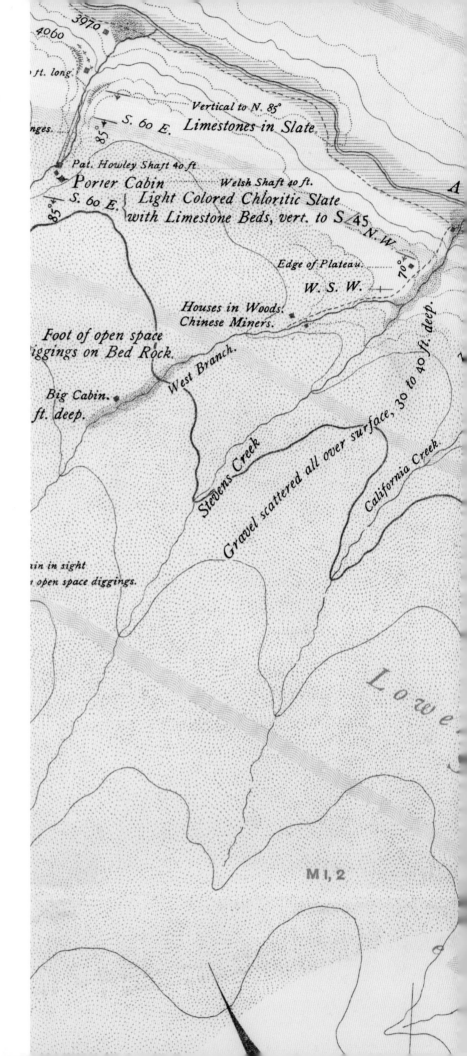

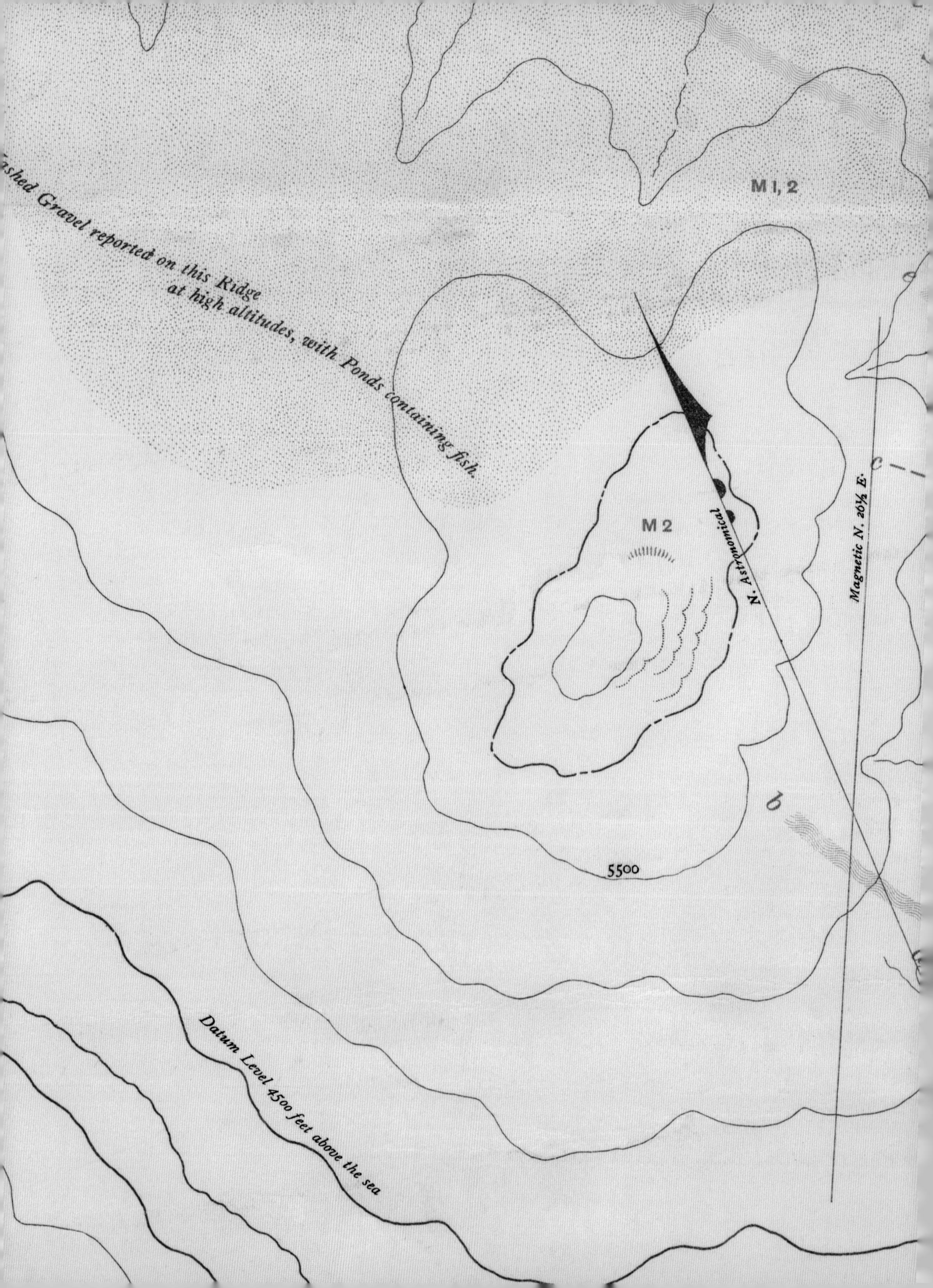

M 1, 2

Washed Gravel reported on this Ridge
at high altitudes, with Ponds containing fish

M 2

N. Astronomical

Magnetic N. 20½ E.

c

b

5500

Datum Level 4500 feet above the sea

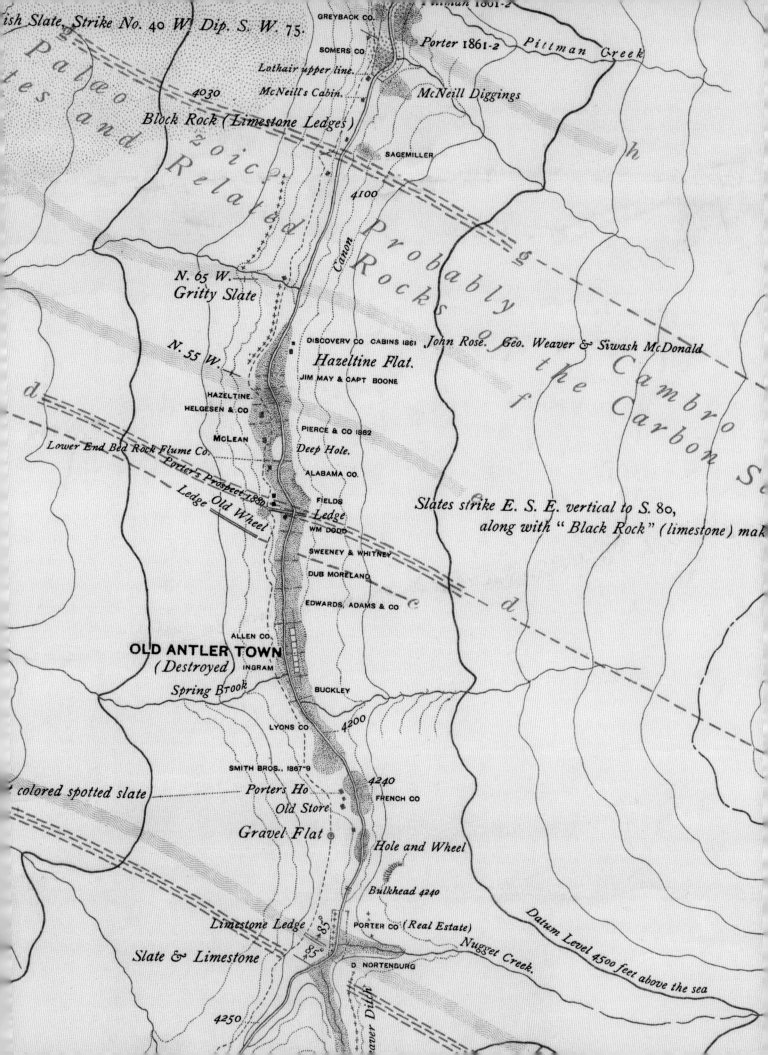

Williams Creek, Cariboo

Williams Creek, named for Wilhelm Dietz and easily the most important and richest digging in the Cariboo goldfields, gave birth to the towns of Richfield, Barkerville, and Camerontown, which collectively were also known as Williams Creek. Barkerville and Camerontown were named for William Barker and John Angus Cameron, respectively, Barker being the most famous and at one time richest of the Cariboo gold miners. Dietz's claim, though, was not a money-maker, and he died in poverty.

In the early 1860s, when placer gold production peaked, the search began for lode gold deposits. The Black Jack, Home Stake, Cornish, and the Wintrip were among the first claims to be staked in the area.

Isaiah Frederick Diller, an American miner, found riches beyond his wildest dreams. From Pennsylvania, "Young" Diller joined forces with two other men and secured a thirty-by-ninety-metre (one-hundred-by-three-hundred-foot) claim adjacent to the Billy Barker claim. The men ended up sinking a shaft twenty-four metres (eighty feet) down before reaching bedrock.

Because they encountered "Cariboo slum," a soupy and porridge-like gravel, too thin to dig and too thick to pump, Diller and his pals had to build stout log cribbing all the way down the shaft until reaching

CONTINUED ON PAGE 50

RIGHT AND FOLLOWING PAGE SPREAD

Williams Creek, Cariboo.

GEOLOGICAL SURVEY OF CANADA MAP 364.
NATURAL RESOURCES CANADA

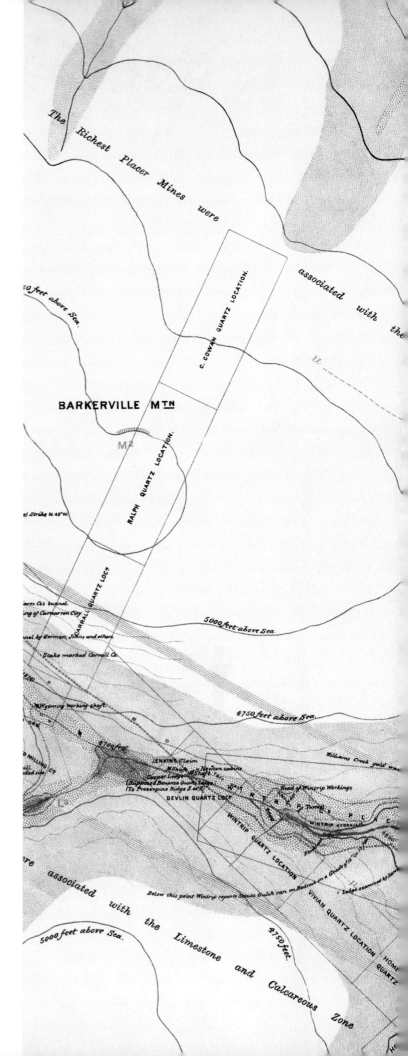

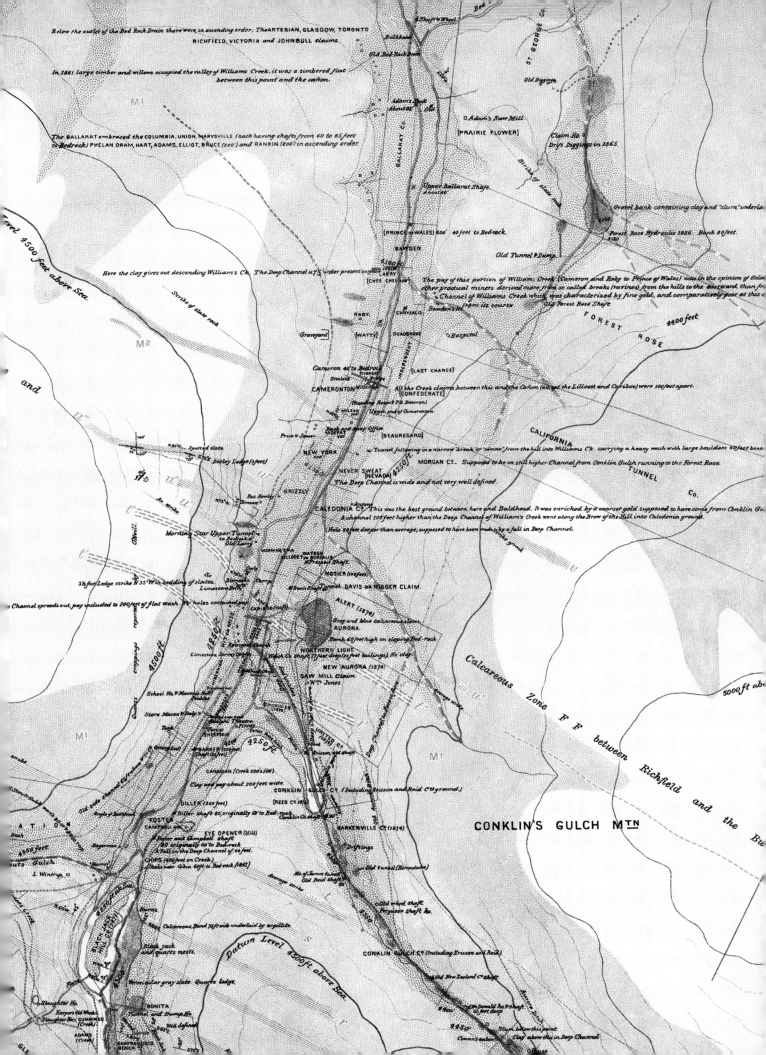

bedrock. Next, they tunnelled or drifted out from the shaft and, by a stroke of good luck, hit fabulously rich pay dirt six metres (twenty feet) into the adit. Reports vary that the men took out between 11.3 and 45.3 kilograms (25 and 100 pounds) of gold in the first one to three days. Diller would not leave the Cariboo until he had his own weight—109 kilograms (240 pounds)—and the weight of his dog—45.5 kilograms (100 pounds)—in gold. Diller invested wisely, and some of the original Cariboo gold still remains in the hands of the Diller family.

Diller's was one of many rags-to-riches success stories that came out of the Cariboo, but the riches-to-rags stories were far more numerous.

From 1877 to 1892, prospecting and testing was done on these major veins: Bonanza (BC) Vein, Steadman Vein, Pinkerton Vein, Black Jack Vein (Westport), Proserpine Vein, Perkins Vein, and Mount Burns Vein. during this time, Black Jack and Burns Company sank a shaft 55 metres (180 feet) deep on the Black Jack claim, from which three levels were established with up to a hundred metres of drifts and crosscuts. Assays greater than $70 per ton were reported.

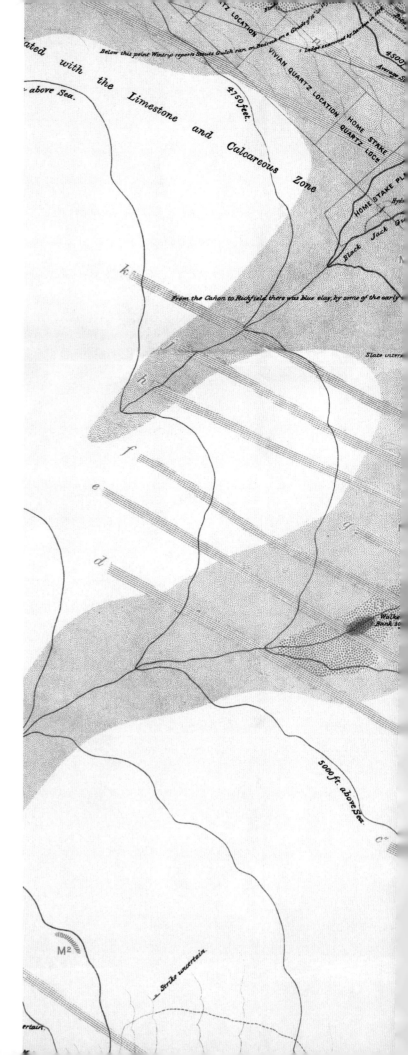

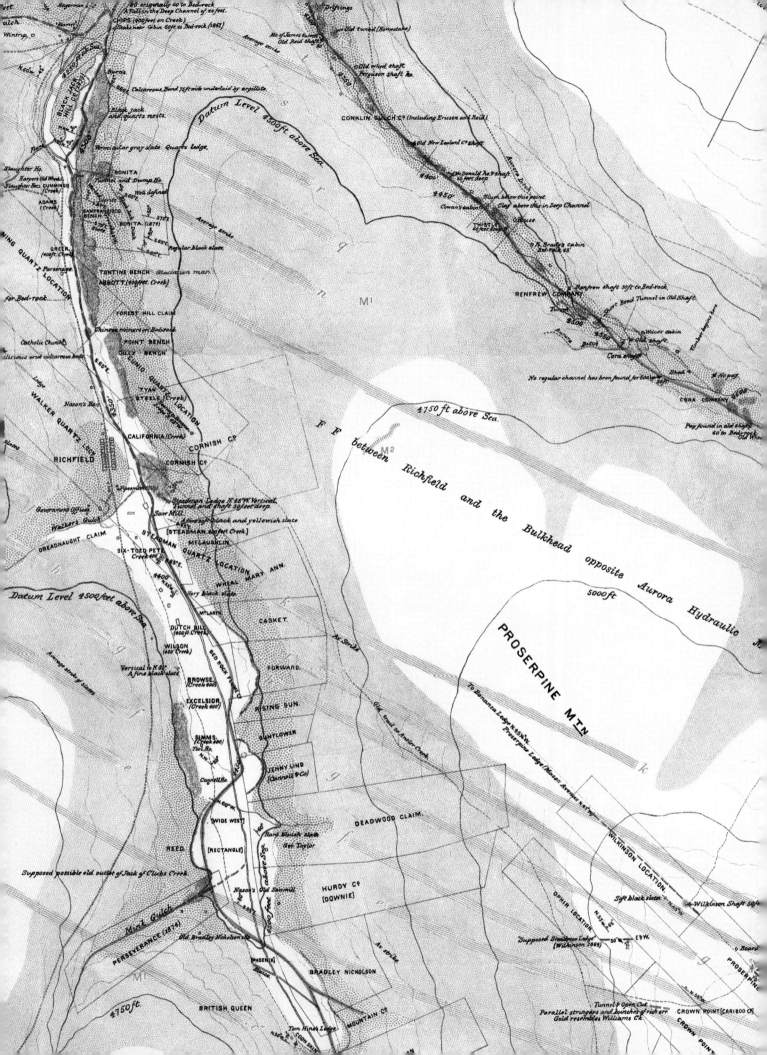

The overshot water wheel in this photograph was six metres (twenty feet) in diameter and modelled after the wheels and pumps of the tin mines in Cornwall, England. The early miners who had dug shafts into the ground were often faced with water seeping into the shaft, causing flooding. They found that the pay gravel often lay twelve to thirty metres (forty to a hundred feet) or more under the surface. The wheels were used to pump the water from the deep workings to the surface and also to lift pay gravel. Water would be fed into cup-like shelves at the top of the wheel, using water transported by a flume from a water source, such as a lake, to make the contraption turn. The wheel would then drive a rocker arm that would pump the water from the bottom of the mine shaft.

When bedrock was reached, shafts or drifts went out in several directions seeking the richest pay dirt, not unlike the spokes of a wheel. The drifts around the bottom of the shaft were usually large enough that a man was able to stand up to fill the buckets. The shafts had to be shored up with lumber to prevent cave-ins. Some of the offshoot drifts were no more than ninety-one centimetres high by ninety-one centimetres wide (three feet high by three feet wide), while some of the richer claims with taller, wider drifts had ore cars and tracks running along them. It was not uncommon for a lengthy drift to pass underground into a neighbour's claim.

Working underground was a dangerous and wet occupation, and many of the early miners succumbed to pneumonia.

A CORNISH WATER WHEEL AND FLUME HYDRAULIC OPERATION AT THE DAVIS CLAIM ON STOUT'S GULCH, WILLIAMS CREEK

The Davis wheel and flume Williams Creek. Cariboo.

The Rocker

Rockers were used to extract deposits of placer gold from alluvial sediment, much like gold pans but on a larger scale. They were called rockers because they were rocked back and forth like a baby's cradle, moving the mixture of water and sediment over the riffles along the bottom in order to separate and trap the denser gold. This rocker was 1.22 metres (4 feet) long, 43 centimetres (17 inches) tall, and 40 centimetres (15.5 inches) wide. The tray on top, into which the gravel is placed is 41 centimetres (16 inches) by 51 centimetres (20 inches) by 20 centimetres (8 inches) deep. The gravel is placed into this tray along with water and rocked, sending the heavier gold through the holes in its bottom. The gold and black sand are captured in the riffles (and on a blanket) at the very bottom of the rocker. By comparison, the gold pan is 41 centimetres (16 inches) in diameter by 10 centimetres (4 inches) deep.

The rocker box was one of the primary tools invented by California's '49ers to extract gold from gravel. Usually set up near the banks of creeks or rivers, the devices were much faster and more productive than gold pans, and a single miner could put through two to three cubic yards of gravel in a single day. An added bonus was that they could be built by the miners from sawn lumber on location and easily packed around on their backs if necessary.

Dirt, gravel, and water would be placed into the cradle's box, which had holes in its bottom. Underneath, the approximately 0.5-by-1.2-metre (2-by-4-foot) cradle sloped downward away from the box. Beneath the cradle were two semicircular boards that permitted the device to be rocked back and forth with one hand while water was added to the gravel mixture with a ladle with the other hand. The rounded surface covered in canvas was called the slide, or apron. As the cradle was rocked, the finer gold and sand would wash through the holes in the top box and be caught by the ridges and canvas on the apron. The larger rocks caught would be thrown out, and the process would then be repeated with a new batch of dirt and gravel.

After the gravel was washed clean in the box, any oversized material was inspected for nuggets and then dumped out. The undersized material went over the apron, where most of the gold was caught, the riffles stopping any gold that got over the apron. At the Cariboo gold camps, the rockers were cleaned every two to three hours or more when rich ground was worked and the gold began to show on the apron or in the riffles. In cleaning up after a run, the water was poured into the box on top and the device was gently rocked to wash away the surface sand and gravel. Then the apron was dumped into a gold pan. The material in the back of the riffles in the sluice was taken up by a flat scoop, placed at the head of the sluice, and washed down gently once or twice with clear water. The gold would remain behind on the boards, from where it was scraped up and put into the pan with the concentrate from the apron. The few colours left in the sluice would be caught with the next run. The concentrate was cleaned in the pan. Skilful manipulation of the rocker and a careful cleanup permitted recovery of nearly all the gold. The overflow drained back to the one at the rear, and the water was reused. A miner with a rocker could process three to five times more gravel than a man with a gold pan.

Bill Phinney uses a hand rocker with a long-handled ladle to separate gold from gravel at the Caledonia Company on Williams Creek.

HISTORICAL PHOTO A-00353, ROYAL BC MUSEUM AND ARCHIVES. PHOTO BY FREDERICK DALLY

Lightning Creek, Cariboo

With Keithley, Antler, and Williams Creeks all solidly staked, the miners of poorer claims began to investigate any unexplored streams within a thirty-kilometre radius of Antlertown. In June 1861, William Wallace Cunningham, Edward Campbell, W. Henry Lightfall, James Bell, and John Hume discovered an incredibly rich stream that began as a trickle on the slopes of Agnes Mountain and flowed westward before emptying into the Swift River. When Cunningham took the first pan of gravel from the creek and saw the prospects, he remarked, "Boys, this is lightning," and the name stuck.

It was Cunningham who announced that gold had been discovered on Van Winkle Creek, a tributary of Lightning. Because Rip Van Winkle Bar near Lytton in earlier days had been prosperous, the new locality was named Van Winkle after it.

In keeping with political tradition, the nearby community of Stanley, which sprang up in 1870 to replace the declining Van Winkle, was named in honour of Edward Henry Stanley, the Earl of Derby and Secretary of State for the Colonies at the time. His brother, Frederick Arthur Stanley, Baron Stanley of Preston, was the Governor General of Canada from 1888 to 1893 and left his name to Vancouver City's Stanley Park (and later the National Hockey League's Stanley Cup).

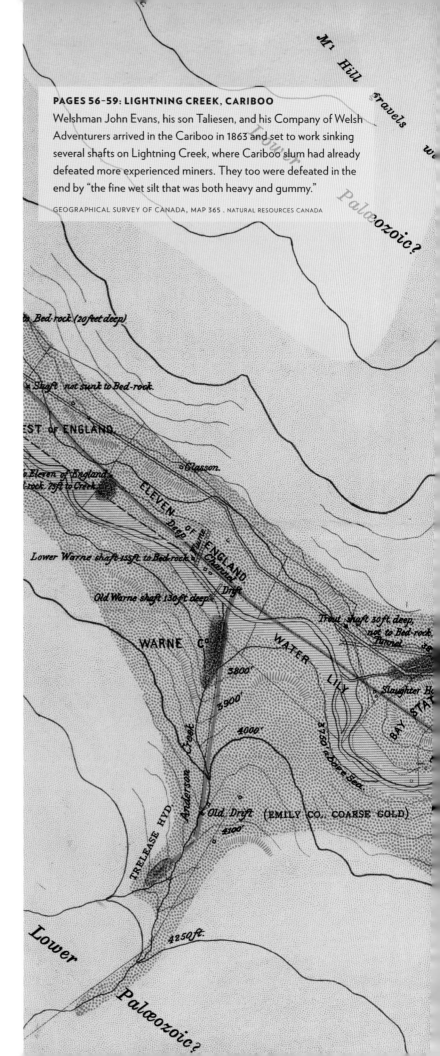

PAGES 56-59: LIGHTNING CREEK, CARIBOO
Welshman John Evans, his son Taliesen, and his Company of Welsh Adventurers arrived in the Cariboo in 1863 and set to work sinking several shafts on Lightning Creek, where Cariboo slum had already defeated more experienced miners. They too were defeated in the end by "the fine wet silt that was both heavy and gummy."

GEOGRAPHICAL SURVEY OF CANADA, MAP 365 . NATURAL RESOURCES CANADA

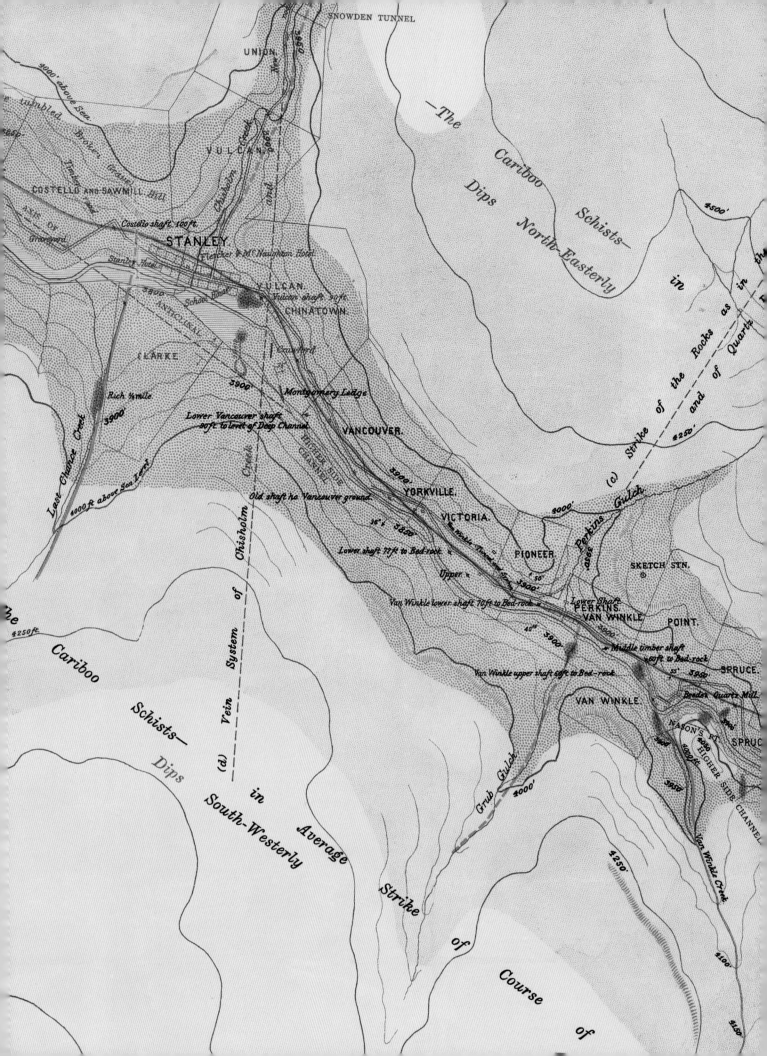

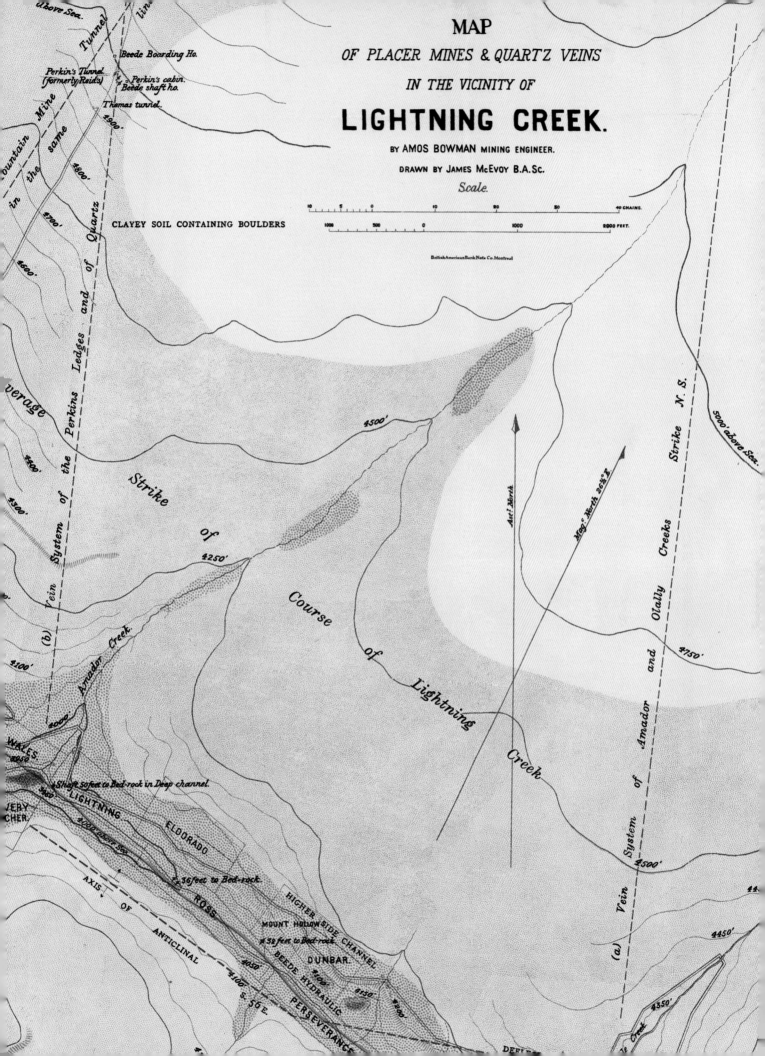

MAP

OF PLACER MINES & QUARTZ VEINS

IN THE VICINITY OF

LIGHTNING CREEK.

BY AMOS BOWMAN MINING ENGINEER.

DRAWN BY JAMES McEVOY B.A.Sc.

Scale.

10 5 0   10   20   30   40 CHAINS.

1000   500   0   1000   2000 FEET.

British American Bank Note Co. Montreal

CLAYEY SOIL CONTAINING BOULDERS

4500'

4250'

Act'l North

Mag: North 26½ E.

Strike N. S.

5000' above Sea.

4750'

Strike of

Course of Lightning Creek

Strike of the Perkins Ledges and of Quartz

Vein System of the

(b)

Amador Creek

Above Sea.

Beede Boarding Ho.

Perkin's Tunnel (formerly Reid's)

Perkin's cabin.
Beede shaft ho.

Thomas tunnel.

4900'

4800'

4700'

4600'

4500'

4400'

4300'

4100'

4000'

WALES.

0950

VERY CHER.

Shaft 50 feet to Bed-rock in Deep channel.

3600

4000' above Sea

LIGHTNING

ELDORADO

ROSS

AXIS OF ANTICLINAL

4050

4100 S. 56 E.

BEEDE HYDRAULIC

PERSEVERANCE

36 feet to Bed-rock.

HIGHER HOLLOW-SIDE CHANNEL

MOUNT

52 feet to Bed-rock

DUNBAR.

4000

4150

4200

Vein System of Amador and Olally Creeks

(a)

4500'

4450'

4350'

Creek

4750'

DEEP

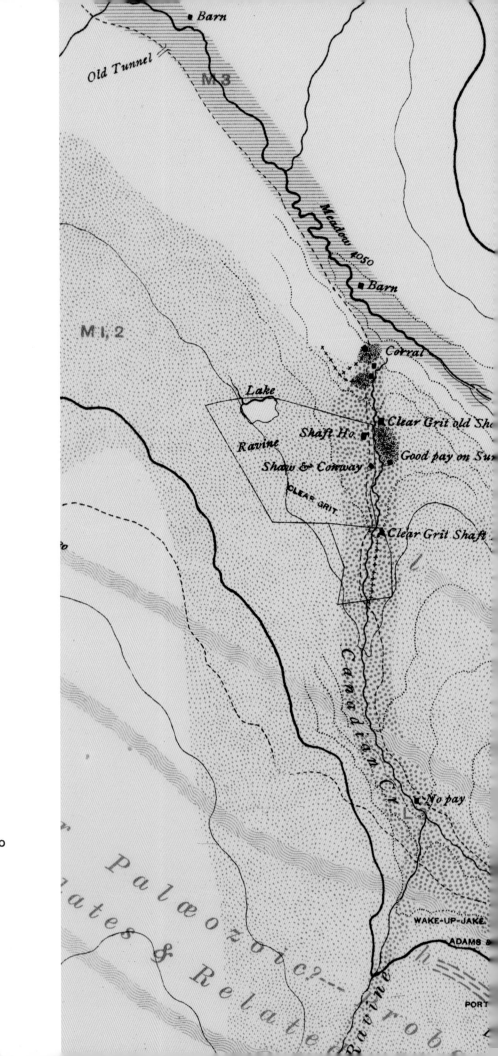

PAGES 60-63: GROUSE CREEK, CARIBOO

GEOLOGICAL SURVEY OF CANADA, MAP 367.
NATURAL RESOURCES CANADA

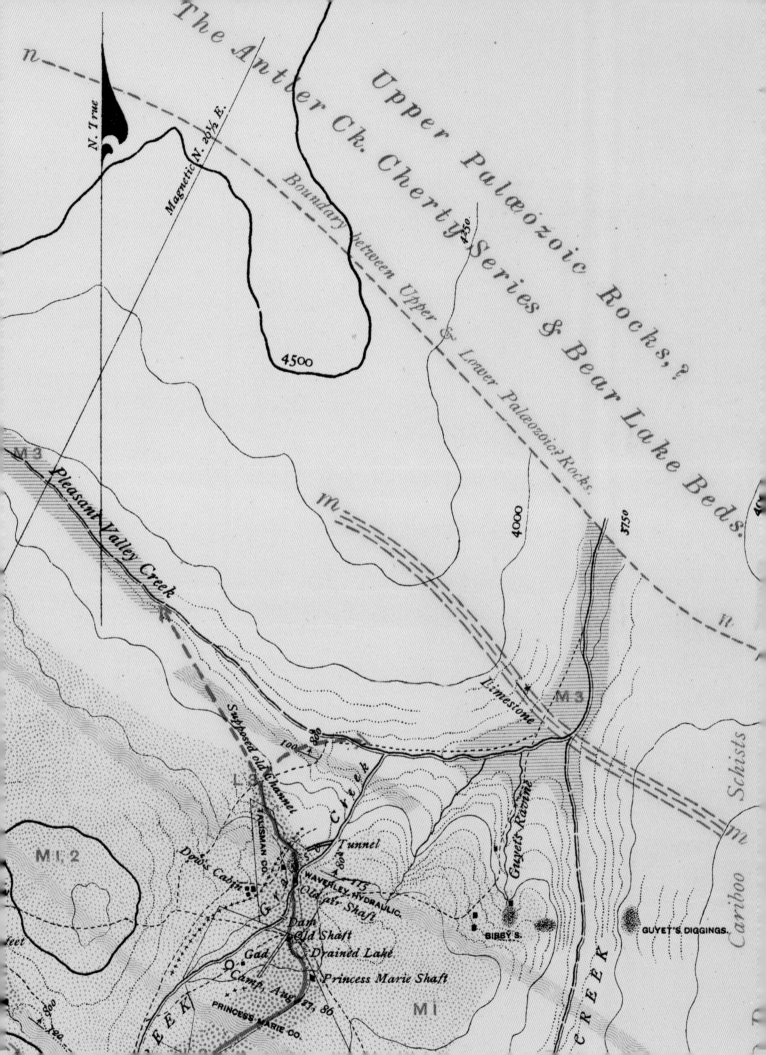

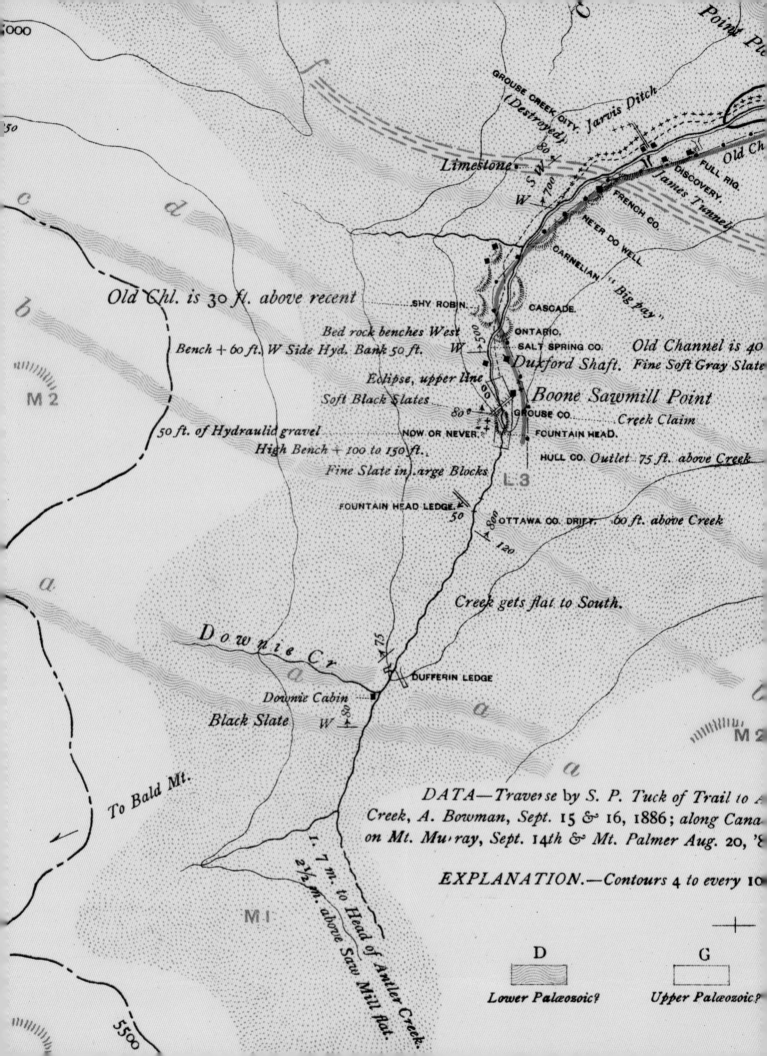

5000

50

GROUSE CREEK CITY. (Destroyed)

Jarvis Ditch

Point Pic

c

d

80

Limestone

S. W.

N. W.

W

700

Jarvis Tunnel

DISCOVERY.

FULL RIG.

Old Ch

FRENCH CO.

NE'ER DO WELL

CARNELIAN "Big Pay"

b

M 2

Old Chl. is 30 ft. above recent

SHY ROBIN.

CASCADE.

500

ONTARIO.

Bed rock benches West

Bench + 60 ft. W Side Hyd. Bank 50 ft.

W

SALT SPRING CO.

Duxford Shaft. Fine Soft Gray Slate

Old Channel is 40

Eclipse, upper line

000

Boone Sawmill Point

Soft Black Slates

80°

GROUSE CO.

Creek Claim

50 ft. of Hydraulic gravel

NOW OR NEVER.

FOUNTAIN HEAD.

High Bench + 100 to 150 ft.

HULL CO. Outlet 75 ft. above Creek

Fine Slate in Large Blocks

L 3

a

FOUNTAIN HEAD LEDGE.

50

800

OTTAWA CO. DRIFT. 60 ft. above Creek

120

Creek gets flat to South.

Downie Cr.

a

75

a

M 2

DUFFERIN LEDGE

Downie Cabin

80

Black Slate

W

a

To Bald Mt.

DATA—Traverse by S. P. Tuck of Trail to

Creek, A. Bowman, Sept. 15 & 16, 1886; along Cana

on Mt. Murray, Sept. 14th & Mt. Palmer Aug. 20, '8

M 1

EXPLANATION.—Contours 4 to every 10

1.7 m. to Head of Antler Creek.

2½ m. above Saw Mill Flat.

5500

D

Lower Palæozoic?

G

Upper Palæozoic?

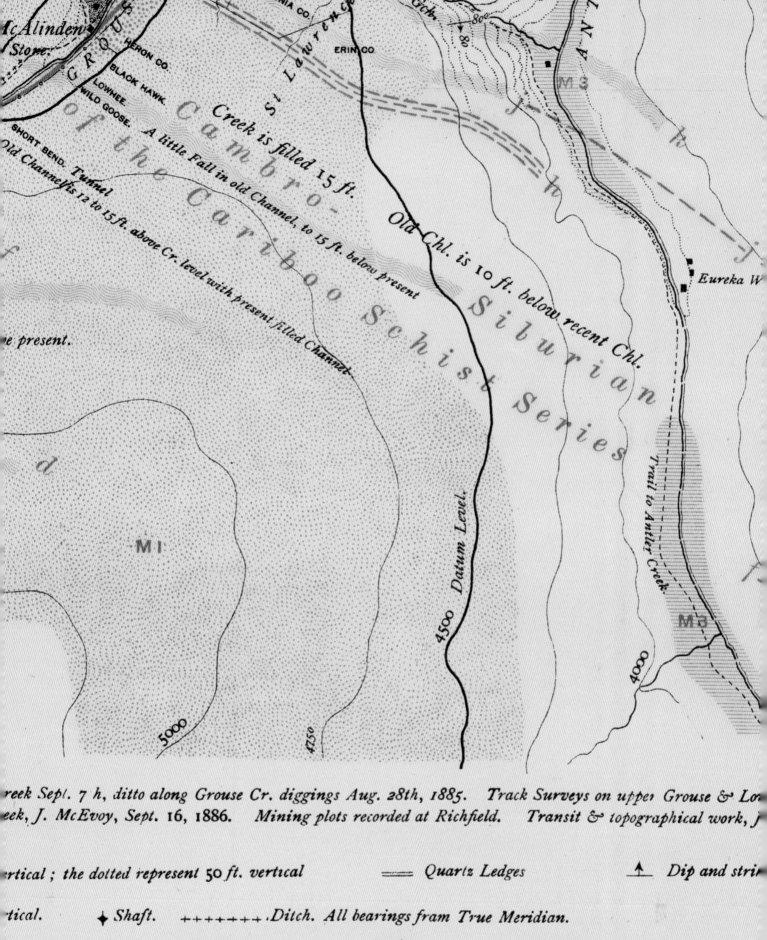

McAlinden
Stone.

GROUSE

HERON CO.

BLACK HAWK.

LOWHEE.

WILD GOOSE.

Cambro-

SHORT BEND. Tunnel

Old Channel is 12 to 15 ft. above Cr. level with present filled Channel

of the Cariboo Schist Series

Creek is filled 15 ft.

A little Fall in old Channel, to 15 ft. below present

St. Lawrence Cb.

ERIN CO

Old Chl. is 10 ft. below recent Chl.

Silurian

e present.

M 1

5000

4750

4500 Datum Level.

M 3

Eureka W

Trail to Antler Creek

M 3

4000

reek Sept. 7 h, ditto along Grouse Cr. diggings Aug. 28th, 1885.   Track Surveys on upper Grouse & Lo
eek, J. McEvoy, Sept. 16, 1886.   Mining plots recorded at Richfield.   Transit & topographical work, j

rtical; the dotted represent 50 ft. vertical

━━━ Quartz Ledges

↑ Dip and stri

tical.   ◆ Shaft.   ╉╉╉╉╉ Ditch. All bearings from True Meridian.

F	L³	M¹ & ²	M³
Limestone	Pliocene & Pre-glacial areas, bluffs and gutters.	Pleistocene areas and Terraces.	Recent Alluvium, &c.

•—•—• High Channel.   o—o—o Deep Cha

A group of miners pose proudly with the tools of the underground gold-mining trade at the Alturas Gold Mining Company on Stout's Gulch, Lowhee Creek, in 1868. Their tools included picks, broadaxes, gold pans, rubber boots, five-pronged forks, crosscut saws, and tool sharpeners. Two men are partially hidden by the rooftop of the main structure, while another sits on the roof over the main shaft. The fourteen people in the front row include two women, two children, and a baby, on the extreme right. Above, a man with a sharpening tool can be seen.

TOOLS OF THE GOLD-MINING TRADE

RICHFIELD

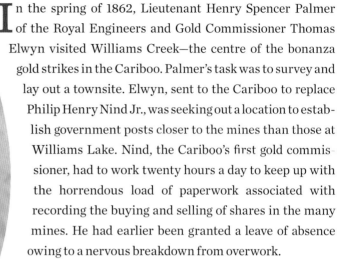

In the spring of 1862, Lieutenant Henry Spencer Palmer of the Royal Engineers and Gold Commissioner Thomas Elwyn visited Williams Creek—the centre of the bonanza gold strikes in the Cariboo. Palmer's task was to survey and lay out a townsite. Elwyn, sent to the Cariboo to replace Philip Henry Nind Jr., was seeking out a location to establish government posts closer to the mines than those at Williams Lake. Nind, the Cariboo's first gold commissioner, had to work twenty hours a day to keep up with the horrendous load of paperwork associated with recording the buying and selling of shares in the many mines. He had earlier been granted a leave of absence owing to a nervous breakdown from overwork.

Elwyn assessed the situation and recommended that the Cariboo be divided into two districts, with a gold commissioner serving each. Governor Douglas agreed and appointed Elwyn to serve the section where most of the activity was taking place, while Peter O'Reilly, previously of the Similkameen, was assigned to the other. The miners liked Elwyn's good judgements in settling mining disputes, and for a time it seemed that the twenty business establishments along the creek might be called Elwyntown. Palmer vetoed the idea and chose the more appropriate name of Richfield, for the riches being brought from the ground.

A letter written at Williams Creek by Elwyn to the colonial secretary in England gives some idea of the fabulous strikes being made in the Cariboo. It read:

> *At Antler five hundred men are preparing to mine but only a few companies are actually at work. There will be, I am satisfied, over one thousand men employed on the creek, and the yield of gold for this season will nearly equal the yield of the whole of the Cariboo last summer. Claims have been taken up on the creek and on the banks for a distance of two miles that will pay $40 to $100 a day to the hand.*
>
> *I paid five shillings per pound for flour and six shillings per pound for bacon at the town of Antler (considered of little importance last year).*
>
> *On my way from Antler to this place I passed within two-and-a-half miles from the mouth of Grouse Creek, but my*

LIEUTENANT HENRY SPENCER PALMER (1838–93)

Palmer came to BC as a Royal Engineer in 1858 and was credited with undertaking several exploratory surveys, laying out trails, and inspecting the construction of the Cariboo Wagon Road. He was also credited with laying out the townsite of Richfield and supervising the construction of government buildings. After leaving the province and retiring from the Royal Engineers, Palmer headed to Japan, where he was hired by the Japanese government to help with the development of Yokohama Harbour. A sculpted bust of Palmer stands in Yokohama's Nogeyama Park, circa 1980.

HISTORICAL PHOTO A-01702, ROYAL BC MUSEUM AND ARCHIVES

presence was so urgently required here that, fearing a delay of some days, I did not go up this creek.

The yield from Williams Creek is something almost incredible and the rich claims have risen to three times their market value of last year. Only six companies are at present taking out gold, but there are between five and six hundred men on the creek, sinking shafts and getting their claims into working order. Cunningham and Company have been working their claims for the past six weeks, and for the last thirty days have been taking out gold at the rate of three thousand dollars every twenty-four hours. In the tunnel owned by this company the average prospect is thirty-five ounces to the set. Messrs. Steele and Company have been engaged for the past ten days making a flume, but during the previous three weeks their claims yielded two hundred ounces a day. These figures are so startling that I should be afraid to put them on paper in a report for his Excellency's information were I not on the spot and know them to be the exact truth.

There is every possibility that before the end of the season there will be fifteen to twenty companies on the creek, the yield of whose claims will equal those mentioned above.

There are at present no provisions for sale here; but the prices hitherto have been about the same as at Antler Creek.

I expect to be detained here for five or six days settling disputes, after which I will go to Lightning Creek.

A great many men, principally Canadians, are returning below. They are as a rule entirely ignorant of mining and came here with a few pounds of provisions on their backs and hardly any money. Considering the exorbitant prices … I have that His Excellency will give consent to Mr. Hankin and my constable receiving some extra allowances, or an increase in salary.

The provisions situation eased dramatically when several cattle drovers from Oregon brought meat "on

THOMAS ELWYN (1837–88)
Elwyn was an early gold commissioner at Richfield on Williams Creek in the Cariboo in 1862. The early miners were so impressed with Elwyn's decisions regarding mining disputes that they wanted to name the town Elwyntown rather than Richfield in his honour. In 1861 he was put in charge of the government gold escorts from the Cariboo to Yale.

HISTORICAL PHOTO F-03767, ROYAL BC MUSEUM AND ARCHIVES

the hoof" to the diggings. The mixed herds of dairy and beef cattle were driven through the mining towns and up into the mountains to good pasture to fatten. On the top of the mountain (afterward called Cow Mountain), corrals, stables, and herdsmen's quarters were erected, and very soon fresh milk was being delivered to the various settlements on Williams Creek. Each day, beef animals were taken down to the mining communities for butchering to provide fresh steaks for the miners.

The gold the miners obtained presented a problem because it required constant vigilance. To help the miners, the government organized a gold escort to

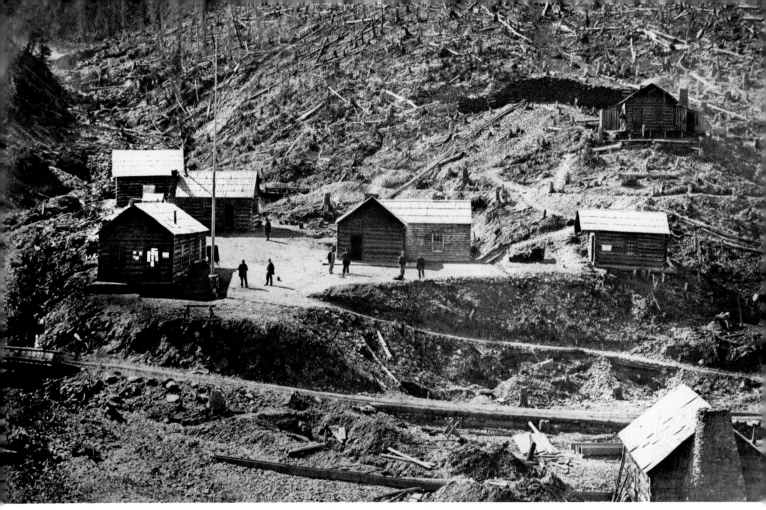

Lieutenant Henry Spencer Palmer supervised the construction of the government buildings in Richfield in 1862.

carry the burdensome booty to the coast for a small fee. Unfortunately, they did not guarantee safe delivery, and rumour quickly circulated that a miner once arrived at a stopping house in the wee hours of the morning and saw an unguarded gold wagon, as its escorts were all sound asleep in the roadhouse. Therefore, few miners used the service but chose instead to send the yellow wealth by Barnard's Express. An early newspaper reported:

> *Mr. Barnard has fitted an iron burglar-proof safe into each of his wagons. He has the chests constructed with detonating powder in the interstices between the plates, and on any attempt being made to open them with a chisel, they would inevitably explode with the force of a bombshell. The safes are also fitted with combination locks, known only to the principals at each terminus.*

The gold escort was a real asset for the miners of the Cariboo, as they could now ship their gold to the coast through the Bank of British Columbia. The miners were secure in the knowledge that their hard efforts in wresting the gold from the ground had paid off. Upon reaching Yale, the gold was either kept in a safe overnight at the Oppenheimer store or placed directly onto a steamboat bound for Langley, New Westminster, or Victoria. Old Fort Langley had a 450-kilogram gold safe. The gold was either exchanged for goods going back up to the Cariboo or forwarded to the nearest mint in New Westminster.

NUGGETS FROM THE JOHN B. HOBBS CLAIM ON LOWHEE CREEK

Richfield. Williams Creek. Cariboo.

A HYDRAULIC OPERATION AT THE CORNISH CLAIM AT RICHFIELD

HISTORICAL PHOTO A-03853, ROYAL BC MUSEUM AND ARCHIVES. PHOTO BY FREDERICK DALLY, 1868

ANOTHER VIEW OF RICHFIELD ON WILLIAMS CREEK

A water pipe can be seen in the foreground. The side hills, as with all the other early mining towns, were completely denuded of timber.

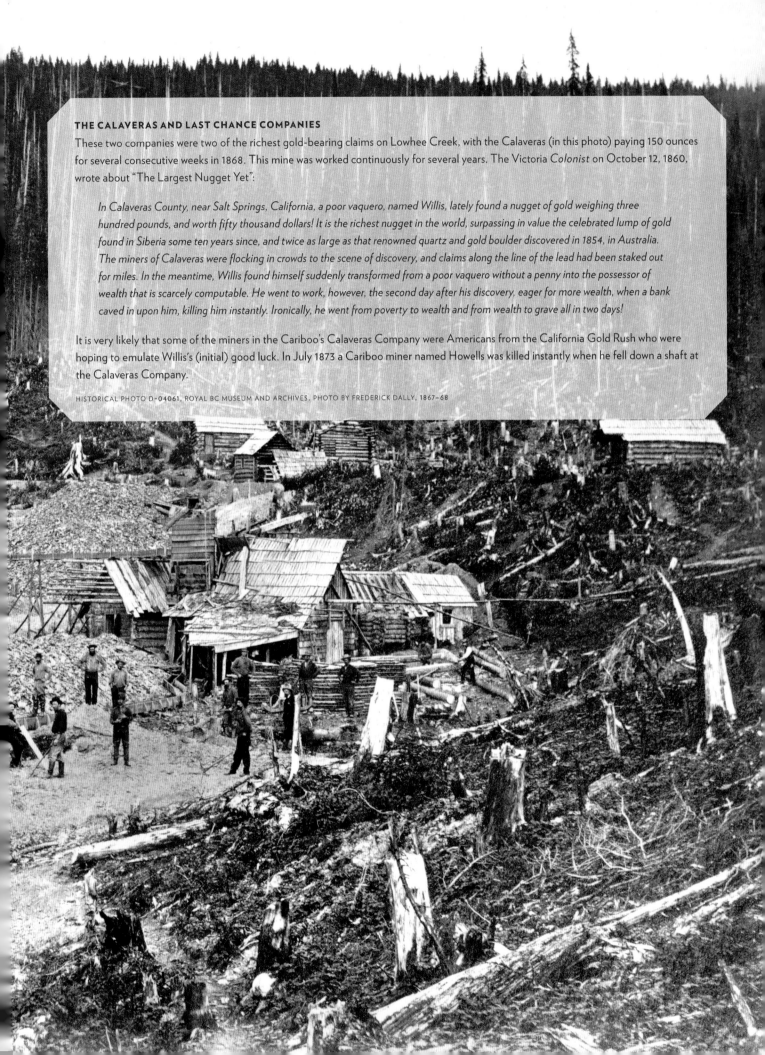

THE CALAVERAS AND LAST CHANCE COMPANIES

These two companies were two of the richest gold-bearing claims on Lowhee Creek, with the Calaveras (in this photo) paying 150 ounces for several consecutive weeks in 1868. This mine was worked continuously for several years. The Victoria *Colonist* on October 12, 1860, wrote about "The Largest Nugget Yet":

> In Calaveras County, near Salt Springs, California, a poor vaquero, named Willis, lately found a nugget of gold weighing three hundred pounds, and worth fifty thousand dollars! It is the richest nugget in the world, surpassing in value the celebrated lump of gold found in Siberia some ten years since, and twice as large as that renowned quartz and gold boulder discovered in 1854, in Australia. The miners of Calaveras were flocking in crowds to the scene of discovery, and claims along the line of the lead had been staked out for miles. In the meantime, Willis found himself suddenly transformed from a poor vaquero without a penny into the possessor of wealth that is scarcely computable. He went to work, however, the second day after his discovery, eager for more wealth, when a bank caved in upon him, killing him instantly. Ironically, he went from poverty to wealth and from wealth to grave all in two days!

It is very likely that some of the miners in the Cariboo's Calaveras Company were Americans from the California Gold Rush who were hoping to emulate Willis's (initial) good luck. In July 1873 a Cariboo miner named Howells was killed instantly when he fell down a shaft at the Calaveras Company.

HISTORICAL PHOTO D-04061, ROYAL BC MUSEUM AND ARCHIVES. PHOTO BY FREDERICK DALLY, 1867–68

BARKERVILLE

BILLY BARKER (1817–94)

The young miner poses for a postcard portrait for a studio photographer in Denver, Colorado. The handsome, mustachioed Billy worked in a silver mine before venturing into the Cariboo District and becoming the name-giver of Barkerville.

BRANWEN P. PATENAUDE

William Barker was a river man from Norfolk, England, who had left behind his wife, Jane, and daughter, Emma, in order to participate in the California gold rush and then later in a silver rush in Denver, Colorado. It was while he was in California that he learned of his wife's passing.

Hearing about the fortunes being made in the Cariboo, Barker arrived on Williams Creek and obtained Free Miner's certificate No. 9 under the new Goldfields Act from Thomas Elwyn, the Cariboo's gold commissioner. He almost immediately registered a claim along the crowded banks of Williams Creek. This claim proved productive, and Barker was able to buy into other claims by selling shares in his own claim. As bad weather started to set in, he joined the hordes of miners who migrated to the more temperate climate of Victoria.

Barker and six other miners headed back to the diggings in the spring of 1862 and in August founded the Barker Company, staking seven claims downriver from Stout's Gulch. Although it has never been proven, rumour had it that Judge Begbie had helped grub-stake the stubborn Englishman. Urged on by Ned Stout, Barker's men kept digging until August 17, 1862, when they struck pay dirt that yielded an ounce of gold for every three pans of dirt at twelve metres (forty feet) below the surface. They had found the gold in a blue clay. They kept digging deeper, and at twenty-four metres (eighty feet) reached bedrock, taking sixty ounces of gold from one tiny crevice. The bedrock of the 30-by-210-metre (100-by-700-foot) rectangle of ground that the seven claims totalled eventually yielded $600,000 in gold at a time when gold was worth $16 an ounce. The rewards from their labours had hardly commenced when winter settled in and all work stopped. Billy, now prosperous, decided to again winter in Victoria and enjoy some much-deserved rest and relaxation. On January 13, 1863, Barker married London widow Elizabeth Collyer. She had arrived from London, England, a short time earlier aboard the ship *Rosedale*.

The following spring, Mrs. Barker accompanied her husband back to the Cariboo. Barkerville, a new town of saloons and stores that had sprung up beside the creek, had been named in honour of Barker, and the town soon touted itself as the largest city west of Chicago and north of San Francisco.

Elizabeth loved the rip-roaring life of the gold-camp towns, where men outnumbered women 250 to 1, and the forty-five-year-

The sheepshead shaft. Williams Creek Cariboo.

THE SHEEPSHEAD COMPANY ON WILLIAMS CREEK

This company was adjacent to the Billly Barker Company. As the ground was uneven, this early photograph clearly shows the cribbing that would have lined the "well," or shaft. The sloped roof provided the men some protection from the rain and sun. The windlass, a type of pulley system, lowered a hand-riveted iron ore bucket down the 1.8-by-1.8-metre- (6-by-6-foot-) diameter well to one or two workmen with pickaxes and shovels, who then filled it with gold-laden gravel to be hauled to the surface. The men in the bottom of the shaft either climbed down a series of ladders or were lowered to the bottom by standing in an ore bucket. It was not uncommon for debris to fall from buckets of dirt back into the hole and onto an unfortunate miner.

A wheelbarrow, shovel, and scoop shovel can be seen at the left-hand side of the shaft. Some of the deeper shafts went down anywhere from twelve to sixty metres (forty to two hundred feet) or more before reaching bedrock.

Two of the men in this photograph are identified by last name only. On the left is Mr. McLehanie; the man in the centre is unidentified, while on the right is Mr. Hance (perhaps Orlando Thomas Hance of Hanceville, in the Chilcotin).

HISTORICAL PHOTO A-02049, ROYAL BC MUSEUM AND ARCHIVES. PHOTO BY FREDERICK DALLY, 1868

THE BARKER COMPANY ON WILLIAMS CREEK

On August 17, 1862, William Barker and his seven partners found rich gold deposits at a depth of twelve metres (forty feet).

BILLY BARKER'S GRAVE MARKER IN VICTORIA'S ROSS BAY CEMETERY

William (Billy) Barker
1817 - 1894

Baptized: March, Cambridgeshire, England
June 7, 1817
Died: Victoria, B.C., Canada
July 11, 1894

On August 17 of 1862, Barker struck gold
at 52 feet on Williams Creek, Cariboo.
The town of Barkerville bears his name.
Like many miners he was soon broke,
but Barker continued to mine and prospect
throughout the Cariboo for the rest of his life.

The fabulous wealth of the Cariboo mines
laid the foundation for British Columbia.
With this monument, Billy Barker is honoured
as a builder of the Province.

He died poor in wealth but forever rich in friends.

old Billy soon found himself competing for her attention with men half his age. In his efforts to please her, Barker allowed his wife a fairly free rein with his money and became one of the biggest spenders in the town's saloons, to the point where he had to hire an ex-fighter to look after him when he became too drunk to look after himself. Their spending habits forced him to occasionally sell off shares in his company.

For a little while, he sold candles to miners of other claims. Meanwhile, the Barker claim began yielding less pay dirt and showed signs of running out of gold completely. Good fortune, it seemed, had turned its back on Billy Barker, and with the aid of a few good friends who "passed the hat" to collect his fare, Billy and his wife boarded a stage and left the Cariboo. He later prospected near Beaver Pass.

Eventually he was offered a job in a government road camp whose workers were upgrading the Cariboo Wagon Road. In his later years, Barker lived at the Dominion Hotel in Clinton. He died in 1894 in Victoria and was buried in the Ross Bay Cemetery.

CARIBOO CAMERON'S STORY

John Angus Cameron's rags-to-riches-to-pauperism story is undoubtedly the most bizarre tale to come out of the Cariboo. Cameron was born in 1820 in Lancaster, near Cornwall, in the county of Glengarry, Upper Canada (now Ontario). His father, Angus, was an immigrant farmer who could trace his ancestry to Donald Cameron, chieftain of Lochiel. In his youth, John worked on a farm for an uncle near Summerstown on the St. Lawrence River. He hated farming and by 1852 had reached the goldfields of California. His two brothers, Roderick and Allan, followed two years later, and all three worked the diggings in California for the next seven years.

In 1859, John Cameron returned home to marry fiancée Margaret Sophia Groves, who lived in the nearby town of Wales. Soon after the wedding, the couple returned to California, where John overextended his resources to construct a flume to bring water to an already exhausted mine. Before long he was broke and his wife was pregnant. It was during this period that he heard about the fabulous gold discoveries of the Cariboo. In the spring of 1862, John, his wife, and daughter Alice set off for British Columbia along with 750 other passengers aboard the sidewheeler *Brother Jonathan*. By the time they reached Victoria, their child was critically ill and they were down to their last $40. Their circumstances were desperate, but the final blow came five days later when Alice died. It was during these bad times that Cameron cemented his lifelong friendship with Robert Stevenson. It came as a surprise to both of them that they had been born and raised only a few kilometres from each other and were now about to cast their lot together in life.

When news of the Fraser River gold discoveries first reached Glengarry, Bob Stevenson was a young lad working on his father's small farm at Vankleek Hill. In March 1862, father and son left the farm and travelled through New York State to catch an Atlantic ship bound for Panama. The two later took another ship from San Francisco destined for BC. Shortly after their arrival, the senior Stevenson decided to return home, but the son, finding the Fraser River prospects rather dull, joined an expedition of Americans who were heading off for the exciting new gold discoveries at Rock Creek in the Similkameen country of southern BC. Instead of prospecting, Bob Stevenson took a government job as a customs officer. He quit his $250-a-month position after homeward-bound Americans told him about the incredible gold discoveries being made in the Cariboo. The shrewd youth, learning that pack animals were in great demand in the gold country, bought a hundred horses that he drove as far as Lillooet. He netted a handsome profit of $10,000 from this venture. He then proceeded to Antler, where he purchased a supply store before deciding to come out to Victoria for the harsh winter.

He was staying in the Royal Hotel in Victoria when he met Cameron. He liked the big Scotsman and agreed

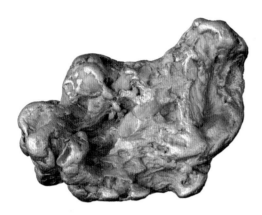

A STEVENSON CREEK NUGGET
A great deal of quartz indicates that this specimen was found not far from the motherlode.

CANADIAN MUSEUM OF NATURE, 10424

MINING CANDLE
Used by miners to stick into a shaft wall or to shore up timbers for the purpose of holding a candle in a spring clip, this gadget permitted a miner to work underground with hands free in the dark and dank deep mines.

ROSSLAND HERITAGE MUSEUM AND ARCHIVES

to put up the security for $2,000 worth of goods that Cameron was to pack to the Cariboo. Stevenson left for the diggings in April, and upon reaching Antler engaged in the commission business, advancing money to packers and getting 10 percent for selling their goods. By the time Cameron and his wife arrived there in July, Stevenson had cleared another $11,000 on this new venture. Among the goods that Cameron brought in were boxes of candles. Stevenson took them around to several mining companies and was able to get a hundred dollars for a nine-kilogram (twenty-pound) box.

Nails sold for $5 per pound in a 100-pound keg; butter for $5 per pound; wax matches for $1.50 per box; a five-pound bag of salt for $7.50; flour for $2 per pound, when there was any; and potatoes for $115 per hundred-pound sack. The inflation of these prices was incredible, considering that in eastern Canada, the average labourer earned a dollar a day. Stevenson sold his store at Antler, and immediately after disposing of most of his supplies headed for Williams Lake, intent on purchasing shares in a gold mine.

Stevenson purchased a one-fifth share in Barker's claim before being tipped off by Dr. Samuel Crane about some good vacant ground below the Billy Barker Company. It was this piece of land that eight partners staked in August. This new company originally consisted of Stevenson, Crane, Cameron and his wife, Allan MacDonald (Ranald's half-brother), Richard Rivers, and Overlander brothers Charles and Richard Glendinning.

When staking, Cameron and Stevenson disagreed over the location, but Stevenson finally gave in to his older partner, and as a result Henry Beatty and John Wilson were able to acquire the neighbouring ground. Beatty's Tinker claim yielded almost as much gold as the Cameron claim, and Beatty returned to Toronto to invest his booty in shipbuilding. He went on to become a millionaire. His son, Edward W. Beatty, became the president of the Canadian Pacific Railway from 1918 until his death in 1943.

John Wilson left Yorkshire, England, at the age of seventeen and spent two years working as a farm hand in Logansport, Indiana. He then participated for five to six years in the California rush on the American and Russian Rivers before going on to Petaluma. He mined Fraser River bars before pressing upriver to the Cariboo. Wilson took his nuggets and went with a man named Lewis Campbell to Oregon, where he purchased a good-sized herd of cattle that they drove over the mountains and back to Kamloops. This was the beginning of the stock that later increased to such proportions that Wilson became known as the "Cattle King."

John Cameron and Sophia Groves at the time of their marriage at Cornwall, Ontario.

HISTORICAL PHOTOS D-07951 AND D-07952, ROYAL BC MUSEUM AND ARCHIVES

Wilson married three times, each wife bearing him three children. Unfortunately, Wilson's third wife, when widowed, married his bookkeeper, who mismanaged the very large estate. Subsequently, most of the family fortune vanished.

After staking their ground, Cameron and his partners sat down for a naming ceremony. Dr. Crane suggested it be named after Stevenson, but Stevenson objected and proposed that it be named for his friend Cameron. Each partner was given an equal share in the company. Crane soon afterward got into a barroom brawl in which he drew a gun and took a potshot at an antagonist. Judge Elwyn sentenced him to thirty days in jail and a heavy

fine. Crane's partners did not approve of his actions and asked him to sell his share in the company.

Shortly after her arrival in July, Mrs. Cameron had given birth to a second daughter, but the child was still-born. She never fully recovered from the ordeal, and in the first week of September she became critically ill. Her husband spent all of his time at their cabin in Richfield trying to nurse her back to health.

During this time, the two Glendinning brothers, Rivers, and Stevenson began work on a shaft, but it flooded at nearly seven metres (twenty-two feet) and on the September 22, it collapsed. By now there was snow, and the Glendinning brothers, thoroughly

ROBERT STEVENSON, JOHN CAMERON'S PARTNER

In this formal portrait, Stevenson is wearing three nuggets for stud earrings.

CITY OF VANCOUVER ARCHIVES, 677-674

discouraged, refused to continue work or leave any funds for the sinking of a new hole. Instead, they called it quits and departed for the milder climate of Victoria.

Mrs. Cameron's condition worsened, and she died on October 23. Her death was attributed to typhoid fever. Two days after the funeral, Rivers and Stevenson began sinking two separate shafts, but after a few days Rivers abandoned his and came over to help his associate. At four metres (fourteen feet), they hit water and had to hire carpenters to build a flume to divert the creek water away from the shaft. Stevenson's memoirs best tell what happened next:

> On 22 December we struck it very rich at 22 feet. It was 30 below and Dick Rivers was in the shaft, and Halfpenny and I were on the windlass. Rivers called up from the shaft: "The place is yellow with gold. Look here boys," at the same time holding up a flat rock the size of a dinner plate. I laid down on the platform and peered into the shaft. I could see the gold standing out on the rock as he held it. He sent the piece up and I got one ounce of gold.
>
> Then Cameron started down the shaft, and while he was down I took my pick and went through some of the frozen stuff that had been sent up that morning and got another ounce before he came up again. Out of three 12-gallon kegs of gravel I got $155 worth of gold.
>
> Sinking, we found bedrock at 38 feet. It was good all the way down to there, but the richest was at 22 feet, strange to say.

Although the partners had perhaps the richest claim in the Cariboo, little could be done to get the gold out of the ground until the spring thaw. Cameron, haunted by a deathbed promise to return the bodies of his wife and infant daughter back to Ontario, decided to leave the diggings and take his wife's body to Victoria, where his first daughter was buried. Cameron approached Charles C. Hankin, Judge Elwyn's ex-assistant and a shareholder in the Billy Barker Company, and offered him part interest in his company for a fifty-pound sack of gold. Thus enriched, John offered any of the ninety men wintering on the creek $12 per day plus a bonus of $2,000 to assist him in transporting Sophia's body to Victoria.

On January 31, 1863, Cameron and Stevenson left Williams Creek on snowshoes, hauling a toboggan into which was roped the casket containing Sophia's remains. Twenty miners volunteered to help them over the worst section of the trail, and they spent eleven days travelling the 116 kilometres (72 miles) to Beaver Lake. From

here, Cameron and Stevenson went on alone. At Lac la Hache, Cameron bought a horse for $300 to haul the toboggan. The harsh winter claimed the life of this horse and also the next, so a third horse was needed for the last leg of the journey over the Douglas Trail. At Williams Lake, Stevenson counted 120 First Nations snow graves, the result of a recent smallpox epidemic. The road leading into Port Douglas was lined on each side with tents containing dead or dying Natives, and only one in ten of those dying could hope to be spared.

At Port Douglas the men caught the little steamer *Henrietta* to New Westminster and from there took the seagoing vessel *Enterprise* to Victoria, thus completing their epic 965-kilometre (600-mile) journey. Cameron immediately arranged to have his

wife's body preserved in alcohol and interred temporarily with her daughter in the Quadra Cemetery. This, Mrs. Cameron's second burial, was attended by eight hundred miners who were wintering over in the island city.

On March 19, the two men left Victoria on horseback, and were back at Williams Creek on April 4. While in Victoria, Cameron had wired his family about the death of his wife and the rich strike. He requested that his brothers, Roderick and Allan, join him at the diggings.

It was during the months of July, August, and September that the Cameron Company yielded up its enormous hoard of nuggets. Since Cameron could not legally hold more than one claim, he asked James Cummings to stand proxy for him on a second mining interest. During these hectic months, Cameron employed seventy-five men to work around-the-clock shifts. The community that housed the miners first acquired the name Cameron's Town, but this was later shortened to Camerontown.

It was during this period that pneumonia took one of his men. Peter Gibson, from Stevenson's hometown of Vankleek Hill, died on July 24; he was thirty-one years old.

On October 22, 1863, two British tourists, Dr. Walter Butler Cheadle and Viscount William Fitzwilliam Milton, visited the goldfields after crossing the prairies and Rockies. On their trip into the mines from Quesnel Mouth, Dr. Cheadle wrote in his diary:

> *We met a small bullock wagon escorted by about 20 men on foot. This proved to contain 630 pounds of gold, the profits of Mr. Cameron, and the principal shareholder in the noted Cameron claim. The gold, worth about 30,000 pounds, had been amassed in the short space of three months and represents less than one-half of the actual production of the mine during that time.*

Upon reaching the diggings, the visitors were given a tour of the shaft. Dr. Cheadle described this in his diary:

> *The shaft was about 30 feet down through gravel and clay to bedrock of slate.* [There were] *numerous shafts all supported by timber and very closely roofed in with flat crosspieces.* [It was] *wet, damp, dark and gloomy, the shafts* [drifts] *being in many parts very low, the pay dirt not being extensive perpendicularly.*
>
> *They kindly helped us wash out two pans that yielded*

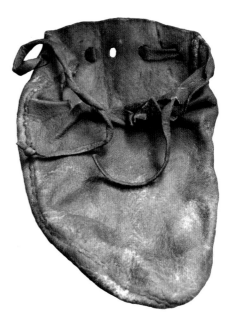

A MUCH-USED LEATHER GOLD POUCH
WERNER KASCHEL

OPPOSITE—CAMERON CLAN, CIRCA 1867
Standing, left to right: Robert Stevenson, Samuel Montgomery. Seated, left to right: Allan, John Cameron, Roderick Cameron.

HISTORICAL PHOTO G-03767, ROYAL BC MUSEUM AND ARCHIVES

ABOVE

A sculpture of John Cameron, at Cameron's home, Fairview House, in Summerstown, Ontario.

AUTHOR PHOTO

BELOW

The intertwining initials "J.A.C." above the main entrance to John Cameron's house in Summerstown, Ontario.

AUTHOR PHOTO

some beautiful gold to the value of $21, nearly 1⅓ ounces. We could see nuggets lying in the gravel before loosening out by the pick. Steele showed me about $1,000 in gold in a bag, and the company's books, showed weekly expenses averaging $7,000 and the yield generally from 40 to 112 ounces per shift, of which there were three per day, or on to $29,000 a week. Over 100 feet of claim yet quite untouched.

Immediately after the cleanup, Cameron, henceforth known as "Cariboo" Cameron, left the Cariboo for Victoria and arranged to have his wife's and daughter's remains exhumed from the Quadra Cemetery. The three Cameron brothers and Stevenson then took the casket and their gold and embarked on the first ship heading south. The men accompanied their strange cargo down the California coast, across the Isthmus of Panama, and then took another ship up the Atlantic coast to New York. From here, they took a train to Ontario, arriving back in Glengarry just before Christmas. A few days into the New Year, Mrs. Cameron was buried for the third time, with Cameron refusing to permit a viewing of the body. Stevenson, a short time later, returned to the Cariboo.

Cameron bought his uncle's farm at Summerstown, where he built a showpiece home called Fairfield in 1865. He then married Christina Emma Woods, a daughter of John R. Woods, who operated a large foundry and machine shop at Lunenburg. Christina was twenty-two years his junior.

For the next ten years, rumours circulated that the casket Cameron had brought home did not contain the body of his wife, and in 1873 a New York newspaper came out with a story claiming that Cameron had taken his wife into the wilds of northern BC and sold her to a wealthy Native chief for a large sum of gold that was placed in the casket. To stop the gossip, Cameron was forced to exhume the body for a third time for a public viewing. When the lid was removed, the dead woman's mother recognized the almost perfectly preserved face of her daughter. Under her head was a woollen shawl that had been given to her as a wedding present by a sister and had been bought at a local store. After the viewing, Cameron instructed the gravediggers to pour off the alcohol before placing the coffin back in the ground, giving his wife a fourth, and thankfully final, burial.

A short time later, many of Cameron's investments began to sour as none of his gold properties in Ontario, Quebec, or Nova Scotia ever paid dividends, but the final blow came when a disgruntled employee set fire to his uninsured sawmill on Lake Superior that held two million board feet of dressed lumber. By 1885, Cameron had lost his entire fortune. In 1886, he returned to BC on the newly completed Canadian Pacific Railway to visit his old chum Stevenson and to return to the Cariboo to seek a second fortune. This time Lady Luck failed to smile on the old prospector, and he died in a hotel at Barkerville in 1888 at the age of sixty-eight. He was buried in the cemetery he had founded twenty-five years earlier. His second wife, who accompanied him out to the Cariboo, moved to Chicago, Illinois, and then later to Vancouver, BC, where she remained until her death in the 1920s.

Robert Stevenson, Cameron's partner, remained in the Cariboo until 1876, when he opted to try his luck in the Cassiar goldfields. The following year, he purchased 160 hectares (400 acres) of prime farmland at Sardis (near Chilliwack) in

Sophia Cameron's grave at Summerstown, near Cornwall, Ontario.

JOHN WILSON (1833-1904)

Wilson, an early partner in the Cameron Claim, later became known as the "Cattle King" in Kamloops.

ASHCROFT MUSEUM

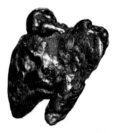

Rust-coloured nugget recovered from the Cariboo Cameron Claim is on permanent display at the Royal BC Museum in Victoria.

AUTHOR PHOTO

the Fraser Valley before marrying Caroline Eliza Williams with the intention of settling down. Unable to get mining out of his system, he staked seventy square kilometres (twenty-seven square miles) of coal lands in the Princeton area of the Similkameen but was not able to interest James Dunsmuir, the coal magnate in Victoria, into developing the lands. He also staked claims near Osoyoos, a small community directly south of Kelowna, close to the Canada–US border. One of Stevenson's wishes in later life was to have his partner's body exhumed from the Barkerville cemetery for a final burial beside his first wife at Summerstown. Stevenson died in 1922 before he could complete this last favour to his partner.

Brothers James and William Wattie returned to Williams Creek in the spring of 1863 and purchased the claim adjoining the Cameron Company. The claim was successful and was incorporated with the Cameron Company and came to be known as the Wattie and Cameron Company. In 1884, James left for his home in Huntington, Quebec, where he operated a woollen mill for several years before selling it to the Montreal Cotton Company. He retired in 1890 and died in 1907. William returned home in 1865 to resume his trade as a machinist. He later became superintendent of Knowles Loom Works, in Worchester, Massachusetts, during which time he invented and patented over sixty devices relating to weaving machinery. A world traveller, he revisited the Cariboo on a sentimental journey in 1893.

THE OVERLANDERS

The Douglas Trail and the Cariboo Wagon Road were the most feasible, but they were not the only means of reaching the goldfields. About 250 gold seekers trekked overland in several parties from Ontario and other eastern parts of Canada through the Rockies. Brothers Thomas and Robert McMicking, from Stamford Township, Welland County, led one group of so-called Overlanders from Upper Canada to the BC interior, responding to an invitation from the Reverend Robert C. Brown, the Anglican rector at Lillooet. The first parties arrived at Quesnel Mouth in the fall of 1862. Once in the Cariboo goldfields, these brave pioneers planned to help transform the area from wilderness to settled homeland.

The main parties had set out from Upper and Lower Canada (Ontario and Quebec) in the spring of 1862 and travelled by rail and by steamer across the US, then crossed up into Canada south of Fort Garry (Winnipeg). Here they paid $8 each for Red River carts, $40 a head for horses, $25 to $30 for oxen, and $4 for a set for harnesses before continuing fourteen hundred kilometres (900 miles) over open prairie to Fort Edmonton. One party left Fort Garry on June 2 and travelled in 97 carts with 110 animals, most of which were slow-plodding oxen whose speed was only 4 kilometres (2.5 miles) an hour. They averaged 40 kilometres (25 miles) a day and reached Fort Edmonton July 21.

Here the carts were sold and the supplies loaded on the backs of oxen and horses. At the Rocky Mountain foothills, progress slowed to sixteen kilometres (ten miles) or less a day. The food gave out, and the Overlanders had to live on chipmunk, squirrel, porcupine, berries, and whatever else they could scrounge up. They even had to kill some of their horses and oxen for food before they met Aboriginal people with whom they bartered for fish. Before leaving the mountains, the party split up. The majority wanted to head southward to the Thompson River and Kamloops, while the rest decided to come down the Fraser River to Quesnel Mouth and the goldfields. Included in the first group was the only woman, Catherine O'Hare Schubert, her husband August, and their three children. Although several men drowned and the entire party suffered extreme hardships, Mrs. Schubert reached Kamloops, where she immediately gave birth to a daughter. Schubert Drive in Kamloops is named after this Overlander family.

To those Overlanders travelling the Fraser to Quesnel Mouth, the most dangerous obstacle was a huge canyon, where the river

This old plaque is located beside the Thompson River beside Highway 5 south of Barriere. It commemorates the men and women who came from Fort Garry (Winnipeg) to Kamloops in 1862. A new plaque, in Kamloops, also acknowledges the feats of these brave pioneers.

AUTHOR PHOTO

A SELF-PORTRAIT BY WILLIAM G.R. HIND (1833–89)

ROYAL BC MUSEUM AND ARCHIVES, PAINTINGS, DRAWINGS AND PRINTS PDP00027

Hind is holding a meerschaum pipe like this one.

YALE MUSEUM. AUTHOR PHOTO

was compressed into a fraction of its normal width. To challenge the river, the parties built twelve-metre- (forty-foot-) wide rafts onto which were loaded the oxen and supplies. One of these rafts was caught in a whirlpool and spun around and around, sinking lower and lower, until only the horns of the oxen could be seen by observers on shore. Luckily, the raft was too large for the suction to pull it completely under, and it emerged safely. Those on the other rafts ran the rapids in safety. Some of the party decided to travel in dugout canoes. This proved to be a disastrous mistake, as the canoes swamped upon entering the water; one man drowned.

These Overlanders arrived at Quesel Mouth on September 11, 1862. Although they were only 96.5 kilometres (60 miles) from the goldfields, the majority of them were too disillusioned and discouraged to care about gold and instead continued on to Victoria. One of the expedition leaders summed up their desperate trip with the wry comment, "Our mining tools were the only articles that we found to be unnecessary."

The Overlanders' walk was extremely dangerous. A smallpox epidemic was rampant and the Chilcotins were now hostile to the white men, who they blamed for the rapid spread of the disease among the Native population. Unconscionable miners had robbed several First Nations graves, taking the HBC blankets in which the corpses had been wrapped and trading them back to the Native people. Thus the highly contagious pestilence spread like wildfire.

British-born painter William George Richardson Hind had immigrated to Canada in 1851. He set out with a party of Overlanders in 1862 from Toronto. During the trip, Hind made himself so obnoxious to his comrades that he was temporarily ostracized from their company. He just couldn't make the other Overlanders understand that his purpose for making the trip was to sketch the journey for posterity. In 1865, Victoria's *Colonist* praised his paintings, which were later placed on display in England to encourage immigration to British Columbia.

OPPOSITE, TOP

Hind's painting, "The Bacon Is Cooked," circa 1862, depicts a miners' cabin on the Fraser River.

PAINTING BY WILLIAM G.R. HIND. MCCORD MUSEUM M5828

OPPOSITE, BOTTOM

This Hind painting, circa 1865, shows a bar in a mining camp.

PAINTING BY WILLIAM G.R. HIND. MCCORD MUSEUM M605

The Overlanders pass through the Rocky Mountains en route to the Cariboo goldfields.

JOHN INNES PAINTING, NATIVE SONS OF BRITISH COLUMBIA POST NO. 2

PROSPECTING FOR ALLUVIAL GOLD IN BRITISH COLUMBIA

Overlander William Hind was noted for a style of painting known as *trompe l'oeil*, involving the use of very realistic imagery to create an optical illusion that makes the depicted objects in the foreground appear three-dimensional. Hind used the technique in this painting of a gold miner panning for alluvial gold in the Cariboo in 1864.

Chinese Miners in the Gold Rush

ABOVE

Overlander William Hind sketched these Chinese miners sluicing for gold on the Fraser River in 1864 but never did a final painting.

ROYAL BC MUSEUM AND ARCHIVES. PAINTINGS, DRAWINGS AND PRINTS, PDP05418

BELOW

A Chinese bamboo hat provided shade for the men as they worked their rockers, seeking gold.

VERNON MUSEUM. AUTHOR PHOTO

A SHORT-HANDLED TIN LADLE FOR POURING WATER INTO A ROCKER

FORT LANGLEY NATIONAL HISTORIC SITE. AUTHOR PHOTO

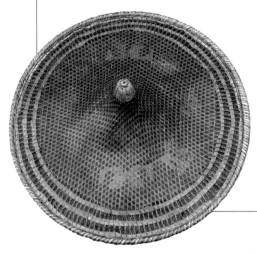

A CHINESE BANJO MADE WITH RATTLESNAKE SKIN

VERNON MUSEUM. AUTHOR PHOTO

CAPTAIN EVANS AND HIS COMPANY
OF WELSH ADVENTURERS

WELSHMAN JOHN EVANS AND HIS SON, TALIESEN
Evans and his Company of Welsh Adventurers arrived in the Cariboo in 1863 and set to work sinking several shafts on Lightning Creek, where Cariboo slum had already defeated more experienced miners.

HISTORICAL PHOTO A-01314, ROYAL BC MUSEUM AND ARCHIVES

Welshman John Evans and his twenty-six-man "Company of Welsh Adventurers" travelled halfway around the world in order to reach the Cariboo diggings in the summer of 1863. Evans's small amount of knowledge about mining had been gained by working for three years in a Welsh slate quarry. Henry Beecroft Jackson, a Manchester industrialist who befriended Evans when the pair worked together in the cotton industry, financed Evans's venture in the Cariboo.

Upon their arrival at the diggings, Evans chose to stake a quarter section (64 hectares, or 160 acres) of ground on Lightning Creek where the infamous Cariboo slum had already defeated more experienced miners. After they levelled some uneven ground on which to pitch their tents, Captain Evans had his men form a circle and bow in silent prayer before initiating the sod-turning ceremony. His men immediately set to work and built a 5.5-by-11-metre (18-by-36-foot) bunkhouse. In a very short period of time, the company had whipsawed several hundred trees, dug drainage ditches, and installed flumes to bring water from half a kilometre away to a shaft site.

On the August 6, the Welsh miners began sinking their shaft. Some of them were assigned the construction of a Cornish wheel and two log pumps. These cumbersome wooden pumps were made from logs that were 3.5 metres (12 feet) long and 41 centimetres (16 inches) in diameter. Each was first drilled lengthwise with an auger and redrilled with a larger auger, made from curved knives, that removed another inch of wood so that the finished hole was fifteen centimetres (six inches) in diameter. The tops and bottoms of these logs were shaped so that they could be mortised one inside the other in order to reach far down into the shaft. To prevent wooden pumps from breaking apart from water pressure, they were generally bound with iron bands, but Evans, in an effort to keep expenses down, omitted the bands. He also refused to buy steel with which to tip his men's picks. Consequently the shaft men working in gravel or hardpan soon blunted their picks, which greatly slowed work. The men became so desperate that they scrounged scrap steel from abandoned sites.

By early October, the Welsh miners had sunk their shaft some nine metres (thirty feet) when water rushed in and drenched the men working at the bottom of the shaft. The two log pumps were put to work but kept splitting and clogging up. At this point, the miners relied on an iron hand pump and old-fashioned bailing by bucket and windlass. Although they worked continuously day and night, the cold water kept pouring into the shaft. To prevent the shaft from being totally flooded, the men quickly constructed a third pump, but Evans ordered a halt to the work until after the Sabbath before it could be installed. The men were sure all would be lost, especially since the nights were getting colder and Evans would not even allow further work to divert water away from the water wheel to keep it from coating up with ice. On Monday, work was to be resumed, but that Sunday night the waterwheel became so heavy with ice and snow that it simply fell apart under its own weight. Work on the shaft ceased until spring.

The men repaired the machinery during these winter months and also started work on several tunnels in other areas of their claim. Captain Evans, upset by the financial disaster he was faced with, decided to cut expenses—this time on the company food, by reducing the menu to little more than beans. This "prison diet" was the final straw for the disgruntled Welsh miners, and they approached Evans with an ultimatum: the rules would be changed to suit the men, or they would all leave. The furious captain jumped to his feet and told the men that they all knew where the trail was and pointed to the door. Every man, including Evans's own son, Talieson, was outside in seconds. Captain Evans quickly followed and begged them to stay, agreeing to their terms.

By early January, the men of the Company of Welsh Adventurers were striking "coloured" ground, but they were becoming sick. Evans's first thought was that they had rheumatism, but a passing prospector informed them that it was scurvy and delighted Captain Evans by telling him that the cure could be found right outside the door. The prospector instructed them to boil spruce branches and drink the resulting "tea," and without spending a single penny for medicine, Evans soon had all the men back in good health and back to work.

Although the men had been able to stockpile much pay dirt from the tunnels, they had to wait until spring to wash it to separate the gold from the tailings.

When spring arrived, they continued their efforts to successfully sink another shaft on Lightning Creek but were again defeated. Lightning Creek, meanwhile, had provided the companies upstream from the Welsh miners with deposits of gold, with one particular nugget weighing over close to a kilogram (thirty ounces). By fall, the men had concluded that Evans was a loser because of his bull-headedness and inexperience with mining in the Cariboo, and so they dissolved the company. Theirs was not the only failure on Lightning Creek, as Cariboo slum was the bane and defeat of many companies that struggled to get the gold that lay on the creek's bedrock.

A BARREL OF CRANBERRIES

Cranberries were a most valuable commodity to the miners of the Cariboo; they provided much-needed vitamin C, which prevented scurvy. Miners who could not afford cranberries could get the vitamin by drinking tea made by boiling spruce boughs.

FORT LANGLEY NATIONAL HISTORIC SITE. AUTHOR PHOTO

John Evans went to work a claim on Davis Creek, a tributary of Lightning Creek, and was hired on as a surveyor by several mining companies. In the summer of 1875, the government requested that he write up a report and draw a map of the mining claims on Lightning Creek. This map was done so well that it was considered the best in the Cariboo. That fall, Evans was elected to the BC legislative assembly as the representative for the Cariboo District. In 1877, he married Catherine Jones, who became his third wife; he had already been married and widowed twice. Catherine brought him great happiness. Two years later, he was re-elected to the legislature and remained an MLA until he died in 1879. Remembered by all as a man who was honest and forthright, he was greatly respected for having the courage to always express what he believed was right. He was buried in the Stanley, BC, cemetery, close to where his Company of Welsh Adventurers had established their camp on Lightning Creek.

OPPOSITE—A MAP DRAWN BY JOHN EVANS SHOWING SOME OF THE RICHEST GOLD-BEARING CLAIMS IN THE WORLD, BELOW BARKERVILLE

UNIVERSITY OF BRITISH COLUMBIA RARE BOOKS AND SPECIAL COLLECTIONS, MAPS G_3514_B37_H36_BARKERVILLE

Harry Jones, one of the Company of Welsh Adventurers, brought some of the members of the original group to successfully run this operation.

THE BURNING OF BARKERVILLE

FREDERICK DALLY (1838–1914)

Dally, the official photographer to Governor Arthur Kennedy, visited the Cariboo goldfields in 1867 and 1868. He had his own studio in Barkerville, but it, like the rest of the town, went up in flames on September 16, 1868. Dally afterward sold his photography business and decided to become a dentist in the US. He eventually returned to Staffordshire in England. Dally, who is wearing his Masonic regalia in this photo, took the majority of the photographs that appear in the Cariboo gold rush section of this book.

HISTORICAL PHOTO B-00883, ROYAL BC MUSEUM AND ARCHIVES. PHOTO BY HENRY JOSEPH WHITLOCK AND SON LTD., BIRMINGHAM, ENGLAND, CIRCA 1888

Frederick Dally, one of Barkerville's photographers, composed the only known written account of the great Barkerville fire of September 16, 1868:

The eve of the great fire of Barkerville was remarkable for the grandeur of the Aurora Borealis so often to be seen in these high northern latitudes. It commenced at 8 p.m. by the shooting up of upright parallel rays in the west and shortly after by the same appearance in the east, also the same in the north.

Whilst viewing this grand spectacle, my attention was drawn to the town . . . dancing and revelry was going on . . . the number of stove-pipes very close together coming through the wooden roofs of the buildings at every height and in every direction . . . were sending forth myriads of sparks, and numbers of them were constantly alighting on the roofs, where they would remain many seconds before going out, and from the dryness of the season I came to the conclusion that unless we shortly had rain or snow to cover the roofs . . . the town was doomed.

When I mentioned the probability of a fire to the businessmen of the place, they answered me and said, it had become their settled opinion that the wood the town was built of was different to other wood and that it would not burn, otherwise the town would have been burnt long since, for, said they, see the number of small fires that have occurred and not one of them sufficiently destructive to destroy a house, and so they remained passive in their fancied security and had nothing done to guard against so dire a calamity.

The morning of the fire was bright and clear and the sluice boxes . . . bore traces of a hard frost as the icicles that were descending from the flumes were two or three yards in length by several feet in depth, looking very beautiful.

I had occasion to go down street to make a call on a young man, Patterson, who had formerly been a steward on the passenger ship "Cyclone" that I came to the country in. He showed me over his large and well-built premises containing a large stock of goods and, as he informed me, all paid for. I congratulated him most cordially as I felt he deserved it for his industry, steadiness and perseverance, but little did

I think that in less than two hours not a vestige of the town would remain but a burning mass of ruins. I gave him an invitation to visit my new building, just finished and nicely furnished.

I returned to my house and seated myself in a chair and again meditated on the probability of a fire when I heard several running on the plank sidewalk and heard one exclaim, "Good God! What is up?" I ran instantly to see the cause of the alarm, and to my astonishment beheld a column of smoke rising from the roof of the saloon adjoining the steward's house. I saw the fire had a firm hold of the building and, as there was no water to be had, I felt certain that the town would be destroyed. So I collected as much of my stock of goods as possible together and hastened with them to the middle of the creek and left

them there, whilst I made several journeys after other goods. The fire originated in a small room adjoining Barry & Adler's Saloon. One of the dancing girls was ironing and by some means or other, the heat of the stove-pipe set the canvas ceiling on fire, which instantly communicated with the roof and [in] no less than two minutes the whole saloon was in flames, which quickly set the opposite business in the Bank of British North America in flames.

So the fire travelled at the same time up and down the sides of the street, and as fast against the wind as it did before it, and although my building was nearly fifty yards away from where the fire originated, in less than twenty minutes, it together with the whole of the lower part of the town was a sheet of fire, hissing, crackling, and

CONTINUED ON PAGE 109

THE MAIN STREET THROUGH BARKERVILLE, SHOWING THE BOARDWALK AND BUSINESSES BEFORE THE FIRE

HISTORICAL PHOTO A-02050, ROYAL BC MUSEUM AND ARCHIVES. PHOTO BY FREDERICK DALLY

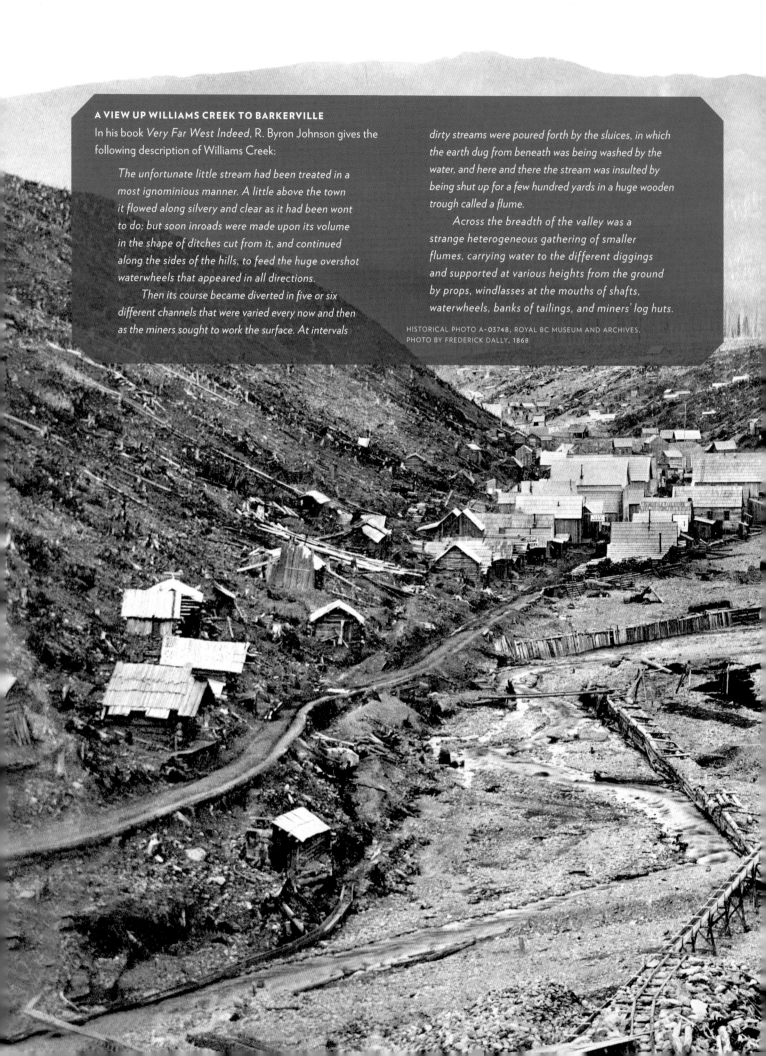

A VIEW UP WILLIAMS CREEK TO BARKERVILLE

In his book *Very Far West Indeed*, R. Byron Johnson gives the following description of Williams Creek:

The unfortunate little stream had been treated in a most ignominious manner. A little above the town it flowed along silvery and clear as it had been wont to do; but soon inroads were made upon its volume in the shape of ditches cut from it, and continued along the sides of the hills, to feed the huge overshot waterwheels that appeared in all directions.

Then its course became diverted in five or six different channels that were varied every now and then as the miners sought to work the surface. At intervals

dirty streams were poured forth by the sluices, in which the earth dug from beneath was being washed by the water, and here and there the stream was insulted by being shut up for a few hundred yards in a huge wooden trough called a flume.

Across the breadth of the valley was a strange heterogeneous gathering of smaller flumes, carrying water to the different diggings and supported at various heights from the ground by props, windlasses at the mouths of shafts, waterwheels, banks of tailings, and miners' log huts.

HISTORICAL PHOTO A-03748, ROYAL BC MUSEUM AND ARCHIVES.
PHOTO BY FREDERICK DALLY, 1868

A VIEW DOWN WILLIAMS CREEK JUST BELOW THE CANYON, WITH BARKERVILLE TO THE RIGHT OF CENTRE

Dozens of small miners' cabins line both hillsides, which are denuded of trees, most of the timber being used for building construction and cribbing for the mine shafts. A flume in the lower centre carries water to a Cornish wheel that in turn runs a pump to keep a shaft dry and to raise and lower the buckets of dirt—and the men. A couple of abandoned water wheels can be seen near the centre of the photo. The wing dam in the centre of the photo was built to keep the creek from flooding the town. On the right is an extension of the Cariboo Wagon Road. In the lower centre and lower right can be seen a pile of tailings and a miner's cabin with a chimney of stone and one of tin. The entire creek bed is a mass of tailings from the various claims that follow both sides of Williams Creek. This photo was taken on a Sunday, when all work was stopped for worship. In 1868, Barkerville was said to be the largest town west of Chicago and north of San Francisco.

A VIEW UP WILLIAMS CREEK TO BARKERVILLE FROM CAMERONTOWN THE DAY AFTER THE FIRE

On the afternoon of September 16, 1868, a fire swept through Barkerville, wiping out most of the town. On the left-hand side of this photo, Williams Creek is diverted away from Barkerville by a wing dam. Also, the centre left-hand side of the photo shows a flume on stilts bringing water to at least one but possibly two Cornish water wheels. In the lower right foreground are piles of tailings from the many claims. The Cariboo Wagon Road is visible coming into Barkerville in the lower right-hand corner of the photo.

HISTORICAL PHOTO A-00355, ROYAL BC MUSEUM AND ARCHIVES, PHOTO BY FREDERICK DALLY, SEPTEMBER 17, 1868

Origins of Cariboo Freemasonry

THE AURORA GOLD MINING CLAIM ON CONKLIN'S GULCH, A TRIBUTARY OF WILLIAMS CREEK
The day this photo was taken—on June 15, 1867, near Barkerville—the mine (named after the Roman goddess of the dawn) had a wash-up of 485 ounces of gold. The foreman of the claim was Jonathan Nutt, an Englishman who had been a miner in California and who, on reaching the Cariboo goldfields, initiated a movement to form a Masonic Lodge at Barkerville.

HISTORICAL PHOTO A-00782, ROYAL BC MUSEUM AND ARCHIVES. PHOTO BY FREDERICK DALLY

By 1866, miner Masons realized that Barkerville had taken on an air of permanency and that the separation of the gold from the gravel of the creeks was going to take much longer than had been anticipated. Jonathan Nutt is credited with the movement to form a Masonic Lodge in Barkerville. Nutt was the foreman of the Aurora Claim on Conklin's Gulch, a tributary of Williams Creek. Nutt was an Englishman who had been a miner in California and while there, in 1854, became a Freemason in Tehama Lodge No. 3 in Sacramento. Later, he was affiliated with Western Star Lodge No. 2 in Shasta, California.

Nutt called (and chaired) a meeting on October 13, 1866, that was attended by thirteen Masons: W.W. Hill, George Grant, Joshua Spencer Thompson, Alexander C. Campbell, W.M. Cochrane, John R. Price, George Duff, Carl Strouss, John Patterson, John B. Lovell, W.E. Boone, and William Bennett.

The men decided to establish a Masonic Lodge in the Cariboo and to build a Masonic hall. Each person pledged a certain amount each week toward this end—the amounts ranged from fifty cents to a dollar. Soon, another twenty members were added to the original thirteen.

W.M. Cochrane, referred to as "An Irish Gentleman," was apparently a man of money and loaned the lodge a considerable sum of cash. Alexander Campbell, a cousin of John Cameron, owned the Foster-Campbell Claim on Williams Creek. He was also a blacksmith.

Many of the Cariboo Masons had participated in the California gold rush. Joshua Thompson had been a member of San Francisco Lodge No. 7, in California.

The minutes of Vancouver Lodge record that on January 16, 1867, Brother Jonathan Nutt presented a petition to the Grand Lodge of Scotland for the establishment of a Masonic lodge at Barkerville, to be named Cariboo Lodge.

roaring furiously. There was, in a store not far from my place, fifty kegs of blasting powder and had that not been removed at the commencement of the fire and put down a dry shaft, most likely not a soul would have been left alive of the number that was then present. Blankets and bedding were seen to be sent at least 200 feet high when a number of coal oil tins (5 gallons) exploded, and the top of one of the tins was sent five miles and dropped at the sawmill on Grouse Creek.

Every person was thinking of his own property and using desperate efforts to save it.

The town was divided by the "Barker" flume crossing it at a height of fifty feet, and as it was carrying all the water that was near, it kept the fire at bay for a short time from the upper part of the town, but the hot wind soon drove those that were standing on it away. The fire then quickly caught the other half of the buildings, also the forest on the mountain ridge at the back, and as the sun set behind the mountain the grandeur of the scene will not be quickly forgotten by those who noticed it. Then the cold frosty wind came sweeping down the canyon, blowing without sympathy on the houseless and distressed sufferers, causing the iron-hearted men to mechanically raise the small collars of their coats (if they had been so fortunate as to have one) as a protection against it. Household furniture of every description was piled up along the side of the creek, and the people were preparing to make themselves as comfortable for the night, under the canopy of heaven, as circumstances would allow. And in the early morning as I passed down the creek, I saw strong men rise from their hard beds on the cold stones, having slept wrapped in a pair of blankets, cramped with cold and in great pain, until a little exercise brought renewed life into their systems. At a quarter to three p.m. the fire [had] commenced; at half past four p.m. the whole town was in flames, and at 10 o'clock the next morning signs of rebuilding had commenced. Lumber was fast arriving from the saw-mill and was selling at one hundred and twenty five dollars per one thousand feet, the number of houses destroyed was one hundred and sixteen

The fire was caused by a miner trying to kiss one of the girls that was ironing, and knocking against the stove displaced the pipe that went through the canvas ceiling, and through the roof, which at once took fire. This information I got from an eye witness, who never made it generally known thinking that it might result in a lynching scene.

CARIBOO LODGE NO. 4, "ANCIENT FREE AND ACCEPTED MASONS," AT THE AURORA GOLD MINING CLAIM ON WILLIAMS CREEK:
John Weill; Paul Manetta; John Williams Edward Pearson; Edwin Johns; Joseph F. Clarridge; Charles J. Paulson; Robert Patterson; August Hoffman; David T. Price; Joseph H. St. Laurent; William Fraser; James Amm; William Rennie; John L. Muir; James Carson; Ninian F. Foster; Joshua Spencer Thompson; William H. Hill; William Mckenzie; Jonathan Nutt; James S. McMillan; George Grant; Alexander C.M. Campbell; John McLaren; John Bruce; Samuel Kahn.

HISTORICAL PHOTO A-03782, ROYAL BC MUSEUM AND ARCHIVES. PHOTO BY FREDERICK DALLY

THE CARIBOO WAGON ROAD

JOHN MARSHALL GRANT (1822–1902)

As a captain in the Royal Engineers, Grant took on the challenge of building the most difficult section of the Cariboo Wagon Road through the Fraser Canyon. His daughter Alice, a professional painter, did this study, circa 1890, of her dignified-looking father long after he had left British Columbia.

HISTORICAL PHOTO A-01315, ROYAL BC MUSEUM AND ARCHIVES

Mining successes in the Cariboo goldfields necessitated the further improvement of the roads to the Cariboo. In May 1862, Colonel Richard C. Moody advised Governor James Douglas that the Yale-to-Cariboo route through the Fraser Canyon was the best to adapt for the general development of the country and that it was imperative its construction start at once.

The governor concurred. Planners of the road decided it would be a full 5.5 metres (18 feet) wide in order to accommodate wagons going and coming from the goldfields, and thus it came to be known as the Cariboo Wagon Road. The builders were to be paid large cash subsidies as work progressed, and on completion of their sections were to be granted permission to collect tolls from travellers for the following five years.

Captain John Marshall Grant of the Royal Engineers, with a force of sappers, miners, and civilian labour, was to construct the first ten kilometres (six miles) out of Yale, while Thomas Spence was to extend the road the next eleven kilometres (seven miles) to Chapman's Bar, at a cost of $47,000. From here, Joseph William Trutch, Spence's partner, was to tackle the section to a point that would become Boston Bar, a distance of nineteen kilometres (twelve miles), at a cost of $75,000. From here, Spence would continue the road to Lytton. Walter Moberly, a successful engineer, with Charles Oppenheimer, a partner in the great mercantile firm Oppenheimer Brothers, and Thomas B. Lewis accepted the challenge to build the section from Lytton to where the road joined a junction with the wagon road to be built by Gustavus Blin Wright and John Colin Calbreath from Lillooet to Watson's stopping house. As well, Trutch was to build a bridge across the Fraser River at Chapman's Bar, while Spence was to place one across the Thompson River, at the site of Cook's ferry.

Wright, from Burlington, Vermont, had arrived in BC on February 28, 1862, aboard the *Brother Jonathan* and almost immediately formed partnerships to operate a line of vessels between San Francisco and New Westminster. At Port Douglas, his associates began hauling freight by mule train to the goldfields. He saw great financial advantages in the construction of an improved wagon road into the Cariboo, since this would enable him to profit not only on the building of the road but also in the future enterprises along the new highway.

Calbreath, born in New York in 1826, had left home in 1849 for the California goldfields. He married Carolyn Smith, and a son

James was born in 1857 in LaGrange, California. Shortly after the baby's birth, the young couple departed for the Cariboo to run a boarding house, trading post, and farm at Soda Creek. Shortly after Gustavus Blin Wright's arrival in BC, Calbreath joined him in his ventures and became his partner in the building of roads.

The construction partners of Moberly, Oppenheimer, and Lewis ran into trouble even before the first shovel of dirt was turned on their section of the road. They had advertised for a thousand men and were confident that their first thirty-four kilometres (twenty-one miles) between Lytton and Cook's Ferry would be done in time to meet the government's deadline of July 15, 1862. When Moberly and Oppenheimer arrived at Yale, they found their workforce stranded and unable to get beyond that point as they were without food, money, and proper clothing. By this time, Moberly had already spent between $2,000 and $3,000 in boat fares to get the men from New Westminster to Yale. Now he was faced with the additional cost of advancing money to these labourers so they could outfit themselves for the walk to Lytton.

Before leaving Victoria, David Oppenheimer had arranged to have large quantities of supplies and tools forwarded to his brother's mercantile firm in Yale. Now the pack trail between Yale and Lytton was impassable, which made it necessary to transport all freight between those partly by water through the dangerous canyons and partly by pack trains. There were not enough boats on the river to meet the demands of this task, which resulted in long delays. The partners soon discovered that the mule packers were demanding tremendously high rates for the haul from Yale to Lytton. The firm wound up hiring Native people to pack supplies in on their ponies at a lower, but still outrageous, rate.

Moberly made his headquarters in the courthouse at Lytton before establishing his first road camp a short distance out of town. As the men arrived, he set them to work, and for several weeks the road building progressed at a great rate.

According to the government contract, the firm from Victoria was to be paid well. The money did not arrive, so Moberly and Oppenheimer began buying supplies on their personal credit from the HBC.

During the first few months of road work, many reports about the fabulously rich strikes occurring in the Cariboo reached their labour force without any apparent impact. This changed as soon as the men received their first pay: many of them, entirely disregarding the terms of their contract to work for the entire season, and

A ROYAL ENGINEER'S BUCKLE & BUTTONS
WERNER KASCHEL

THE *ONWARD* AT EMORY'S BAR, FIVE KILOMETRES BELOW YALE, WITH THE CASCADE MOUNTAINS IN THE DISTANCE

HISTORICAL PHOTO A-00102, ROYAL BC MUSEUM AND ARCHIVES. PHOTO BY FREDERICK DALLY, 1867–68

all of them indebted for clothes and other necessities, threw down their shovels and headed for the goldfields.

The situation was desperate when Oppenheimer left for Victoria for an audience with Governor Douglas, who told him the British government had denied a request for money to build the wagon road and that any forthcoming money would have to be obtained through taxation. Oppenheimer returned to Lytton, and when he conveyed this news to partners Lewis and Moberly, a heated discussion resulted in Moberly agreeing to purchase Lewis's interest in the company.

Oppenheimer agreed to leave for San Francisco to try to negotiate a $50,000 loan by mortgaging the revenue that they would soon be able to obtain from tolls. Unfortunately, rumours began to circulate among the labourers that Oppenheimer planned to pick up the money advanced by the government and skip the country, and that caused much distress in the road camps. As a result, Moberly decided to travel to New Westminster and request an interview with Moody and Douglas. Douglas had good news for him: the government had negotiated a $50,000 loan from the newly established Bank of British Columbia. The governor advanced Moberly $6,000 from the bank's New Westminster and Yale treasuries to pay the men's wages.

Upon his return to Yale, Moberly met a large number of his disgruntled workers who had stopped work after hearing that he too had skipped the country. These men were broke and hungry. Moberly, after feeding them a hearty breakfast, explained the circumstances and persuaded them to return to work.

Shortly after his return to the camp, he discovered, to his great consternation that smallpox had broken out in a nearby Aboriginal village. Given this news, the only way to keep his labourers from leaving was to make immediate payment of their wages to date. To do this he used the $6,000 advanced money and the remainder of his own personal fortune, placing himself in debt to his suppliers and personally destitute.

Meanwhile, the government announced that the contract time was up, and since Oppenheimer and Moberly had failed to complete their section, they were not entitled to any further payments. On hearing this, Oppenheimer stopped negotiating for his loan but remained in San Francisco. One creditor, to whom they were indebted for supplies, issued a warrant for Moberly's arrest if he failed to pay in full. Fortunately, a friend came to his aid and loaned him enough money to keep him from being imprisoned. Moberly signed over his contract to the government, and the government in turn offered him the job as supervisor until the completion of his section. William Hood, a contractor from Santa Clara, California, took the contract to complete their section from Spence's Bridge to Clinton. It took Moberly seven years to pay off his debts.

Joseph W. Trutch and Thomas Spence experienced a few problems on their sections between Yale and Lytton as well, but the situation changed dramatically for Spence on the Thompson River. In summer of 1863, Spence began to build a bridge across the Thompson River at Cook's Ferry. A capable foreman ensured that the bridge opened on schedule in 1864, but unfortunately a spring freshet soon took out the entire bridge, and Spence's only way to avoid bankruptcy was to rebuild. In the autumn of 1864, with the same foreman and work gang, Spence began work on the second bridge, which opened in spring 1865.

By the fall of 1863, Gustavus (Gus) Wright and John Calbreath had completed the road from Lillooet to Clinton, the name given by Douglas to the vital junction where Watson's stopping house was located. (Henry Clinton was Earl of Newcastle and the Colonial Secretary from 1859 to 1864). Because of the efficiency with which Wright and Calbreath had completed their sections, they won the contract, at $1,700 per mile, to extend the wagon road from Clinton north to Alexandria.

ABOVE– DAVID OPPENHEIMER (1834–97)
David Oppenheimer was one of five brothers —the others were Charles, Meyer, Isaac, and Godfrey— who participated in early gold rushes in British Columbia. The brothers had warehouses in Fisherville, Yale, and Barkerville. This photo was taken at the Imperial Gallery portrait studio in San Francisco. David later became the second mayor of Vancouver.

HISTORICAL PHOTO A-02384, ROYAL BC MUSEUM AND ARCHIVES

RIGHT–CHARLES OPPENHEIMER (1834–97)

HISTORICAL PHOTO A-02383, ROYAL BC MUSEUM AND ARCHIVES

YALE AT THE BEGINNING OF THE GOLD-RUSH ERA
Originally called Fort Yale in 1848 by Ovid Allard, the manager of the new post, Yale honours James Murray Yale, the HBC's chief factor of the Columbia District. In its heyday the town reputedly earned epithets such as "the wickedest little settlement in British Columbia" and "a veritable Sodom and Gomorrah" of vice, violence and lawlessness. At the head of navigation, Yale was the best location for the start of the Cariboo Wagon Road to the goldfields. In this photograph, taken in 1867 or 1868, a paddlewheeler is tied up, disembarking miners and cargo destined for the Cariboo goldfields. The buildings running parallel to the river are on Front Street.

HISTORICAL PHOTO A-00902, ROYAL BC MUSEUM AND ARCHIVES. PHOTO BY FREDERICK DALLY

GUSTAVUS BLIN WRIGHT (1832–98)

A Cariboo Wagon Road builder and promoter, Wright participated in both the Cariboo and Omineca gold rushes. Wright built the sternwheelers *Enterprise* and *Victoria* to ferry passengers along parts of the Fraser River to the goldfields. This portrait was taken circa 1870.

HISTORICAL PHOTO B-00667, ROYAL BC MUSEUM AND ARCHIVES

While work was progressing out of Clinton, Wright contracted out the building of a steamboat named the *Enterprise* at Alexandria to run as an extension of his road up the Fraser to Quesnel Mouth. The lumber for its construction was cut on location, while its boiler, engine, and ironworks were packed in on mules over the Douglas Trail. The *Enterprise*'s maiden run took place in 1864. Wright and Calbreath also opened the 70 Mile House, thirty-seven kilometres (twenty-three miles) north of Clinton, to cater to the needs of the miners.

The road-builders convinced the government that the road could end at Soda Creek, thirty kilometres (twenty miles) closer than Alexandria, since the Fraser River was navigable beyond that point. They also persuaded the government to allow them to bypass Williams Lake, where Thomas Manifee had a stopping house, thereby eliminating the competition for Calbreath's stopping house at Soda Creek.

Even before the road neared completion, speculators began arriving to open businesses. In 1861 two enterprising brothers, William and George Boothroyd, left California for the Cariboo. Midway between Boston Bar and Lytton, the two became sidetracked from their original mission and instead started farming. One day, William and a son left Yale with a large wagonload of gunpowder to be used as blasting powder on the Cariboo Wagon Road. After they did not arrive at their destination, searchers found a big hole in the road and surmised that there had been a hole in one of the kegs that allowed the powder to drip down onto the road. A spark, likely from the wheel, likely caused the powder to ignite, blowing father and son, horses, and wagon to bits. Boothroyd was named in their honour.

In time, the Boothroyd Hostelry came to be known as Forrest House, after George's wife's maiden name. This stopping house became a welcome retreat to the many teamsters using the Cariboo Wagon Road over the years. In 1873, George sold his interests in the roadhouse and moved with his wife to New Westminster. He later took up property in Surrey Centre.

Mule packers made good use of the road, even while it was under construction. William T. Ballou was the first pioneer express man to use the highway to get to the goldfields. This wild waif of French descent had arrived on the Fraser in 1858, coming straight from the California rush. Using a canoe and mule teams to carry letters, newspapers, coins, and gold dust to and from the interior, he entered into direct competition with the government service. His Pioneer Fraser River Express held supremacy on the mainland for about three years; his fame was such that Chartres Brew, chief inspector for police for the colony, wrote to Colonel Moody: "There are many complaints here of the irregularities and uncertainties of the mails. Merchants would rather send their letters by Bellors [Ballou's] Express at a cost of half a dollar than put it in the post at a cost of 5 cents and remain in the uncertainty when it would reach its destination."

By May 1862, Francis Jones Barnard had won the government mail contract and snuffed out Ballou. The pioneer express man retired from the road, momentarily broken in health and finances. Barnard brought in mules and soon had a string tied head to tail, with him trudging alongside the animals. It was hard work, requiring him to be up at the crack of dawn to load the pack animals and then get them moving. Barnard did have competition from others besides Ballou.

In May 1864, J.W. Trutch surveyed a route for the extension of the Cariboo Wagon Road from Quesnel Mouth to Williams Creek. James Douglas, in one of his last acts as governor, instructed that the road be built in sections under the supervision of Walter Moberly.

Gus Wright was awarded the contract for the lower section from Quesnel Mouth to Cottonwood (a new settlement located where the road crossed the Cottonwood River) for $85,000. Wright hired a force of 300 Chinese labourers and 240 white labourers to tackle the project. He later built a bridge across the Cottonwood River under a separate $9,000 contract.

In April of 1865, Malcolm Munroe, the road-builder from Victoria who built the road into Leechtown on Vancouver Island, secured the contract to complete the road from Cottonwood to Williams Creek. A stipulation in the agreement ruled that the work had to be finished by October or the $45,000 contract would be forfeited. Munroe reached Van Winkle before bad weather forced his workers to shut down operations. He wrote Trutch, now the chief commissioner of Lands and Works, requesting an advance to pay his creditors and men with the understanding he would complete the last portion of his section in the spring. Trutch refused, and Munroe, having failed to meet the terms of the agreement, received no payment and was sent to

debtor's prison in New Westminster. His portion of the road was completed in the spring at a total cost to the government of only $500.

In July 1865, Robert T. Smith, under the supervision of Thomas Spence, took the contract to upgrade a sleigh trail that paralleled the Fraser River between Soda Creek and Quesnel Mouth. Before he could finish his road, heavy freight wagons, hauled by six- and eight-horse teams, began cutting it into deep ruts. Worse damage was done by sixteen-yoke spans of slow-plodding oxen that hauled two freight wagons in tandem. When Smith refused to keep the road in good repair for one year, he forfeited his contract, and Spence assumed the responsibility for carrying out the necessary repairs. With the completion of the last section of the Cariboo Wagon Road, both Gus Wright's steamer *Enterprise* and the Deep Creek stopping house decreased in importance.

In 1875, Gus Wright married Julia Sutton of Portland, Oregon, and moved to Nelson. He died in 1898 at Ainsworth.

Wright's partner, Calbreath, sold his holdings in the Cariboo in 1873, shortly after his wife left him for another man. That same year he established a trading company that expanded by the turn of the century into general merchandizing, packing, forwarding, and warehousing, with offices throughout the Cassiar. In 1890, Calbreath raised money in Astoria to build the Astoria and Alaska Packing Company cannery at Point Ellice, Alaska. He superintended that company's operations until it burned down in 1892. The following year he started Alaska's second salmon hatchery, which operated until 1905—about the time he became blind from cataracts. Calbreath lived in Wrangell, Alaska, for several years but eventually moved to Seattle, Washington, where he died in 1916.

On February 28, 1871, the legislative council granted Barnard and Josiah Beedy the right to operate R.W. Thompson's newly patented "road steamers" between Yale and Williams Creek. Barnard, like Trutch, also had an in with the government (his son became lieutenant-governor). Six of the English steam engines arrived complete with Scottish drivers, and the first machine was quite a sight chugging along Grant's section of the highway out of Yale. Its wheels, though only thirty centimetres (twelve inches) in diameter and cushioned with thick India rubber padding, still managed to chew up the Royal Engineers roadwork. Pulling six tons of freight, the steamer reached Spuzzum the first day, Boston Bar on the second, and Jackass Mountain on the third. Here, it refused to climb the hill. To add further embarrassment, investigation revealed that the horse-drawn freight wagons were just as fast and far less trouble and expense. As a result, five of the engines were shipped back to England, while the one that remained was acquired by pioneer logger Jeremiah Rogers to be used to haul spars and logs from Vancouver's forests to the water's edge.

SEVERAL FREIGHT WAGONS ROLLING THROUGH BOSTON BAR EN ROUTE TO THE CARIBOO

Located nineteen kilometres (twelve miles) above Yale, Boston Bar was named after American miners from Boston who took up the challenge to seek gold along the Fraser River at the beginning of the Fraser River gold rush. In this early-morning landscape, teams of oxen pull single and double wagons of goods destined for the goldfields. The five wagons are being pulled by oxen, while in front of them pack mules are being loaded. These covered wagons without proper suspension were used to transport goods over the rough roads. A teamster or drover usually walked on the left side of the team and directed the oxen with verbal commands and whip cracks. The term "prairie schooner" was a fanciful name sometimes applied to the covered wagon because the white canvas was reminiscent of sails of a ship at sea.

Instead of prospecting, Fraser Valley pioneer Edward Julius Muench packed freight for several years, using oxen, over the 1,287-kilometre (800-mile) return trip from Yale to Barkerville. He made his West Langley farm his headquarters for his animals. The oxen were excellent for freighting because, unlike horses, they would feed at night on twigs and grasses. Despite this, the beasts of burden were only capable of making two trips a year and would return as skin and bone to the farm each fall, to be fattened over the winter for the next year's trip.

The wires of The Russian–American Telegraph, also known as the Western Union Telegraph Expedition and the Collins Overland Telegraph, are clearly visible in this landscape. Portions of the telegraph route became part of the Ashcroft Trail used by gold seekers during the Klondike gold rush. Of all the trails used by the stampeders the Ashcroft was among the harshest. Of the over fifteen hundred men and three thousand horses leaving Ashcroft, BC, in spring 1898, only six men and no horses reached the goldfields.

HISTORIC PHOTO A-03876, ROYAL BC MUSEUM AND ARCHIVES. PHOTO BY FREDERICK DALLY, CIRCA 1867

Despite errors such as the steamers, the BX, as the Barnard Express with its brightly painted red-and-yellow stagecoaches came to be called, prospered. Barnard began hiring men like Stephen Tingley, soon to be known as the "best whip on the road," to make the trips back and forth to the Cariboo. On one occasion, Barnard sent Tingley to Mexico to negotiate the purchase of 250 unbroken horses for the Barnard line. Tingley drove the horses overland through the US and up into BC in order to keep costs down. Once these animals were broken, Barnard was able to keep a team of fresh horses at every roadhouse so that changes could be made every twenty-two kilometres (fourteen miles).

On one occasion, Tingley made the 611-kilometre (380-mile) trip from the Cariboo to Yale, transporting a prisoner charged with murder, in the record time of thirty hours. His run, although requiring changes at every roadhouse, still managed to average twenty-six kilometres per hour on the winding, twisting road.

When the Cariboo goldfields were at their height of productivity, it was Barnard's Express, complete with an armed guard, that brought the yellow wealth to the coast. An early newspaper reported:

Mr. Barnard has fitted an iron burglar-proof safe into each of his wagons. He has the chests

ABORIGINAL FISH CAMP AT THREE MILE CANYON, FOUR MILES ABOVE YALE ON THE FRASER RIVER

HISTORICAL PHOTO A-04283. ROYAL BC MUSEUM AND ARCHIVES. PHOTO BY FREDERICK DALLY, 1867

A six-horse team destined for the goldfields stands hitched to a Barnard Express stage in front of Barnard's Express Line Stages office at Yale, or Mile Zero. Stephen Tingley holds the reins while James Newlands rides guard.

HISTORICAL PHOTO A-01559, ROYAL BC MUSEUM AND ARCHIVES. PHOTO BY FREDERICK DALLY, 1868

A jerk-line of horses stands hitched to a loaded freight wagon in front of Barnard's Express Line Stages. A huge volume of cordwood is stacked at the river's edge, waiting for the steamers plying daily between New Westminster and Victoria to Yale.

HISTORICAL PHOTO A-3618, ROYAL BC MUSEUM AND ARCHIVES. PHOTO BY FREDERICK DALLY, 1868

constructed with detonating powder in the interstices between the plates, and on any attempt being made to open them with a chisel they would inevitably explode with the force of a bombshell. The safes are also fitted with combination locks, known only to the principals at each terminus.

Wright's partner, Calbreath, sold his holdings in the Cariboo in 1873, shortly after his wife left him. That same year, he established a trading company that expanded by the turn of the century into general merchandizing, packing, forwarding, and warehousing, with offices throughout the Cassiar.

ABORIGINAL CACHES ON THE FRASER RIVER ABOVE YALE, FEATURING TWO POLE NETS FOR CATCHING SALMON
HISTORICAL PHOTO C-09266, ROYAL BC MUSEUM AND ARCHIVES. PHOTO BY FREDERICK DALLY

Chapman's Bar Bluff was part of the first ten-kilometre (six-mile) section of the Cariboo Wagon Road north of Yale built by the Royal Engineers between May and November 1862. The road had to be blasted from rock or suspended over the many tributaries into the Fraser River on cribbing and bridges. Note photographer Dally's horse and buggy on the road.

Built in 1863 over the Fraser River twenty-one kilometres (thirteen miles) above Yale, the Alexandra Suspension Bridge, located between Spuzzum and Chapman's Bar, was the first suspension bridge in BC. Begun in June 1862 and completed in September 1863, it was built with a span of nearly a hundred metres (three hundred feet) at a cost of $45,000. Joseph Trutch contracted with the government to build it with the understanding that he could collect tolls for seven years. The original bridge, subcontracted by Trutch to Andrew S. Halladdie of San Francisco, was an engineering feat for the time. This bridge was destroyed by the great flood of 1894 and was rebuilt on the same site in 1926. The present bridge, farther downstream from the original location, was built in 1962.

THE CARIBOO WAGON ROAD AT NICARAGUA BLUFF (OR 17 MILE BLUFF) IN THE FRASER CANYON

Built through the Fraser Canyon by Native and miner labourers under the supervision of Joseph Trutch, this section of the Cariboo Wagon Road was twenty-seven kilometres (seventeen miles) above Yale. It was imperative that this first section of road be completed as quickly as possible to allow road-builders to work on sections of the road farther up the Fraser River.

This portion of the road had to be blasted from solid rock, and then cribbing had to be placed over tributary creeks that flowed into the Fraser River, with added bridges. Despite the difficulty, the road-builders were able to accomplish the first forty kilometres (twenty-five miles) out of Yale in a record seven months in 1862.

Trutch went on to become BC's first lieutenant-governor from 1871 to 1876. Some contractors like Trutch were successful, but others went bankrupt for want of men, materials, and government funds.

At points, there was barely room for a wagon's wheels on twisting ledges; at others, masses of sheer rock had to be moved with gunpowder blasts and human ingenuity. Chasms were bridged with cribbing filled with stone. When civilian workers defected to the lure of the nearby goldfields, Chinese labourers finished the job successfully.

HISTORICAL PHOTO A-03868, ROYAL BC MUSEUM AND ARCHIVES.
PHOTO BY FREDERICK DALLY, 1867–68

GEORGE SALTER'S ROADHOUSE, SIXTY-EIGHT KILOMETRES ABOVE YALE, WITH FRED DALLY'S BUGGY IN FRONT OF THE ENTRANCE

HISTORICAL PHOTO D-01289, ROYAL BC MUSEUM AND ARCHIVES. PHOTO BY FREDERICK DALLY, CIRCA 1867

NATIVE CHIEF'S GRAVE AT LYTTON

HISTORICAL PHOTO C-09264, ROYAL BC MUSEUM AND ARCHIVES. PHOTO BY FREDERICK DALLY, 1867–68

JACKASS MOUNTAIN

Early freighters on the Cariboo Wagon Road sometimes referred to Jackass Mountain as "the hill of despair" because it was the steepest portion of the route and a difficult climb. Before the Cariboo Wagon Road was built, the best mode of transportation to the interior was the mule train. Stronger and more sure-footed than a horse, a mule could pack much more weight. It cost a dollar per pound, and it took a month to transport goods from Yale to Quesnel.

Legend has it that a jackass owned by packer Joseph Deroche, after whom Deroche was later named, had a stubborn animal that committed suicide by jumping off the trail with a full load into the Fraser River.

Teams of oxen were also useful for pulling heavy loads. However, the slow, plodding animals could only make two trips a year.

Sometimes as many as twelve horse teams hauled two loaded wagons in tandem up and down Jackass Mountain. For the heaviest loads, trees would be cut and attached to the rear wagon so that the branches could act as a crude breaking system to prevent runaways.

In 1871, six road steamers were imported from England to use on the Cariboo Wagon Road, but the grade of Jackass Mountain was impossible for the steam engines to overcome. At this point, the Cariboo Wagon Road was 366 metres (1,200 feet) above the Fraser River.

HISTORICAL PHOTO A-03879, ROYAL BC MUSEUM AND ARCHIVES. PHOTO BY FREDERICK DALLY, 1867–68

Lytton at the junction of the Fraser and Thompson Rivers, ninety-two kilometres (fifty-seven miles) above Yale.

THE THOMPSON RIVER A SHORT DISTANCE ABOVE LYTTON It was here that a Native man first discovered gold while taking a drink of water.

HISTORICAL PHOTO A-03575, ROYAL BC MUSEUM AND ARCHIVES. PHOTO BY FREDERICK DALLY

LEFT AND OPPOSITE— SPENCES BRIDGE

This elaborate truss bridge was built by Thomas Spence. The first bridge he built was taken out by early spring freshets and had to be replaced. Spence was allowed to collect a toll on the bridge for five years after its completion.

HISTORICAL PHOTO C-05541,
ROYAL BC MUSEUM AND ARCHIVES.
PHOTO BY FREDERICK DALLY, 1867

HISTORICAL PHOTO A-03568, ROYAL BC MUSEUM AND ARCHIVES. PHOTO BY FREDERICK DALLY, 1867

Freight wagons ascend the Great Bluff on the Thompson River thirteen kilometres (eight miles) above Spences Bridge. This photo shows the poles and wires of the Collins Overland Telegraph, part of an ambitious attempt to lay an electric telegraph line from San Francisco, California, to Moscow, Russia. Although the project died on the vine, the telegraph did connect New Westminster with Barkerville. The bluff was 142 kilometres (88 miles) above Yale.

INSTALLING CRIBBING ON THE CARIBOO WAGON ROAD

This painting by Rex Woods shows a party of Royal Engineers installing cribbing on the Cariboo Wagon Road above Spences Bridge. Dress for the officers was a scarlet tunic with dark blue trousers, featuring a scarlet strip along the seams; yellow cord on the shoulder straps, collar, and sleeve cuffs; blue collar and cuffs; blue pillbox hat with a yellow band and red piping; and a buff white belt. The sappers wore grey shirts with their uniform.

A wall of rock has been breached, and a cleft is being cribbed and filled as horses drag heavy logs on "goboy" skids or sleds. Workers toil in the background. Their assignment completed, the detachment of Royal Engineers was disbanded in 1863. Many remained as settlers in the expanding west.

REX WOODS, PAINTINGS AND DRAWINGS POP 03696, ROYAL BC MUSEUM AND ARCHIVES

Twenty-six members of the Nincumshin tribe, including two women carrying newborns in baskets, gather for a group photo near Spences Bridge on the Thompson River.

Originally known as 47 Mile House because it was seventy-five kilometres (forty-seven miles) from Lillooet, Clinton was named in honour of Henry Pelham Fiennes Clinton. Here, William Bose's fourteen oxen stand harnessed and ready to haul two heavily laden wagons in tandem to the Cariboo goldfields in 1868.

HISTORICAL PHOTO A-00346, ROYAL BC MUSEUM AND ARCHIVES. PHOTO BY FREDERICK DALLY, 1868

This photo shows Clinton in 1868, with the Cariboo Wagon Road in the left foreground with a toll gate, the Smith General Store and the Clinton Hotel all just to the left of centre. The numerous barns contain hay and grains for the animals coming and going to the Cariboo and provided shelter as well. In the spring of 1861, brothers George and Robert Watson began to build a new log structure that came to be the famous Clinton Hotel. In 1863, the Watsons placed an advertisement in the *Victoria Colonist*, stating that they had "built a new building that had a large bar, a private sitting room and free beds to people that brought their own blankets." The Watsons apparently leased their new hotel to William McKinnon, and when the lease ended, they sold the land to Mary and Joseph Smith and their partner, Thomas Marshall.

Across the road from the Clinton Hotel, Gustavus Blin Wright installed a toll booth to collect tolls for the work he had done as a road-builder. Tolls were collected from 1863 until 1868.

For nearly one hundred years, the Clinton Hotel was a landmark on the Cariboo Wagon Road. It burned down on May 15, 1958.

HISTORICAL PHOTO A-03504, ROYAL BC MUSEUM AND ARCHIVES.
PHOTO BY FREDERICK DALLY

Seen here are the Sternwheeler *Enterprise*, the Exchange Hotel, the Colonial Hotel, and Dunlevey's Store, in 1868 Soda Creek. The *Enterprise* took passengers and freight upriver eighty-seven kilometres (fifty-four miles) to Quesnel. The boilers for the tiny craft were brought nearly five hundred kilometres (three hundred miles) from Port Douglas.

SODA CREEK

HISTORICAL PHOTO A-03909, ROYAL BC MUSEUM AND ARCHIVES. PHOTO BY FREDERICK DALLY, 1867–68

Seven gold-rush pioneers relax in front of the Colonial Hotel at Soda Creek. The two men at left are Peter Dunlevey and Robert McLeese, owners of the town's side-by-side hotels.

HISTORICAL PHOTO A-03910, ROYAL BC MUSEUM AND ARCHIVES. PHOTO BY FREDERICK DALLY, 1867–68

FERRY RIDE ACROSS THE QUESNEL RIVER
A mule train, belonging to "Red-Headed" Davis, waiting to make an early morning ferry ride across the Quesnel River. Each mule knew by smell the pack that it carried the previous day.

THE GOLDEN CITY OF ROSSLAND

QUARTZ SAMPLES CONTAINING GOLD TAKEN FROM IN AND AROUND ROSSLAND

AUTHOR PHOTOS

After 1865, the portion of the Dewdney Trail from Wild Horse Creek to Hope was little used, except for a few berry-gathering Native families. By the early 1880s, a few former '49ers began using the overgrown trail to travel to the coast from Wild Horse, where they had been prospecting. American gold hunters, venturing north across the border, used the old trail intermittently. Ironically, none of the original Argonauts looked twice at a red mountain a short distance off Dewdney's trail.

George Bohman and George Leyson discovered the first interesting outcroppings of ore not far from the trail and named their discovery the Lily May claim in 1887. However, they allowed the claim to lapse. Two years later, Oliver Bordeau of Colville and Newlin Hoover of Nelson restaked the claim. In March 1890, Bordeau decided to do assessment work on the claim. It was a painstaking task, according to his employee, Joseph Moris, who later wrote:

> We left Colville on the 17 March 1890 and went as far as the Little Dalles by sleigh, and there Mr. Bordeau hired a boat and two men to help us up the river to the mouth of Trail Creek. Here Mr. Bordeau expected to have horses to do the packing from the river to the claim, but we found too much snow on the trail so we could not use horses for the packing. So Mr. Bordeau and I had to pack everything on our backs and as I remember it now, it was very hard work as we had to travel over five feet of snow and in the afternoon it was impossible to get over it at all. It was not until we were very near through with the assessment work that the snow had gone off enough so I could see some bare patches of ground on the south slope of Red Mountain which showed the surface to be very red and which attracted my attention at once.

Moris endured pure hell putting in an entrance to an underground mine with a sledgehammer, drill rods, and a few sticks of dynamite. Work was painstakingly slow, as he had to sharpen his drill bits nightly to prepare for the next day's work.

Only after the assessment work was done did Bordeau inform Moris that he didn't have the money on hand to pay him but did have money in Nelson. On his way to Nelson, Moris found an interesting-looking cropping and set up the Homestake claim. Unfortunately for Moris, money seemed to elude him, for Bordeau reneged on making any payment even after the pair reached Nelson.

To get some quick cash for supplies, Moris went to work in the Silver King Mine on Toad Mountain above the Nelson for a few weeks. With his pa, he bought supplies and headed back to the Homestake claim to do assessment work when he happened to meet George "Bushway" Bourgeois. An experienced miner, Bourgeois persuaded Moris to abandon his discovery and go with him to explore the side of a mountain that had been burned by a brush fire, leaving a red scar. It was then that they dubbed the site Red Mountain. On July 2, 1890, the two men discovered five claims: Centre Star, War Eagle, Idaho, Virginia, and Le Wise. (Since the two men were only allowed two claims each, Moris put two stakes on the extension of the Centre Star and called it the Le Wise.)

The next morning, the two men left for Nelson. They arrived on July 4 and had their ten samples assayed. Since the results were not that promising, Bourgeois, although he had $700 in the bank, was not interested in having the claims put on record at a cost of $6.25 each. Moris, the inexperienced miner, almost broke with only $18, disagreed. Bourgeois suggested they discuss their discovery with Eugene Sayre Topping, the deputy mining recorder at Nelson. They told Topping about their find and offered him the Le Wise claim if he'd pay the recording fees on all five claims, which he agreed to.

Bourgeois and Moris left Nelson on July 17 and were joined by Topping three days later. Topping examined the Centre Star extension and finally remarked to his companions, "I'll keep it. We'll call it the Le Roi and next month I will go down to Spokane and raise money to work it."

Thus Topping purchased what would become one of the richest mines in the world, earning him the name of "The Father of Trail." Born in New York State in 1842, Topping changed occupations frequently. He was a sailor, railway builder, trapper, scout, miner, and newspaper reporter. In 1883, he wrote *Chronicles of the Yellowstone,* a comprehensive history of the country drained by the Yellowstone River.

True to his word, Topping, with ore samples from his claim, left for Spokane on the Spokane Falls and Northern Railway. This rail line, built by Daniel Chase Corbin, ran north from Spokane Falls to Colville. On

AN ORE CAR ON DISPLAY IN FRONT OF THE PRINCETON MUSEUM

A VIEW SOUTH OF THE LE ROI MINE

ROSSLAND HERITAGE MUSEUM AND ARCHIVES , 45-746. PHOTO BY CARPENTER AND MILLAR

the train or while overnighting at Colville, Topping happened to meet Colonel William W. Ridpath and lawyer George Forster.

Ridpath and Forster were influential businessmen from Spokane and they were very interested in Topping's ore samples. They told six associates about their chance meeting with Topping, and a deal was struck. The six newcomers were brothers George and W.W. Turner, Oliver Durant, Alexander Tarbet, F. Graves, and Isaac Peyton. Topping would sell a 51 percent share to the eight Spokane businessmen. The new partners would each get a one-fifteenth interest in the mine for $2,000, and Topping would retain a $14,000 interest.

The new syndicate agreed to do assessment work in the amount of $3,000 by June 1, 1891. William

Harris, owner of a hostelry in Spokane, became a member of the group by accepting shares in lieu of payment of debts owed to him by members of the syndicate. Peyton later purchased Topping's remaining shares and sold them to friends in Spokane. The new owners wasted little time in registering their purchase as the Le Roi Mining and Smelting Company of Spokane. The new owners now decided to issue 500,000 shares at a par value of $5, providing there were buyers. But there would soon be a glitch: the company was registered in Washington State, but the mine was on Canadian soil. After a great deal of court time in both countries, the company was eventually incorporated in BC.

In the spring of 1891, Topping took Durant and Harris to the Le Roi claim, and before long they had a cabin and an inclined shaft on the property. By fall, the men at the Le Roi had seven tons of high-grade ore ready to be packed down the eleven kilometres (seven miles) of trail from their camp to the Columbia River, where it was unloaded onto a boat for transportation south to the Little Dalles. From here, the ore was prepared for transshipment to a far-off smelter belonging to American copper king Marcus Daly in Butte, Montana. The ore was incredibly rich: 5 percent to 20 percent copper, and yielding three to ten ounces of silver and from two to twenty ounces of gold to the ton.

The lengthy freight and costly smelting charges, however, ate up all the profits. The entrepreneurs quickly realized they would need a smelter much closer to the mine site to be profitable. By now, the word was out that a rich ore body had been discovered in the Kootenay district of British Columbia, and the local inhabitants prepared for the inevitable rush.

Joe Moris sold his Centre Star claim to Oliver Durant of the Le Roi syndicate, while George Bourgeois allowed his War Eagle to be bonded to Durant and Tarbet.

Topping invested his money in real estate, and together with Frank Hannah, a blacksmith-prospector, laid out a townsite where the trail from the mining camp connected with the Columbia River. The pair called the place Trail Creek Landing, later shortened to Trail.

In January 1892, miner Ross Thompson, only twenty-seven years old, had a vision for the future and decided to pre-empt a 65-hectare (160-acre) townsite not far from the gold claims. He wanted to call the place Thompson, but since a town by that name already existed, he settled on the name Rossland.

Two rich Americans, Fritz Augustus Heinze and David C. Corbin, cast their sights on Rossland's mines. Heinze had heard rumours that Corbin, an American railroad magnate, was considering building a smelter in northern Washington, at Northport. Heinze became one of BC's most flamboyant industrial pioneers. Born in 1869 in Brooklyn, New York, he graduated from the School of Mines at Columbia University, then went to work as an engineer with the Boston and Montana Copper Company in the wide-open town of Butte. He studied American mining laws, and his shrewd mind began to find loopholes in the system. Heinze was not long with his employer before being let go to make room for the relative of a large shareholder. Now he held a grudge. He raised money to buy an abandoned water-filled mine adjacent to a rich Boston and Montana property and built an onsite smelter. He began doing underground raids on rich neighbouring copper-bearing mines, bringing the ore

ROSS THOMPSON (1865-1951)
The founder of Rossland, Thompson initially wanted to name the town Thompson, but a town by that name already existed—hence the name Rossland.

ROSSLAND MINING MUSEUM

MINING COMPETITION

Two brawny miners compete in a drillers' competition in 1897 Rossland.

HISTORICAL PHOTO D-01628, ROYAL BC MUSEUM AND ARCHIVES

out through shafts on his own mine. To hide his thievery, he dynamited the shafts once the ore was brought to the surface and smelted. The big players went after him, but because he had powerful friends in high places, he was able to keep his enemies at bay.

It was during this turbulent time that Heinze heard about the Le Roi Mine at Rossland. Now twenty-six and a self-made millionaire, Heinze sent emissaries to Rossland, who reported back that he could make big money honestly by building a smelter. The provincial government offered inducements, and Eugene Topping offered him a third of his townsite for a smelter. Heinze quickly agreed and immediately built a tramway from the mine down the long hill to Trail. Heinze's men contracted with the Le Roi management to treat 75,000 tons of ore: the first half of the ore was to be treated for $11 a ton and the remainder at a lower price, if possible.

On September 13, 1895, ground was broken for his new smelter just above Trail on the Columbia River. Two hundred men worked on the buildings, and the smelter was ready for the first ore on February 1, 1896. The growing success of the smelter led Heinze to replace the tramway with a eleven-kilometre- (seven-mile-) long narrow-gauge railroad from the mine down to Rossland. It was during this time that two of his smelter managers at Trail defected and built a competing smelter at Northport, Washington.

ABOVE

Three heavily loaded ore wagons cut deep groves into the road upon leaving Rossland around 1895.

FOLLOWING PAGES—MAP SHOWING THE MANY CLAIMS AT ROSSLAND

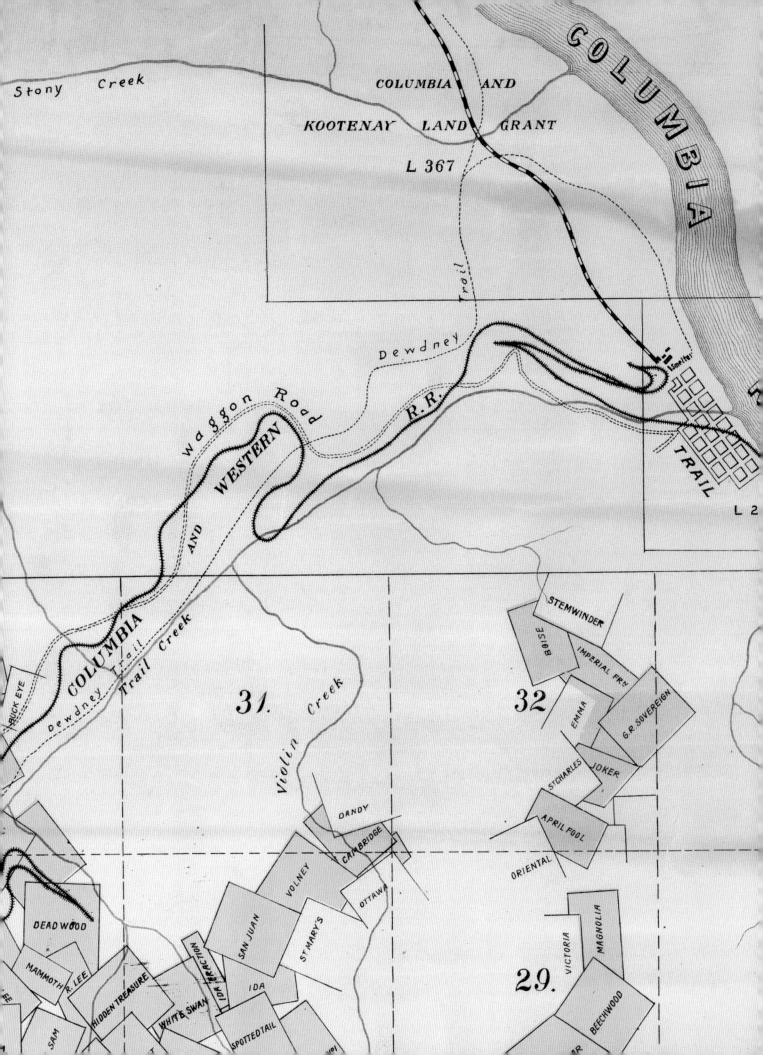

Stony Creek

COLUMBIA AND

KOOTENAY LAND GRANT

L 367

COLUMBIA

Dewdney Trail

Waggon Road

WESTERN

AND

R.R.

Smelter

TRAIL

L 2

COLUMBIA

Dewdney Trail Creek

BUCK EYE

31.

Violin Creek

32

STEMWINDER

BOISE

IMPERIAL FR'N

EMMA

G.R. SOVEREIGN

ST CHARLES

JOKER

APRIL FOOL

ORIENTAL

DANDY

CAMBRIDGE

VOLNEY

OTTAWA

ST MARY'S

DEADWOOD

SAN JUAN

IDA FRACTION

IDA

MAMMOTH R. LEE

HIDDEN TREASURE

WHITE SWAN

SPOTTEDTAIL

SAM

VICTORIA

MAGNOLIA

29.

BEECHWOOD

FRITZ AUGUSTUS HEINZE (1864-1914)

This fast-living, unscrupulous American was known as the Copper King of Butte, Montana, before venturing north across the Canadian border to do battle with the directors of the Canadian Pacific Railway.

HISTORICAL PHOTO C-08957, ROYAL BC MUSEUM AND ARCHIVES

Heinze soon learned that the Canadian Pacific Railway's (CPR) executives had decided to run a spur line toward Trail. Now railroad-conscious, Heinze built his Columbia and Western Railway to bring ore from Kootenay Lake to Trail. When copper ore was found in Phoenix Mountain near Grand Forks, the alert developer saw another new opportunity. He went to Victoria to lobby for a charter to extend his railroad west to Penticton. But the thirty-year-old whiz kid made the error of biting off more than he could chew. He became tangled up in legal battles with Marcus Daly, owner of the Acaconda Mines in Butte, Montana, and with John D. Rockefeller, another Montana copper king and the president of Standard Oil.

So Thomas Shaughnessy, the second president of the CPR, turned to a friend to help him select a suitable man to look after his interests in Trail; his friend suggested Walter Hull Aldridge. Shaughnessy was impressed with the young man's impeccable credentials and knowledge of mining. Aldridge had graduated with Heinze from Columbia University's School of Mines. He knew Heinze's idiosyncrasies and seemed the perfect man for the job. Shaughnessy was lucky to get the young graduate engineer, as he'd just been offered a job with the Guggenheim brothers of New York, one of the wealthiest families in the US. Aldridge accepted the CPR's offer to him to assist in the purchase of the Trail smelter and then to stay on and manage the newly named Canadian Smelting Works.

Rumours that the company was ready to sell began circulating in 1897, when owners started to disagree on the management of the mine. The value of the mines escalated when the Honourable Charles MacKintosh, the lieutenant-governor of the Northwest Territories (and later of Alberta), travelled to London, England, looking for wealthy Englishmen to invest in Canadian ventures. MacKintosh met with school chum J. Whitaker Wright, the top figure in the London and Globe Finance Company. A true gambler with other people's money, Wright didn't hesitate to launch a new company with Mackintosh to acquire mining properties throughout BC and Alaska. It would be known as the British America Corporation. As the managing director in Canada for the new company, MacKintosh left London and was very soon in Rossland, buying up property around the Le Roi Mine. At the same time, Colonel Peyton and W.W. Turner were in London for the express purpose of selling the Le Roi. Peyton met with Wright contacts, arranging the sale of the Le Roi for $3 million. Unfortunately, his price was $2 million short of what some of the other mine owners wanted for their gold mine. The case ended up in a Spokane courtroom. The position of Washington State was that no alien could hold property within the state. As mentioned earlier, however, the property was in Canada, even though it was registered in the US. As a result, the lawyer representing British interests gathered together as many documents as possible and fled across the border back into BC.

Heinze was also having problems with his Trail smelter. He wanted to charge higher rates to process than originally negotiated, with the result that other smelters started cropping up on both sides of the border. Heinze heard that Shaughnessy was interested in buying his smelter, but at a very low price, so Heinze bought a newspaper and instructed the publisher to write derogatory editorials about the greedy railroad

magnate, but to no avail. He had hoped to get $1 million for his smelter, but in the end sold out to the CPR for only $300,000.

Some of the major players in the Rossland mines came to tragic ends. London-based James Wright was convicted of fraud in 1904 and given a seven-year sentence. Before being taken away, he managed to swallow cyanide pills and died in the courtroom.

In 1907, Heinze moved back to New York and, with his two brothers, became a major player in the financial arena. Their company caused the financial collapse that came to be known as the Panic of 1907. He died in 1914, at forty-four, from cirrhosis of the liver.

These giant boilers for the Le Roi Mine were built by the Ingersoll Rock Drill Company in Montreal and shipped by rail across Canada to Rossland. A Red Mountain Railroad spur line transported the heavy equipment to the entrance to the mine.

The Dufferin Coach

Marquis of Lorne

The following information is taken from the New Westminster Museum, where the Dufferin Coach is on display:

This coach was built in San Francisco in 1876 by N.H. Black and Company especially for the purpose of carrying Lord Dufferin, Governor General of Canada, and Lady Dufferin on their trip to the Cariboo goldfields.

The splendid Dufferin Coach, its specially chosen horses—a four- to six-horse team—and the accompanying coach attracted much attention on their journey.

The springs are made of sixteen-ply leather and the body is solid oak. The outer iron rims on the wheels were heated and shrunk down and the only way to get them off is to break the spokes out of them. The seating capacity of the coach is six to nine inside and three on the box, including the driver. The total cost of such superior quality construction came to $1,200, a very high price. After the coach was built it was transported to Yale on a steamer ahead of Lord and Lady Dufferin to await their arrival.

ABOVE

Lord Dufferin is mistakenly identified as the Marquis of Lorne in this archival portrait, done in 1873. He became a well-known figure following the publication of a best-selling account of his travels in North America. In 1872 he became the third Governor General of Canada, a position he held until 1878. By a strange twist of fate Lord Dufferin's downfall came when he gave both moral and financial support to the London and Globe Financial Corporation—headed by England's financial wizard Whitaker Wright, the man who persuaded him to invest heavily in a mine in British Columbia. The mine, located in Rossland, eventually became the largest lead, zinc, gold, and silver mine in the British Empire and morphed into Cominco (Consolidated Mining and Smelting Company).

NEW WESTMINSTER MUSEUM AND ARCHIVES

THE WAR EAGLE MINE IN ROSSLAND BEFORE THE WIDESPREAD USE OF HARD HATS, 1913
ROSSLAND HERITAGE MUSEUM AND ARCHIVES, 50-1762

THE LEGEND OF THE SPANISH MOUND

by Stan Copp, Ph.D.
Department of Archaeology, Simon Fraser University

According to this old legend, the Spanish Mound is a grassy hill in which the armour, weapons, and remains of an ill-fated Spanish expedition are buried.

The legend relates the story of a heavily armed expedition that came into the Similkameen Valley long before the Hudson's Bay Company of "King George" men came to the region looking for furs. One version of the legend indicates that a Spanish ship came to grief on the sandbars of the Columbia River. The conquistadors abandoned the ship and commenced a trek up the Columbia River before turning north into the Similkameen watershed. Oddly, if, as the legend suggests, the Spaniards, with a nose for gold, were looking for an "Eldorado" or "Lost City of Gold," they passed a fortune as they proceeded up the Similkameen River, as a later gold rush would prove.

The First Nations version, according to oral history, states that a band of men with white faces and much hair and wearing "metal clothes" marched into the Similkameen Valley from the south and camped near the Keremeos Native village. The sight of the conquistadors must have been both puzzling and terrifying, since never before had the Similkameen First Nation ever seen anyone riding atop an "elk dog." The Spaniards remained at Keremeos until an altercation erupted between a Similkameen brave and a soldier. The quarrel quickly escalated into a no-contest battle between the heavily armed Spaniards, professional soldiers all, and the Natives. After this bloody affray, in which the Similkameen suffered heavy losses, the Spanish took several Similkameen captive and used them as carriers as they retreated up the valley of Keremeos Creek. Continuing up that stream, the Spanish crossed over the divide and marched down the Shingle Creek draw. At the foot of Okanagan Lake, they crossed to the eastern side near present-day Penticton, followed the old eastside Native trail and established a camp close to a little creek a few kilometres north of the present-day site of Kelowna. There they threw up a large log building to house both the men and the horses through the winter.

The following spring, most probably because their numbers had been cut by either disease or Native hostility, they left their outpost and retraced their steps southward. At any rate, the group, with numbers considerably reduced, made their appearance near the upper reaches of Keremeos Creek.

Several days later, so the story goes, they marched out of the hills and camped on a small flat overlooking Keremeos Creek, evidently close to the area where the stream enters the valley proper. Forewarned, the vengeful Similkameen kept close watch on the column. Finally the Spaniards struck camp and moved off down the valley, and somewhere between Keremeos and Olalla they were ambushed by overwhelming numbers of Similkameen braves. A sharp and vicious battle ensued in which the weakened and outnumbered Spaniards were annihilated.

After this epic struggle, according to legend, the Similkameen then buried the despised white strangers with all their armour and weapons on a low grassy mound somewhere between the last Spanish camping place and the Native village called Keremye'us. And there, so they claim, they remain to this day in the long-lost and unmarked burial place.

The legend is intriguing because there is considerable evidence that tends to corroborate the story. Old steel weapons have been recovered in various parts of the valley and especially in the areas close to Keremeos. They could have been trade items that were brought to the Similkameen, but why were they concentrated almost exclusively around Keremeos?

The pictographs in the valley provide other clues, especially the "prisoner paintings" that seem to depict four Native warriors roped or chained together and surrounded by quadrupeds, seemingly dogs. It was a common Spanish custom to chain their captives together and guard them with vicious dogs. It is an interesting theory.

The discovery of rare Native armour: hammered copper plate in an old Native burial near Keremeos also lends credence to the Spanish story. The armour is perforated and amazingly similar to old Spanish mail. Where did the Similkameen First Nation get the idea of armour plate? It was singular to the Keremeos region, and some historians contend that the Natives simply copied the Spanish mail they had seen, which was nearly impenetrable to arrows during the battles.

Finally, in 1863, a large building that had been constructed for both horses and men was discovered in the Kelowna area. The size of the massive structure, estimated at around ten by twenty-two metres (thirty-five by seventy-five feet), indicated that it had once been a wintering quarters. Even in 1863, it was very old. Was this the building used by the Spanish when they purportedly wintered in Kelowna?

Although the smallest, another piece of evidence is perhaps the most impressive of all. Several decades ago, a pendant of highly polished and beautifully worked turquoise was recovered from a very old Native burial site at Okanagan Falls. Archaeologists state that this is the only documented instance of turquoise found in a Native grave in the province. Was this precious stone originally in the possession of one of the Spaniards in the ill-fated expedition of the seventeenth century?

The clues are fascinating but by no means conclusive, and the mystery of the "Spanish Mound" remains unsolved. Only the discovery of this long-lost burial place would solve this centuries-old puzzle.

Prisoner paintings east of Hedley.

DAVID GREGORY PHOTO

A pictograph, possibly of a helmeted Spanish conquistador mounted on a horse.

DAVID GREGORY PHOTO

A pictograph, possibly of a pair of swords.

DAVID GREGORY PHOTO

Tulameen Canyon and the Similkameen River

Granite Creek *by Gino Del-Ciotto*

Once regarded as British Columbia's third-largest town (sometimes mistakenly referred to as city), Granite Creek was quite literally born out of chance. The legend of the gold-boom town starts with a horse rustler with a reputation for laziness and his chance discovery of gold on Granite Creek. His name was Johnny Chance, and in the summer of 1885, he was herding horses across the border through the Similkameen Valley. He made a short stop at the Allison Ranch. From there, Johnny Chance made the odd decision to head through the Tulameen Valley toward the Coquihalla trail rather than the more often travelled Dewdney Trail. This decision was the beginning of several that led to the birth of a bustling gold-rush town.

Stopping in a quiet little valley delta formed at the confluence of what are now known as Granite Creek and the Tulameen River, Johnny Chance was with the other men in his herding crew when he chose to beat the July heat and head over to a meandering creek. While he was lazing the afternoon away there, the sun shifted position, creating a golden glimmer at the creek bottom. The rustler filled his pouch with coarse gold nuggets, and upon bragging of his discovery to his friends and co-workers, he went from lazy zero to hero. Word about gold discoveries spread fast in those days, and by the time the snow came down in the winter, the new Granite Creek gold rush was in full gear, with over 2,200 souls gathered to reap the little creek's golden harvest. In five short months, Granite City was BC's third-largest city. Of note, the saying "found by chance" was coined on the shores of Granite Creek due to the name of the discoverer.

With over forty homes, six saloons, hotels, and eight stores built in its first five months, the town was well on its way to being established. There were sixty-two known mining companies plying the shores of the creek and surrounding area. Over $500,000 worth of gold, at a value of $18 per ounce, were found in this little creek, along with a strange grey metal that was unfamiliar to the prospectors; it sat heavy with the gold and was difficult to separate. It was gathered and thrown away by many prospectors and cached for later recovery by many Chinese miners. The metal was platinum—the Tulameen River with its surrounding creeks is one of only two river systems on earth that carry placer platinum nuggets.

"Alas 'twas not to last," says the inscription on a memorial standing on the remains of the former gold-rush town, now a ghost town. As is the story with many towns of the era, another gold discovery was made elsewhere, and many left to chase their dreams. Those who stayed remained in the area until fire decimated what was left of the town in 1907. It is rumoured that a man by the name of Johannson buried a large cache of platinum within sight of his cabin, and many treasure seekers have attempted to locate this valuable cache, with no reports of its recovery. Although gone, the town is not forgotten. About one hundred people live at the Granite Creek townsite today.

PLATINUM SAMPLES FOUND ON A TRIBUTARY OF THE TULAMEEN RIVER
AUTHOR PHOTO

GOLD IN QUARTZ SAMPLES FOUND ON GRANITE CREEK
AUTHOR PHOTO, NUGGETVALLEYPROSPECTINGADVENTURES.COM, EUREKAGOLDSANDS.COM

BELOW, LEFT—THE RUINS OF AN ORIGINAL CABIN ON GRANITE CREEK
In the 1970s, seekers of gold, platinum, and artifacts visited the site with excavating equipment and dug up the area around the buildings.

BELOW, RIGHT—THE GRANITE CREEK GRAVEYARD OVERLOOKING THE MINING COMMUNITY DIRECTLY BELOW, CIRCA 1880S
Nestled in the Jack pines, these unidentified graves, encircled by painted white rocks, lie interspersed with the graves of the named dead, which are contained within the white-picket-fence enclosures.

GOLD SAMPLE FOUND ON GRANITE CREEK, ENLARGED FIVE TIMES
AUTHOR PHOTO, NUGGETVALLEYPROSPECTINGADVENTURES.COM, EUREKAGOLDSANDS.COM

The Life of a Hard Rock Miner

There were two methods of hand drilling in the mine shafts and adits. One was called the "single jack" and involved a single miner using a 1.8- or 2.2-kilogram (four- or five-pound) hammer to strike the drill steel that was turned after each blow to keep the hole round. The other method was the "double jack," and it involved two miners. In this case the hammer weighed 3.5 (8 pounds) and had a longer handle than the single jack. The two men worked as a team, one wielding the sledgehammer that struck the steel while the other turned the bit. The miners would drill the holes into the rock to provide a place for a stick of dynamite prior to blasting. It was dangerous work.

At July 1 and July 4 celebrations, contests were held to see which team of miners could drill the deepest hole in fifteen minutes. The drillers would change positions after the first and second minute and in thirty-second intervals thereafter. A Rossland team competing in Spokane in fall 1901 broke the record before three thousand spectators by drilling 1.3 metres (51 inches). The names of the two winners were W.M. Ross and George S. McLeod.

A 3.5-kilo sledgehammer.

PENTICTON MUSEUM AND ARCHIVES

This historic rock received its large boreholes in a drillers' competition in Princeton in 1913.

AUTHOR PHOTO

THE BRALORNE GOLD DISCOVERY

by Arthur Raymond (Bud) Ryckman

Gold was first discovered near Lillooet, at the confluence of the Bridge and Fraser Rivers, by prospectors heading north in 1858 for the Cariboo gold rush. Many of the gold seekers—or Argonauts, as they were sometimes called—had worked the gravel bars in the lower reaches of the Fraser, where the gold dust was so fine, it had to be amalgamated with mercury to be extracted. The miners knew that fine gold dust would have travelled a considerable distance from the motherlode, so the goal was to move upstream to find the primary source. Many of the Argonauts worked up the canyon from Yale to Lillooet, and many more followed the Port Douglas route. Either way, they arrived at Lillooet, and in proceeding upstream, they all passed the confluence of the Fraser and Bridge Rivers between 1858 and 1860. A few tested the gravel bars at the mouth of the Bridge River and discovered showings of placer gold in the gravel bars, coarser than the fine dust found in the lower Fraser River. Some of the miners chose to work the area with rockers and sluices, and some believed that they were near the motherlode. A camp town (mostly tents), named Bridgeport, was set up, and by May 1859 two hundred miners were working the waters of the Bridge River with some promise of success.

Apparently the name Bridge River was given to the stream because the local Native people had built a bridge across the Fraser River where the Bridge and Fraser meet. This bridge had collapsed, but two business partners named Fraser and Davis built a new bridge across the Fraser and operated it as a toll bridge, charging travellers twenty-five cents to cross the bridge.

By 1861 the gravel bars located in the estuary of the Bridge River had been worked out, and none of the miners made any attempts to prospect the depths of the Bridge River valley. The fact that the Native people had let it be known that they didn't want any intruders to enter their territory and would be ready to kill anyone who tried may have played a role in this. The word among the miners was that the big motherlodes they were seeking were farther up the Fraser. That winter, the toll bridge was wrecked by ice floes, so Bridgetown was soon abandoned, and the majority of the gold seekers headed upstream.

Some miners stayed and continued to work the bars in the area, with limited success. For thirty-eight years, no serious attempts were made to prospect the upper reaches of the Bridge River.

In 1896 a prospector named Harry Atwood, who was grubstaked by William Allen, owner of the Pioneer Hotel in Lillooet, discovered a rich pay streak on Cadwallader Creek. The ground was staked with several claims and named the Pioneer, after Allen's hotel. Fred Kinder partnered with Harry Atwood, and together they worked the claim until Atwood sold out to Arthur Noel. Noel and Kinder set up a water-powered mill on Cadwallader Creek and continued to work the claim until 1911, when the property was sold to a group consisting of Arthur Noel, Adolphus Williams, Frank Holten, and brothers Peter and Andrew Ferguson. They bought the claim and equipment for $26,000. Holten and Noel sold their equity, and in 1915 Pioneer Gold Mines Ltd. was incorporated. A mill was constructed, and mining continued for the next three years. Pioneer Gold Mines managed to produce four thousand troy ounces of gold.

Many attempts were made by mining companies to acquire financing to fund the development of a major underground lode mine in the area. In 1920, an opportunity to purchase was granted to a mining company for $100,000. The company defaulted on payment, so a Vancouver group represented by A.E. Bull and A.H. Wallbridge bought out the option. Operations were stopped after a further $50,000 was expended without success. A.E. Bull then contracted David M. Sloan, a mining engineer, to examine the property and advise on the feasibility of a mining venture. Should Sloan decide the property was worth developing, he had been instructed to seek further capital for that purpose. Sloan was convinced that the property was sound and viable but was unable to locate an investor. Finally he and his partner, J.I. Babe, took over the option from Bull and Wallbridge. In 1928, Babe sold out his 50 percent interest to Colonel Victor Spencer, and Pioneer Gold Mines of British Columbia was incorporated.

With David Sloan as general manager of operations, work proceeded at all levels. When the Pioneer townsite was completed, it had two bunkhouses, a machine shop, store, and recreation hall with a dance floor. It also featured a poolroom, library, barbershop, theatre, school, and twelve private homes. Pioneer continued to operate as a profitable and independent company until 1959, when Bralorne and Pioneer were united to create Bralorne and Pioneer Mines Ltd.

In 1897, prospectors John Williams, Nat Coughlin, and William Young, working the gravel bars of Cadwallader Creek, found sufficient coarse gold to stake three claims, which they named the Golden King, the Marquis, and the Lorne. Subsequently, forty-nine other claims were staked in the adjacent area, but the Lorne turned out to be the richest of the claims. The various holders of these fifty-two claims worked their own ground in their own way. In 1900 they amalgamated their properties, totalling about 485 hectares (1,200 acres), into one company, the Lorne Gold Mines.

The principal owner of the Lorne mine was William Sloan, a member of the BC Legislature from 1916 to 1928 and the minister responsible for mines. Sloan had made his original fortune in the Klondike. He had the property assessed by mining engineers in 1916, and as the report was negative, Sloan sold his equity to Arthur Noel, who had been partners with Fred Kinder in the Pioneer Mine. Arthur Noel worked the Lorne mine until 1928, when he sold out to the Stobie Furlong Company, which also bought the adjacent properties. They named their new company Lorne Gold Mines Ltd. The Stobie Furlong Company hired Harry Clinton

Wilmot to supervise operations, which included opening adits and driving tunnels into the main ore body. A sawmill, townsite, machine shop, stamp mill, and crew accommodations were constructed. By 1930, the Stobie Furlong Company was in financial difficulty. Bralco Development, a Vancouver company headed by William W. Boultbee, Austin Cottrell Taylor, George Kidd, and Neil McQueen bought out Stobie Furlong and—by combining the two names Lorne and Bralco—renamed the company Bralorne Mines Ltd.

The new corporation commenced mining immediately. In March 1932, Bralorne Mines poured its first ingot, with a weight of 393 troy ounces. Bralorne continued to operate for forty years, producing more than 4 million troy ounces of gold.

The mine was still in use in 1971, but with the price of gold fixed at $35 per ounce, operating costs growing, and the fact that the mine had now reached down to six hundred metres (two thousand feet) below sea level where the rock pressure and heat is extreme, it became uneconomical to continue. Ed Hall, manager of operations in 1971, said there was still some spectacular ore at the bottom level. However, since they were now what he referred to as being "one mile in and one mile deep," with shafts, drifts, and tunnels extending for a total of close to 160 kilometres (100 miles), it would cost more to mine the ore than it would be worth.

* * *

AUSTIN COTTRELL TAYLOR, a major player in the creation of Bralorne Mines, was born in Toronto in 1889. He made his first million playing the stock markets before reaching his twenty-first birthday. He was a "man's man," an excellent amateur polo player, happiest outdoors with his dogs and horses, fishing or hunting. He married Kathleen Elliott, a graduate of the University of Manitoba, and the couple had a son and two daughters.

In 1917, when he was twenty-eight, Taylor came to BC as the director of the aeronautical department of Britain's Imperial Munitions Board, in charge of harvesting the straight, tough, fine-grained Sitka spruce from the Queen Charlotte Islands for the manufacture of training aircraft for the war effort. This so-called "airplane spruce" was used in the fledgling aircraft. Great Britain's spruce requirements were 8.5 million board feet of timber monthly, and under Taylor's expert organization, the portion of that requirement filled by BC went from 1.36 percent in January 1917 to 12 percent by June and 80.6 percent by November. With the fir shipments added in, Canada's contribution reached 97 percent of Great Britain' lumber requirements.

Taylor's greatest business venture came when he raised the necessary capital to take over the failing Lorne gold mine north of Pemberton, turning it into Bralorne Mines Ltd. The mine became one of Canada's leading gold producers and provided large-scale employment in the Depression years in this part of the country. It also made him a multi-millionaire.

An avid horseman and now wealthy, Taylor became interested in horse racing and started raising thoroughbred stock at his own breeding stables at Milner, in the Langley area. He also used some of his fortune to buy sugar magnate Benjamin T. Rogers's showplace home, Shannon, at 57th Avenue and Granville Street in Vancouver. He spent time at Milner during the summer, but his year-round residence was Shannon.

During the Second World War, the federal government made him a "dollar-a-year man." Among other posts, he was chairman of the BC Security Commission. He was responsible for security matters during the war, and as such was involved with the regrettable decision in 1942 to move Japanese families from the coast and into internment camps, ostensibly for both their safety and for the country's welfare during the war.

In 1947, Taylor was awarded the Order of the British Empire for his wartime civilian service. A modest, humble man, generous and kind and with a wry sense of humour, Taylor never sought publicity for his accomplishments, even though he held directorships in a number of corporations. He was offered the post of lieutenant-governor of BC several times but each time refused the honour.

Taylor suffered from arteriosclerosis and died after a long illness in 1965 in Vancouver at the age of seventy-six.

* * *

ANOTHER GOLD MINE in the Bridge River area was at Minto, which developed from claims staked by prospector Warren A. Davidson near the junction of Gun Creek and Bridge River in 1931. The Minto Camp employed forty men and had a bunkhouse, cookhouse, and a diesel-powered electric generator. The nearby

These are taken from Taylor's Bralorne Gold Mine. The specimen on the left is over 80 percent gold.

CANADIAN MUSEUM OF NATURE, 56706 AND 06706

AUSTIN COTTRELL TAYLOR (1889-1965)
TAYLOR FAMILY

Wayside Mine had its own hydroelectric power plant and a bunkhouse with facilities for sixty men. In 1936, 33,000 tons of ore were milled at Minto Mines, with a recovery of 4,300 troy ounces of gold and 13,000 ounces of silver. The mine closed in 1942, but Minto didn't become a ghost town. The model community created for a population of eight hundred was turned into an internment camp for the Japanese who had been evicted from the coast in 1942. In 1969, the town of Minto disappeared under the man-made Carpenter Lake, created by a BC Hydro dam on the Bridge River.

THE HEDLEY GOLD MINE AT NICKEL PLATE

by Marilyn L. (Mrs. Gene) Morris, née Probert, granddaughter of Myron Knox Rodgers

As early as 1894, Edgar Dewdney, builder of the Dewdney Trail, had James Riordan and Charles Allison stake claims on what was later called Nickel Plate Mountain. Allison was the son of John Fall Allison, the first white settler at Red Earth, or Vermillion Forks (present-day Princeton). This site had originally been named after the red ochre used by the Native people for face painting or pictographs. In 1860, it was renamed Prince's Town (Princeton) to honour the visit to eastern Canada of Queen Victoria's eldest son, Edward, Prince of Wales, later to become King Edward VII. Dewdney and Allison married sisters, which made them brothers-in-law.

According to legend, "the greenhorn prospectors" had been panning for gold in the Similkameen Valley floor and had encountered some locals who, as a cruel prank, told them that the best prospects were on the high mountainous ridges above the 1,524-metre (5,000-foot) level. Incredibly, the two men found free gold in a rusty red outcrop near the top of a mountain. As a result, other seasoned miners quickly staked claims on the mountain. Ironically, the claims staked by Riordan and Allison were allowed to lapse and reverted back to the Crown. (Robert Rist Hedley, the manager of the Hall Mine at Nelson, was one of the earliest grubstakers, and the town that afterward sprang up was named after him.)

John Oswald Coulthard, known as Ozzie, had four claims on the mountain but allowed them to lapse. According to Doug Cox's book *Mines of the Eagle Country: Nickel Plate & Mascot*, this occurred because Richard (Dick) Cawston, after whom Cawston was named, and his brother George were moving steers to Rossland on their fall cattle drive. Since Rossland had an assay office, Ozzie gave some of his Hedley ore samples to Dick to have them assayed. When the steers reached the Columbia River, they initially refused to swim across, so Dick reached into his pocket and threw some of Ozzie's samples at the frightened steers to get them moving into the water. It is likely that some rich gold samples still lay on the banks of the Columbia River at the cattle crossing, which accounts for Ozzie letting his claims lapse. Apparently Riordan, a rancher at Olalla, gained knowledge of placer gold locations from a Similkameen man with the anglicized name of Pinto.

The history of the Nickel Plate Mine really began in August 1898, when Francis Woolaston and Constantine Arundel discovered a rich outcrop of ore on the mountain ridges of what would become Nickel Plate Mountain. They first staked the Horsefly, Nickel Plate, Copperfield, Sunnyside, and Bull Dog mineral claims. Late in the fall of that year, the pair took some samples of the surface ore from their Nickel Plate claim to the provincial fair in New Westminster.

Myron Knox Rodgers, one of the leading figures in the history of the Nickel Plate, later saw the samples in Victoria. At the time Rodgers was travelling through the province in the interests of Marcus Daly, the copper-mining magnate of Butte, Montana. Rodgers was so impressed by the samples that he left post haste by steamer, rail, stage, and horseback to reach the discovery claim. His examination proved so satisfactory that in November, Rodgers made a non-refundable $1,000 deposit on the Nickel Plate, Sunnyside, Bull Dog, and Copperfield claims, promising a payout of $60,000 if the claims proved to be as rich as the samples.

Rodgers was born in 1861 at the family homestead at Charleroi, Pennsylvania, the oldest of ten children. He earned his own way through Washington & Jefferson College in Washington, Pennsylvania, and graduated as a civil engineer. He would come home to the family farm at Charleroi, 160 kilometres from the college, sometimes walking most of the way. He was very dedicated to his family, and after he graduated he paid for the education of his siblings. Born with a strong character, he was conservative, close-mouthed, and possessed an unusual talent in his mining work and finance.

Shortly after he graduated as a civil engineer, he travelled to Helena, Montana, where he secured a position as a rodman on one of the locating/engineering parties of James J. Hill, who was then building the Great Northern Railway from St. Paul, Minnesota, to

THE STAMP MILL

Stamp mills used batteries of stamps to crush ore. Each stamp was made up of a round vertical steel shaft approximately 2.5 metres (8 feet) long with a 91-kilogram (200-pound) cast steel foot attached to the bottom. These were fitted with a camshaft that allowed them to fall down under their own weight, pulverizing the ore into a fine sand. The combination of the shaft and steel foot weighed 476 kilograms (1,050 pounds) each.

HEDLEY MUSEUM

GOLD INGOT MOLD

This gold ingot mould was used for pouring gold bricks. The Hedley Gold Mine yielded 73 metric tons (80 tons), or 1,280 bars.

PENTICTON MUSEUM

Seattle. It wasn't long before Rodgers was promoted to transit man of the party and from that position to chief engineer. As the chief engineer, he was responsible for locating a section of the route that involved a tunnel of considerable length, which, when completed, met the other end of steel with remarkable precision.

Hill had been keeping track of Rodgers and told him that Meyer Guggenheim of New York had asked him to recommend a man to take care of their northern explorations in Alaska. Hill recommended Rodgers and asked that he return to New York to see Guggenheim. This he did and came away with a four-year contract. These operations included building 322 kilometres (200 miles) of railroad, exploring of the Bering River coalfields, and building docking terminals and smelter sites.

After the railroad was done, he went to Butte and became employed by Marcus Daly and James Ben Ali Haggin, owners of the great Anaconda Copper Mine. His rise was rapid, and soon he caught Daly's attention. He persuaded Daly to buy two Corliss compound hoisting engines, each with 1,864 kilowatts of power (2,500 horsepower). The machinery weighed over 360 metric tons (400 tons) and was in continuous use for the next fourteen years. They were the largest, most economical hoisting engines west of the Mississippi River, capable of hoisting a load of 23 metric tons (25 tons) of ore at a speed of 1,070 metres (3,500 feet) per minute.

While living in Butte, Rodgers married Lucy Joyner, a Canadian from Saskatoon, in 1892. Lucy's parents were of Irish and Scottish descent. A college graduate, she was a shrewd lady with unusual innate intelligence. The couple had two children: Edwin Leavitt Rodgers, born in 1894, and ten years later, Margaret Elizabeth, my mother. Edwin, although well educated, ran the gauntlet of wild living as a rich man's son, and his father disinherited him.

Rodgers travelled the world on Daly's behalf, scouting out potential mines. He may have had a sixth sense for this, as Albert E. Pennell explains in his article "An Enviable Record," published in the *United States Investor* on February 19, 1910:

Of the 400 properties examined by Mr. Rodgers, he reported favourably upon only five, and each of these properties has since turned out a bonanza, proving the wisdom of Mr. Rodgers' judgement and showing his ability as a mining engineer to grasp a mine when it is a prospect with little or no development work, the Cananea copper mines in Sonora, Mexico, constituting one of the five. In 1897, Rodgers had a bond on

*practically the whole Cananea copper camp, five miles long
and one mile wide for $175,000. After a few months of devel-
opment work, Mr. Daly gave instructions to close down the
property, on account of dullness in copper. This property has
since produced $50,000,000 in copper.*

Although he was a master in his field and soon amassed a fortune, Rodgers's success did not go to his head; all his actions were
fair and "above the table." As Pennell states further in his article,
"In all his twenty years of active mining operations, Mr. Rodgers
has never yet had a lawsuit and has even yet to enter a courtroom."

Rodgers described his travels in search of mines as follows,
quoted in Percy F. Godenrath's 1905 book, *Mother Earth's Treasure
Vaults*:

> *Hardships! You get used to hardships after travelling for
> three and one-half years, covering over 135,000 miles and
> sampling in the neighbourhood of 700 mineral claims, from
> the tropical climes of Guatemala to the inhospitable shores of
> Alaska. And disappointment; yes, mining men have their full
> share, for fortune is never fickle, to one who seeks to unlock
> her treasure chests. One instance in point will suffice before
> I tell you how I ran across the Nickel Plate. I started out from
> Butte in 1895, holding a sort of roving commission on behalf
> of the late Marcus Daly. I first tackled the then little known
> Boundary district, examining the many remarkable low-
> grade ore bodies in the Phoenix and the Deadwood camps.*
>
> *I had just made a flying* [steam or sailing ship] *trip to
> Australia and was in Victoria bound for the Skeena River
> country. Time hung heavily on my hands while waiting for
> the northbound steamer. One day I happened to be in Wil-
> liam Wilson's store on Government Street in Victoria. He
> showed me some striking looking samples of ore that he said
> came from the southern part of the province from a claim
> owned by two prospectors named Woolaston and Arundel.
> I met Woolaston and arranged to see the prospect. We went
> into the Similkameen by a rather circuitous route, down the
> Okanagan Lake to Penticton, then to Fairview* [later Oliver],
> *where we were joined by Arundel, Woolaston's partner, and
> on to Twenty Mile Creek. I made a stay of about an hour and
> a half on the claim and sampled the showing. Intuitively it
> came to me that it had the earmarks of a mine. I sent the
> samples to a Montana assayer. His returns were encour-*

MYRON KNOX RODGERS
Rodgers, working on behalf of Marcus Daly and
James Ben Ali Haggin of Butte, Montana, brought
the Hedley Gold Mine in production in 1904.
Rodgers was perhaps the greatest mine finder
in both North and South America.

MARILYN L. (MRS. GENE) MORRIS, NÉE PROBERT

aging. They looked too good, so later on I went back to the claim myself and resampled the ore. Again I received big results and that determined me to secure the property. I bonded the Nickel Plate, Bulldog, Sunnyside and Copperfield claims for $60,000. Development started and the prospects in time became a mine. That delay at Victoria was responsible for my getting the Nickel Plate.

Early in 1898, Rodgers set out to examine the claims he'd bonded 4,500 metres (5,000 feet) above the valley floor. He first hired local Native men to shovel a trail through the snow to the mountaintop and then hired George Cahill and a partner named William Yates to build a cabin for twenty men before beginning to put in a tunnel on the Sunnyside claim. These men began by stripping off some overburden and driving a wide-open cut to an average depth of about three metres (nine feet), using dynamite. Cahill was in charge of the first pack train that brought in supplies for the men employed at the new camp, arriving from Fairview (near present-day Oliver) in November 1898. Rodgers remained on the site all that winter and the following summer.

At Hedley, many seasoned miners came to check out the new camp and look for any areas that had not yet been recorded. Cahill combed the mountain and discovered sixteen hectares (forty acres) that had been missed by the other Argonauts. Strapped for cash, Cahill sold the claim to Duncan Woods for a reported $15. Woods's land would over time be whittled down to just under three hectares (nine acres) and be called the Mascot Fraction—in time to become the richest gold-producing claim in BC, but that's the second half of the history of the Hedley mines.

The property proved satisfactory to Marcus Daly, so he authorized the funds to build a stamp mill and reduction plant. Unfortunately, Daly died in 1900 and his assets went into his estate.

Rodgers wanted to build a stamp mill and reduction plant as soon as possible along the side of the mountain, just to the southeast of the Hedley Camp.

His first stumbling block was with the Chuchuwayha First Nation, who happened to have a reserve on the property that Rodgers so desperately needed. The mine finder dealt directly with both the Dominion's and province's departments of Indian Affairs, but progress was extremely slow. Eventually, Rodgers swapped 80 hectares (200 acres) for 121 hectares (300 acres) of suitable grazing land. Although Chief Charlie Squakim and most of the Native people seemed all right with the exchange, the medicine man Cosatasket and other braves of the Chuchuwayha of Sixteen Mile Creek were angry and placed a curse on the "palefaces" for annexing their ancestral lands.

Later, Rodgers went ahead and built a large stamp mill, concentrating plant, cyanide plant, office, assay office, hydroelectric ore-haulage road, incline tramway, and all the accessories for a complete mine and milling operation. At nearly 3.2 kilometres (2 miles) long and with a difference in elevation between the terminals of 1,097 metres (3,600 feet), the tramway was the longest of its type in the world. There was also a 4.8-kilometre- (3-mile-) long flume for the hydroelectric plant. The reduction plant was built on the side of a hill above the town of Hedley and about 1,220 metres (4,000 feet) lower than the mine elevation. The hydroelectric plant was powered by a Pelton wheel, and the water came on the flume from Nickel Plate Lake. When they put the dam on the river and shot the water into a turbine downstream, the plant operated until the flume froze and the miners at Nickel Plate were told to leave and come back in the spring. It was not until the 1930s that electrical power came to Hedley and the concentrator ran all year.

The logistics of setting up the mine were enormous. The first challenge was to bring supplies from Fairview on a switchback trail to the site of the original discovery. Later the trail was upgraded to a freight route to the Nickel Plate mine.

A second freight route was also built from Penticton to Hedley Camp, at the base of the mountains. L.A. Clark surveyed a road up to the top of Nickel Plate in 1900, starting on the Green Mountain Road. A second road, referred to as the New Nickel Plate Road, came in 1937, starting at Chuchuwaya and winding up to the Nickel Plate Mine and townsite. This road is still used today.

Although the CPR were building branch lines into other mining camps in BC, Rodgers's former boss, James Hill, had decided to run one of his branch lines from Spokane and Oroville and buy the Vancouver, Victoria and Eastern Railway, a subsidiary of the Great Northern. This line reached Penticton in 1907 and Hedley in 1909.

One of the first steps that Rodgers took was to hire Gomer Philip Jones. Born in Australia, "GP" started mining at age fourteen and earned his chemical engineering degree before he was twenty-one. He later received a mining engineering degree from the Bendigo School of Mines in the State of Victoria, Australia. In 1892, Jones went to New York, where he operated a bicycle shop. Rodgers tracked him down there, and in 1900, leaving his wife and infant child in New York, GP arrived at the Nickel Plate as the mine superintendent.

During the entire development stage of the mine, Rodgers seemed confident he had located a great mine. A remarkable incident took place at this time. Rodgers went over the property, carefully noting the geography, and then placed himself on a particular spot and exclaimed, "There should be great body of ore under here." He constructed a tunnel toward this place and struck a very rich body of ore.

Earlier, Rodgers had offered Woolaston and Arundel $60,000 for only four claims, with a $1,000 non-refundable deposit, paid when he was first taken to discovery site. One story said that just before the expiration of the bond, Arundel had heard nothing about the results of Rodgers's inspection of the claims. Arundel was beginning to feel pessimistic. One day, he was passing the bank when he was tapped on the shoulder. Turning around, he was surprised to see Rodgers, who said he wanted to complete payment on the deal. Rodgers told Arundel that he wanted a couple of other nearby claims as well and instead of giving him a cheque for $59,000, he gave him a cheque for $79,000. A few years later, Woolaston and Arundel sold Rodgers the Iron Duke Fraction, Silver Plate, Copper Plate, Woodland, and other claims for another reputed $60,000. Between 1900 and 1905, Rodgers acquired additional adjacent claims from other prospectors, including the Mound, Coppercleft, Climax, the I.X.L., and the Exchange Fraction.

In 1912, the Hedley Gold Mining Company acquired the Windfall, Morning, Bighorn, Czar, and Winchester Fractions at an estimated cost of $131,000.

ASSAYER'S FURNACE

This assayer's furnace was made by the Morgan Crucible Company of Battersea, England, and used at the Nickel Plate Mine in Hedley. Assayers analyze the composition of the ore samples to determine the quantity, quality, and value of precious metals contained within the sample. Assayer's furnaces such as this are used to heat ore samples to very high temperatures, causing the metals to separate from the encasing rock and other impurities to be extracted and evaluated.

PENTICTON MUSEUM

COUNTER-WEIGHT
PENTICTON MUSEUM

BUCKET
PENTICTON MUSEUM

In his article "The Nickel Plate: 1898–1932," Harry Barnes wrote:

The staff at the Nickel Plate mine in those early years of development consisted of M.K. [Myron Knox] Rodgers, general manger; Wesley P. Rodgers, a brother of M.K. Rodgers, mine manager and surveyor; Gomer P. Jones, who came to the Nickel Plate in August 1900, mine superintendent; and Frank Bragg, store-keeper and timekeeper. About the time the option was taken up on the four original claims a British Columbia charter was obtained for the Yale Mining Company, which became the holding and operating company. A few years later, when it was decided to build a mill at Hedley, it was found that the Yale Mining Company's charter was not broad enough to provide for the building of tramways and power-flumes, or for the expropriation of land for right-of-way. Consequently, a second company, the Daly Reduction Company Limited, was incorporated, and a British Columbia charter obtained for it early in 1903. It became the operating company for both the mine and the mill, the Yale Mining Company existing thereafter only as a holding company.

In 1900, Marcus Daly died and the Hedley Gold Mine went into the Daly estate. In 1904–5, Rodgers undertook to drive an adit—called the No. 4 tunnel—with the portal, or entrance 1,707 metres (5,600 feet) above sea level to cut into the gold-rich ore body. The tunnel went 354 metres (1,160 feet) into the mountain.

In spring 1909, the Daly estate gave an option on their holdings in Nickel Plate to a New York syndicate headed by Isaac Merrill, president of US Steel. Merrill had taken over this largest business in the US after the death of founder John Pierpont Morgan. The new owners called their holdings the Hedley Gold Mining Company Ltd., and Gomer Jones was made general superintendent, while Roscoe Wheeler of Oakland, California, was engaged as mill superintendent.

In 1914, M.K. Rodgers, accompanied by Mrs. Rodgers and their children and Myron's brother, Joseph Henry ("Harry"), and a Miss Taylor of New York, made a trip from the east to the west coast in a large Pierce Arrow car. According to the papers, Rodgers was "virtually a scout for the members of President [Woodrow] Wilson's cabinet." Rodgers visited a number of mining camps in Colorado, Utah, Montana, and BC. At the end of the 9,656-kilometre

(6,000-mile) trip, Rodgers wrote a letter to Secretary of the Interior, Franklin Lane, in Washington, DC. A portion of his letter reads:

> *In British Columbia I inspected the property of the Granby Consolidated Mining, Smelting & Power Company Limited of which I am a director. The plant smelts 3,400 tons of copper ore per day yielding less than 1 per cent copper per ton, in blister copper, at a cost of $1.28 per ton, of which cost 85 cents is for coke. This is the cheapest copper smelting done in the world today.*
>
> *At Hedley I spent three weeks at … the Hedley Gold Mining Company … The property is one of the largest steady gold producers in Canada, and has yielded about $6,000,000 gold in the past ten years, of which 50 per cent has been profit. This property was found after I had travelled for three years hunting a mine over the United States, Mexico, Alaska, Australia and Tasmania; travelling over 135,000 miles and examining over four hundred mining properties.*
>
> *This property has paid over 200 per cent in profits and pays yearly 30 per cent dividends on its capital stock.*

THE RUINS OF MYRON KNOX RODGERS'S HEDLEY GOLD MINE'S 40-STAMP MILL AND CYANIDE PLANT

Designed and built by M.K. Rodgers, hydroelectric generators produced the power for a milled output of tons of ore. At the top level, the complex, huge crushers broke rough ore into fist-sized chunks. Below, forty ten-stamp units broke them further, and the resultant fine mixture was passed through fine screens. Each of the 400 stamps weighed 476 kilograms (1,050 pounds).

The mixture was then dropped onto vanners, oscillating belts that winnowed out the residue. The gold went into amalgamation pans to be "cooked" eight hours with mercury and other chemicals before being transferred into settling tanks, out of which the tailings were flushed. The poisoned tailing ponds eventually had to be cleaned.

AUTHOR PHOTO

While the auto trip ended in Seattle, I had to travel 800 miles further up the Alaska Coast to Anyox, British Columbia (where I am writing this letter) near Portland Canal, Alaska; to the new copper plant of the Granby Consolidated Mining, Smelting & Power Company, Ltd. where this company has just completed a new copper smelter with a capacity of 2,0000 tons per day, and have expended over $4,000,000 on the mine and smelting plant and have on reserves over 10,000,000 tons of commercial copper ore. I took hold of this property fifteen years ago, and have some pleasure now in seeing it developed into one of the largest copper producing mines in the world.

In the fall of 1916, Rodgers was negotiating the purchase of a building in Los Angeles with an asking price of $1 million. At this time, Myron had plans drawn up for a large new home at Puente, California, on the six-hectare (fifteen-acre) place he had aquired. He later built a mansion on an adjacent piece of property.

Rodgers was well on his way to becoming one of the wealthiest mining men in North America had not Bright's Disease (kidney failure) taken his life. He died on July 23, 1917, in Pittsburgh. A year earlier, he had told an acquaintance that he had $5 million in cash (apart from the rest of his holdings in mining properties). He left half of his cash to his wife and the other half to his ten-year-old daughter. His son was not included in his will. By a strange twist of fate, the mining partners, bankers, and lawyers with whom Rodgers had entrusted his money and assets absconded with his entire estate, and the family was left with nothing.

A MODEL 21 EIMCO ROCKER SHOVEL, WITH A CAPACITY FOR 0.28 CUBIC METRES (10 CUBIC FEET), ON DISPLAY IN FRONT OF THE ENTRANCE TO THE HEDLEY MUSEUM

A FLY IN THE OINTMENT

by David Gregory, President, Okanagan Historical Society, and Jennifer Douglass, Hedley Museum Secretary

Duncan Woods, a relentless prospector, was a lone wolf who had wandered all through the Old West. Finally, after two decades of dedicated searching, he located one of the richest mineral claims in BC, a discovery that eventually yielded a Midas hoard of gold.

In 1898, when Woolaston and Arundel accidentally made the first astonishing discovery of free gold in red rusty ore near the top of a steep mountain called Nickel Plate, that find electrified the mining world. Within months, hundreds of prospectors and tramp miners were streaming into the remote Similkameen Valley.

Close on their heels came the mine makers: American financiers from Spokane and the Inland Empire (California); English bankers from the great investment houses of London; and a handful of Canadian speculators from the distant eastern provinces—all with their eyes fixed on Nickel Plate Mountain, and all envisioning another bonanza like the Silver King, War Eagle, Le Roi, and Centre Star mines, or a galaxy of other renowned mines that had been found in southern British Columbia.

But the mining magnates were not alone in their quest. There were others there too, focusing on the prize and equally determined to get their share. Among these hundreds of hopefuls camped along the banks of Twenty Mile Creek was the enigmatic Duncan Woods. In his forties and with few resources remaining, his options were limited. His career had been depressing. A Canadian from Ontario, he had followed the elusive rainbow of prospecting since his twenties, first to the goldfields of the American West; then to South Dakota; then to Montana, Idaho, Oregon, and Washington, but ill luck attended him every step of the way, so finally he turned toward the North Star and crossed the border into southern BC. Once again, bad fortune marched with him, first in the Okanagan district and later in the mineral-rich Boundary Country. But when whispers circulated through the mining camps that massive veins carrying spectacular quantities of gold had been found in the Similkameen Valley, once again he succumbed to the old urge and decided to try his hand in the new mining district.

By 1899 he was at Hedley, a ramshackle booming mining camp tucked into a narrow canyon under the shadows of Nickel Plate Mountain. That fledgling log-cabin town was crackling with

Hand-carved stakes such as this claim marker, probably made of Jack pine, were set up by early prospectors to identify and delineate the boundaries of their mining claims. Once purchased, a mining claim granted the buyer the exclusive rights to explore for and extract minerals from a tract of land.

The Oro Plata claim post consisted of almost twenty hectares (forty-nine acres) and was located 1.5 kilometres (just under a mile) southwest of the Mascot Fraction. The claim had no reported historic gold production. Mining claims in the early days were much smaller.

HEDLEY MUSEUM & ARCHIVES

Duncan Woods standing beside his log cabin with the sod roof at Trout Lake, Summerland.

excitement when he arrived. A motley and colourful crowd milled along its busy streets, where paupers brushed shoulders with princes of finance, clergymen, old hands with greenhorns, gamblers with drifters—all caught up in the unforgettable drama of the stampede.

Nickel Plate Mountain, the key, had already been heavily staked. The nucleus of the claims around the original discovery, with names like Nickel Plate, Mound, Sunnyside, Copperfield, Morning, and Iron Duke were surveyed and would soon become the illustrious Nickel Plate Mine. And in all directions from the main lode, more than a hundred other claims had been staked. While Woods pondered his waning chances, he examined the claims map and noticed there was a gap of open ground west of the discovery claims. Studying the mountain, he saw that it was located on the precipitous western cliffs, the ground being almost vertical.

After weighing the possibilities, Woods decided to claim the unstaked ground on the off chance that the ore body from the rich Nickel Plate lode might eventually trend westward. With his last few dollars, he hired a sometimes packer named George Cahill to stake the cliff side. The following day, the ground was secured. Woods called the claim the "Mascot," not realizing that it would play an historic role in the annals of mining in BC.

By the early 1900s, a steady stream of staggeringly rich gold ore was being shipped from the Nickel Plate Mine, and when a forty-stamp mill was built to process the ore in 1904, Hedley became a bona fide mining town. That year, however, several events occurred that affected the destiny of the camp for decades. The first was the realization by the Nickel Plate management that their ore body was not only massive, but was, as

Woods had speculated, leading to the west, toward the Mascot claim. The officers of the claims then made an unusual request: they asked the gold commissioner to resurvey all of the claims covering the Nickel Plate lode. It was a significant departure from accepted practice and foreshadowed the David-and-Goliath-like struggle that would take place between the powerful mine management and the solitary prospector.

The government official granted their wishes, and after the second survey had been completed Woods's worst suspicions were confirmed. His Mascot claim had, with the stroke of a pen, been reduced from sixteen hectares (forty acres) to just under seven hectares (seventeen acres), and the full claim had suddenly become a fraction. The first round had gone to the mighty Nickel Plate, but their management compounded the situation by sending word to Woods that they would consider purchasing the Mascot Fraction. It was a major error in judgement. They had underestimated Woods's tenacity. He not only turned their offer down, but he also he vowed then and there to never sell his fraction to the Nickel Plate Mine owners.

As the years passed, the Nickel Plate Mine continued to make overtures to the obdurate Woods, and he continued to turn them down. Every month, the bullion bars were shipped out by stagecoach as gold production steadily increased. By 1914, however, the mine's geologists knew that the main ore bodies led directly into the Mascot Fraction and that the fraction was bonanza ground. On the pretext of getting to ore on their Morning Claim, the powerful company asked permission from the gold commissioner to drive a tunnel through the Mascot Fraction. Corrupt officials granted this unheard-of violation of mining law, and the infuriated Woods was forced to stand by hopelessly as his gigantic adversary followed the rich vein into the heart of his fraction. The mine management then brazenly processed the rich ore through their mill and surrendered not one ounce of gold from Wood's fraction, although somewhere between five thousand and ten thousand ounces were stolen from the prospector. It was a thinly disguised theft sanctioned by legal authority.

Virtually penniless, Woods hung on grimly, refusing to surrender his old rights to his precious Mascot claim. As the years passed, the Nickel Plate became one of the most illustrious mines in BC, and the gold it yielded inched up toward the one-million-troy-ounce mark. Although its steady production resulted in impressive profits for its shareholders, the mine's shrewd management never lost interest in the Mascot Fraction and continued in their attempts, some legal, some illegal, to wrest the property from the old prospector. Woods, in turn, never wavered from his vow in 1904 and refused to even consider any proposals from the Nickel Plate. It was a classic stalemate between the singular prospector and the influential mining giant.

Eighteen years later, the price of gold increased to $35 per ounce, mining activity across the province shot up dramatically, and Nickel Plate Mountain and the Similkameen were instrumental in the revival. In short order, a number of mining companies approached Woods with a confusing variety of deals for control of his fraction. Finally, in 1933, more than a third of a century after Woods had obtained his claim, he accepted an offer from a legitimate and newly incorporated company called Hedley Mascot Gold Mines Ltd.

Woods, nearly eighty years old, had finally triumphed over his old adversary; his long battle over, he retired wealthy and respected. The Mascot went on to become one of the richest fractions in Canadian mining history, and by the time it eventually ceased operation it had produced ten tons of pure gold in more than two decades of mining.

Just after it opened, in 1936, the Hedley Mascot Mine ran into difficulties when rumours about its operation caused a severe stock decline. A government investigation discovered that ore samples from the mine had been "salted," and the public had been given false information. The mine was taken over by the provincial government and one of the officials prosecuted. In 1955, the mine was officially closed, and the buildings and tramway became derelict. From the 1950s through to 1986, the mines on Nickel Plate Mountain were inactive. Then, Mascot Gold Mines Ltd. began production from an open-pit mine in 1987. Homestake Mining Company of San Francisco took over the ownership in 1992, but by 1996 ore reserves were exhausted and the company started to wind down its operations on Nickel Plate Mountain.

In the 1990s, the BC government was going to burn the site down because it posed a safety risk, but Bill Barlee, then minister of tourism, intervened and in 1995 allocated about $740,000 to assemble the various portions of the site and start a stabilization program on the wooden structures and decking. In 1998, following a public bidding process, the Upper Similkameen Indian Band (USIB) was given a contract to manage the site. Later, title to the site was transferred to USIB, which created the Snaza'ist Discovery Centre in Hedley to interpret the mine site and serve as a place to conduct tours to the mine. USIB's goal is to turn the Hedley Mascot Gold Mine into a major heritage tourism destination along Highway 3 and to create jobs for USIB and for the wider community.

The aerial tramlines that transported ore from the Mascot Mine (in yellow) and the Hedley Mine (in red) to mills on the valley floor.

WAITE AIR PHOTOS INC. GLOBALAIRPHOTOS.COM

BRITISH COLUMBIA **185**

THE ORIGINAL YUKON GOLD HUNTERS

Historian and judge Frederick William Howay's text on a 1926 plaque regarding Yukon's first gold discovery totally ignored the contributions of First Nations. It simply read:

> Yukon Gold Discovery—to the memory of the indomitable prospectors and miners who, braving extreme dangers and untold hardships, crossed the Chilkat and Chilkoot passes into the

Part Two
YUKON

unexplored valley of the Yukon, and thus paved the way for the discovery of the rich gold fields with which the names of Robert Henderson and George W. Carmack are inseparably associated.

Any mention of discoveries made by Aboriginal men—or, heaven forbid, First Nations women—by the judge was simply out of the question.

The following text is on a Historic Sites and Monuments Board of Canada plaque erected at Carcross (originally Caribou Crossing), Yukon, in 2000:

FIVE DOGS OF ASSORTED BREEDS LIE ABOUT, ALL HARNESSED UP WITH NOWHERE TO GO, CIRCA FALL 1898

Six miners and one boy pose for this photograph with dogs and sled. One important component missing is snow. The walls of the log cabins are chinked with mud, while the roofs are made of thatch that grows fireweed. Most of the men are wearing sealskin clothing. Empty tin cans litter the foreground.

UNIVERSITY OF WASHINGTON DIGITAL COLLECTIONS, HEGG578. PHOTO BY ERIC A. HEGG

James "Skookum Jim" Mason—Kèish (meaning The Lone Wolf) "Skookum Jim," a Tagish of the Dakhtàwèdé clan and the Wolf moiety, found a nugget on Rabbit (Bonanza) Creek in August 1896 that began the Klondike Gold Rush and changed the history of the Yukon. He made the discovery while on a journey down the Yukon River to find his sister Kate and her husband George Washington Carmack. Renowned for his legendary exploits and physical abilities, "Skookum" (strong) Jim believed his Frog Spirit had guided him to the gold. He became very rich but remained a generous man who never forgot his obligations to this community.

In later years, there would be great controversy as to just who made the first discovery. The initial contenders were two whites, Canadian Robert Henderson and George Washington Carmack, an American named in honour of the first president of the USA; and two Native men, Kèish, or "Skookum Jim" (later known as James Mason), and Tagish Charley, or Káa Goox (later Dawson Charley), both relatives of Carmack's Native wife, Shaaw Tláa (later known as Kate).

Henderson, born in Gulf Shore, Nova Scotia, in 1857, left home at fourteen and signed aboard a sailing ship. He prospected in Australia, Africa, and California before his wanderings took him to Yukon and the Forty Mile River at Ogilvie, where he managed to wangle a grubstake out of Joseph F. Ladue. One of the first men to scale the challenging Chilkoot Pass, Ladue had been in the north for fourteen years, and although he was primarily a trader he had prospected for gold in the nearby rivers. He was one of the first men to search for gold in the Throndiuck (later Klondike) River.

Three years younger than Henderson, Carmack had been a sheep herder in California before joining the US Navy. He left the sea life and ended up in Yukon, where he found a coal deposit south of Five Finger Rapids on the Yukon River. Here he set up a trading post that he called Carmack's Post (later Carmacks).

It was during this time that he met Han braves Kèish and Káa Goox, giving them the English names Skookum Jim and Tagish Charley. Both were from the Tagish village located not far from where the annual migration of caribou crossed the Yukon River. This spot was first called Caribou Crossing (Carcross). The three men formed a partnership, and to earn income agreed to pack Dominion of Canada land surveyor (later Yukon gold commissioner) William M. Ogilvie's supplies over the Chilkoot Pass. It was then that Carmack learned Skookum Jim had assisted steamboat captain William Moore in ascending the Skagway River.

HENDERSON'S GOLD SCALES

When Henderson died, these scales were passed down to his son, Grant. When Grant died, the scales were willed to his son, Chester. Chester prospected in the Yukon with partner Frank Burkhard. Following Chester's death, the scales went to Frank, who passed them on to his daughter, Sylvia. Sylvia runs 33 Claim, a gift shop located thirty-three claims below the Discovery Claim. Henry Troemner, a highly reputable craftsman from Philadelphia, Pennsylvania, made the scales.

SYLVIA BURKHARD, CLAIM 33 GIFT SHOP

According to relatives at Carmacks, George's wife, Kate, had fished in a tributary of the Yukon River near its mouth and knew that the creek contained gold, since the Han Nation had used the shiny stones for fish bait. As a result, the couple abandoned Carmack's Post and set out by canoe down the Yukon River to Rabbit Creek. They were prospecting on the creek when Kate's brother Skookum Jim and nephew Tagish Charley found them.

This story of the first major gold discovery on August 17, 1896, does not quite match William Ogilvie's account, as recorded in notes now held in the Yukon Archives:

At the mouth of the Klondike Robert Henderson saw George Washington Carmack, whose story has connected prominently with the discovery of gold on the Klondike. Henderson, in accordance with the unwritten miners' code, told Carmack of the discovery he had made on Gold Bottom Creek, and invited him to come up and stake. Carmack was then engaged in salmon fishing with his Indian friends and associates, the male members of whom were Skookum Jim and Tagish Charley. As Henderson tells the story, Carmack promised to take it in, and take his Indian associates with him, but to this Henderson strongly objected, saying he did not want his creek to be staked by a lot of Natives, more especially Natives from the upper river. Carmack seemed to be offended by the objection so they parted.

I have this story essentially the same from both Henderson and Carmack, the latter, of course, laying a little stress on the objection to the Indians. I have had long interviews with both Jim and Charley, and some of the others camped with them on the Klondike at that time, and reduced the purport of our talks to writing. As I have said, both Henderson and Carmack gave me the same story about Henderson having told Carmack of the new discovery, and the Indians assured me that they knew Bob, as they called Henderson, told George, as they called Carmack, of it and asked him to go and stake on it; that much, therefore, may be assumed without doubt. The stories told me by the Indians may be questioned, but they were very sincere in their tone and assertions when telling me. I took the precaution to interview them separately and afterwards get them all together and criticize and discuss the narrative of each.

Put in as concrete terms as I can frame it, Jim's story tells us that he, Charley, and George were, as we know, camped at

ROBERT HENRY HENDERSON (1857–1933)
This portrait was likely taken when Henderson came "Outside" of Yukon to Vancouver Island in 1923 at age sixty-six.

GEORGE WASHINGTON CARMACK (1860-1922)

Was he the gold hunter who made the first gold discoveries in Yukon, or should the credit have gone to Skookum Jim, his wife's brother—or neither of the men? According to Carmack's wife, Kate, she found the first gold.

the mouth of the Klondike fishing, but as a straight fish diet becomes monotonous in time, in order to procure some variety it was agreed they would get out some logs, take them down to Fortymile, and sell them to the saw-mill there. Much depended on Jim in this work, and he did a good deal of examination of the woods around the place to find the best and most convenient logs. This work took him some distance up a creek afterwards known as Bonanza. He informed me that he found some very good logs at various places, and in order to learn whether or not they could be floated down to the Yukon, he had to make a close examination of the creek bed. In doing this he said he found some colours of gold at various places in the gravel, and particularly at where claim sixty-six below discovery was afterwards located, he found what he considered very fair prospects. He told the fishing camp of this find, but it did not arouse much interest. Jim, according to his own story, was anxious to further investigate, but as George was chief councillor in the camp and did not appear much interested in the matter, it was allowed to drop temporarily.

About twenty days after Henderson called at the camp, George told him to get ready for a tramp to find Bob. The three men started up Bonanza on the quest, with [prospecting] tools . . . for a prolonged stay away from camp, and such provisions as their means afforded.

A short distance below where they afterwards made discovery, both Jim and Charley told me they, while panning during a rest, found a ten-cent pan . . . It was decided (among the trio) that if Gold Bottom trails failed, they would devote further attention to this place.

As they did not find any prospect approaching in value the ten-cent pan on Bonanza, they remained a very short time at Henderson's camp . . . Before they got down far (Bonanza) their provisions were entirely exhausted, and as they prospected on their way down, and Jim was hunting for meat, their progress was slow . . . Jim at last, when they were all too tired and weak to do further prospecting, got a moose.

Jim says he called on the others, whom he had left some distance away, to come to him. While waiting for them to come he looked in the sand of the creek where he had gone to get a drink, taking with him a bit of the moose. He found gold, he said, in greater quantities than he had ever seen before. When the others joined him, the moose was cooked, and they had a feed. Then he showed them the gold in the sand. They *remained two days at this place panning, and testing the gravel up and down the creek in the vicinity. After satisfying themselves that they had got the best spot, and decided to stake and record there, they got into a dispute as to who should stake discovery claim, Jim claiming it by right of discovery, and Carmack claiming it, Jim says, on the ground that an Indian would not be allowed to record it. Jim says the difficulty was finally settled by agreement that Carmack was to stake and to record discovery claim, and assign himself half of it, or a half interest in it to Jim.*

Meanwhile, Henderson was panning a tributary of a small stream that emptied into the Klondike not far from where it flowed into the Yukon River. He found colours and consequently called the stream Gold Bottom Creek; on his way back out to civilization, he told everyone he encountered about his good fortune. It was when returning from Ladue's trading post at Forty Mile with more supplies that he ran into Carmack and his Native relatives. They talked, and Henderson told Carmack about his discovery but made it explicitly clear that his tip should not be passed on to the Native men, because he did not like the way they treated their women. (Henderson refused to either sell or give some of his tobacco to Jim or Charley.)

Perhaps more out of curiosity than excitement, Carmack and his companions decided to check things out on Gold Bottom Creek. According to legend, Carmack promised to send word back to Henderson should he make good finds, to repay him for his kindness. The three men lingered a bit but then moved back to Rabbit Creek, another stream they had already been sampling. Carmack claimed he was the one who had found the first nugget on Rabbit Creek—soon to be renamed Bonanza Creek—on August 17, 1896, though his two companions stated otherwise, claiming it was Jim who made the discovery.

In any event, all three men instantly recognized the significance of the discovery and after a short celebration began panning in earnest.

Another equally plausible story was that Kate Carmack had made an earlier discovery.

It didn't take long for Carmack to fill an expired shotgun casing with flakes of gold. The next day they began staking claims. As discoverer, Carmack was allowed two rim rock-to-rim rock claims of 152 metres (500 feet) each on both sides of the stream. The two other men staked one claim apiece. The two Native miners staked their claims; Jim's claim, immediately above Carmack's two claims, was called One Above, while Charley's, downstream from Carmack's, was called Two Below. They then set off to record them at Forty Mile. Moving downstream, the party of three encountered four Nova Scotians recently arrived from California, and Carmack told them of their good fortune and urged them to stake their own claims on Rabbit Creek. At the mouth of the Klondike, Carmack saw two French Canadians and gave them the same tip. All these men would soon become wealthy as a result. He failed to pass the tip to Henderson, however. The claims recorder at Forty Mile first mocked Carmack but then realized that the gold in the shotgun shell was of a colour and texture never before seen in the North and that just maybe this was the beginning of a strike. Ladue recognized a possible opportunity of a lifetime and immediately staked out a townsite at the junction of the Klondike and Yukon Rivers. He named the spot Dawson City in honour of the Canadian geologist George Mercer Dawson. Ladue then opened a lumber mill for the anticipated building boom. He then returned to the village of Ogilvie and floated his entire sawmill to Dawson City. Many of the early stakers sold their claims for a pittance before even thawing the ground and putting down shafts to bedrock.

George and Kate later moved to a ranch near Hollister, California, and lived with George's sister, Rose Watson. George eventually left California after parting ways with his wife and former partners. He left Kate and their daughter Graphie with Rose, and in 1900 married Marguerite Laimee in Olympia, Washington. Kate, left nearly destitute, began a difficult legal battle to prove that she was George's wife and

TAGISH WOMAN SHAAW TLÁA, LATER KNOWN AS KATE, OR MRS. GEORGE WASHINGTON CARMACK (CIRCA 1862–1920)

According to Kate, she took her husband to Rabbit Creek, a tributary of the Yukon River, and showed him where the Native people had found gold nuggets that they used for fish bait.

entitled to alimony. She eventually dropped the case in the hopes of winning back her husband. When this attempt failed, she settled in Carcross, where Skookum Jim looked after her. Graphie (now married to Marguerite's brother) and his sister, Rose, challenged Marguerite's appointment as the administrator of Carmack's estate. The case was settled out of court.

After Skookum Jim returned to the Yukon, he moved back to the Cariboo Crossing with his wife and daughter, Daisy, and built the finest home in the village. Built with mill-sawed timber, the home consisted of a large living room, a dining room, several bedrooms, and a porch. According to James Albert Johnson's excellent book, *George Carmack: Man of Mystery Who Set Off the Klondike Gold Rush,* Jim furnished his house ornately:

> The chairs for his dining room table had mother of pearl inserts. His silverware was encrusted with gold nuggets taken from his Bonanza mine. On a trip to Vancouver, Jim had spent $2,000 on a Persian rug with an ornate floral design. When the rug arrived and was laid out on the living-room floor, it was two feet wider than the room. Jim was ready to cut the rug, but his wife would not permit it, so he found a better solution: building an extension on the house.

> During the fall and winter months, [Jim] lived at Carcross, where he wore caribou-skin clothing while hunting with his neighbours or participating in the Tagish ceremonial dances. When he returned to the Klondike each year for the spring cleanup, he walked the streets of Dawson wearing a tailor-made suit and a white shirt, a heavy nugget watch-chain draped across his vest and a large stickpin in his tie.

> Following Jim's example, Tagish Charley also built a new home at Carcross. He also bought the Carcross Hotel across the channel from his native village and hired a man to run it for him.

> By this time Skookum Jim and Dawson Charley had sold a half-interest in their claims to a mining partner and left him to look after the day-to-day operations. The richest men in the village of Carcross, they were besieged by relatives and friends looking for loans and handouts and it didn't take long before their fortunes began to dwindle.

> When celebrating the Christmas holiday in 1908 with friends, Dawson Charley may have taken one too many drinks. In the wee hours of December 26, while crossing the

railway bridge at Carcross on his way home, he fell into the open water and was drowned. His body drifted under and ice and he was not found for several days. He was forty-two.

Church officials in Whitehorse, aware of Jim's frailties as well as being concerned for his wife and daughter, persuaded him to sign a series of wills, and to later establish a trust fund.

During the winter of 1915–16, Jim suffered a crippling bladder infection and was hospitalized in Juneau and Whitehorse. In April, using his legal name of James Mason, he signed a final will instructing his trustees to pay $1,000 to his sister Kate, $1,000 to Patsy Henderson, $1,000 to cousin Caribou John and $500 to a Tagish Jim. The trust fund that he set up for daughter Daisy's education was to be known as the Skookum Jim Indian Fund. Aware that his health was failing rapidly, he then went home to Carcross to die. He died on 11 July 1916 at age sixty. A red granite monument marking his grave on the hilltop of the Carcross cemetery bears the name that George Carmack gave him: James Mason.

When the influenza epidemic swept the Yukon, Kate became one of the casualties. The influenza turned into pneumonia, and after a ten-day illness, she died in March 1920 and was buried in an unmarked grave in the Carcross cemetery. Her daughter Graphie left her Berkeley, California, home and returned to Carcross to pick up her mother's few belongings, which included some family photographs and a nugget necklace that her husband George had given her.

In the *Klondike News*, Vol. 1, No. 1, published in Dawson City on April 1, Carmack's full-body portrait graces the front page. The article indicates that the gold output for that year was $40 million.

In 1900, Carmack left Yukon for the last time and settled as a gentleman in Seattle. When Jim and Charley visited Seattle, Carmack greeted them, wanting to square up accounts with the two Native men. According to James Albert Johnson's account, "Carmack led his two partners to his Seattle attorney's office, where the lawyer read aloud the documents transferring Carmack's Discovery Claim and No. 1 Below to Skookum Jim. Four years had lapsed since the three men had discovered the gold that was to make them all rich and [since they] had made the handshake to share and share alike their wealth. Carmack sold his two claims to Jim for a paltry twenty thousand dollars."

Always the promoter, Carmack bought into several business ventures in Seattle and California such as the Microbane Hair Grower—a "guaranteed hair grower" for bald heads. He was a member of the Seattle Lodge of the Yukon Order of Pioneers. Also a Mason, Carmack became the "Worshipful Master" of St. John Lodge in Seattle in 1916. Carmack commissioned a Seattle jeweller to make a telegraph key, embellished with twenty-two gold nuggets on a base of Alaskan marble, that was used by President William Howard Taft during the Alaska–Yukon–Pacific Exposition in 1909.

Shortly before he died, Carmack began to write the "true" story of the Bonanza Creek discovery. Unfortunately, his second wife edited the manuscript and cut out anything that mentioned Kate.

Carmack died in 1922. On August 17, 1975, the seventy-ninth anniversary of the gold discovery in the Yukon, a monument was placed on his grave in Seattle's Evergreen Washelli Memorial Park. The stone reads: "George Washington Carmack Sept. 24, 1860–June 5, 1922. On August 17, 1896, he staked Discovery Claim on Bonanza Creek starting the Klondike Gold Rush."

On November 10, 1900, the *Daily San Francisco News* featured several gripping headlines and an article about Kate Carmack:

TAGISH KATE CARMACK'S STORY

GEORGE CARMACK'S INDIAN WIFE TELLS STRANGE AND PLAINTIVE STORY OF LOVE, MARRIAGE, AND DESERTION

HOW SHE FIRST MET AND LOVED PALEFACE GEORGE

KÈISH (SKOOKUM JIM) MASON, WIFE DAAKUXDA.EIT (MARY), AND DAUGHTER SAAYNA.AAT (DAISY)

Jim's fob, gold-studded chain, and pocket watch were donated to the MacBride Museum in Whitehorse but were stolen in the 1990s.

HISTORICAL PHOTO H-00072, ROYAL BC MUSEUM AND ARCHIVES

KATE'S CAPE

This cape was made by Kate and is a mix of Tagish and European styles: the pattern of the cape is European; however, the beading and felt along the fur hide are First Nations–inspired. Kate probably made this cape after returning from the US in 1900, where she would have seen many capes in this style. The demi-length cape was a common overcoat for women at the time.

MACBRIDE MUSEUM OF YUKON HISTORY

BETRAYED HER BROTHERS

WHITE MAN PRESSED HER HAND WHEN SHE SHOWED HIM GOLD—YELLOW HAIR CAUSED TROUBLE

Mrs. Kate Carmack, the Indian wife of the Klondike Millionaire George Carmack is suing for divorce at Hollister, California, the case being one of very great interest on account of the great wealth of the husband who was the first white man to find gold in the Klondike. The prominence of the case caused the Examiner of this city to devote a full page to its details. The simple story told to the court by the deserted wife was as follows:

White man, George Carmack, have break Tagish Kate's heart. I want white man's divorce because I am white man's wife. I pay white man for his love and he cheat me. My papoose and me he desert. I want white man's justice for me and my papoose. One night at dance in frozen country I first met white George. He talk to me and press my hand. He tell me how he walk about all over big, frozen country many, many moons and he tell me how he never find so much as one little piece of great gold which make white man's heart glad.

Then he press my hand some more and love came into my heart and I remember some things I hear my brother Skookum Jim and my brother Tagish Charley say. I think of what they tell me of a place where gold is as thick as the sand when one digs on the shore of the Meiozikaka, and I say: "Whiteman, meet me by the river at midnight and I tell you something to make your heart glad and love will come to you for Tagish Kate."

White George he shake his head to show me he no believe Tagish Kate, but all same he came to river at midnight. I took him out in my canoe, away out in middle of river where no red man can hear and I whisper in white George's ear: "I know spot where gold is thick like sand."

I tell paleface George he love me, me show him gold. He shake his head and say he no believe Tagish Kate.

Then I tell him how my brothers, Skookum Jim and Tagish Charley, have found place where they get heap much gold, and I tell him how they go and bring me back necklace all made out of little gold stones. When I see paleface George's eye grow bright by light of moon and when he press my hand with his big strong hands I take one, two, three gold stones from under my dress and show them to him. George look at them and his eyes grow big. He swear he love Tagish Kate. I ask him if he make Tagish Kate his squaw? He say yes, yes many, many times. He take me in his arms; he kiss me and say he love me. Tagish Kate believes and is happy, very, very happy. Then comes wedding and plenty much to eat.

Now is September and in frozen country we must wait, wait for summer before we can go and find gold. Then me tell my brothers, Skookum Jim and Tagish Charley, that my white chief George know where gold is. They very mad, but me no care. Me love paleface George, my chief.

Then when summer came we make peace with Skookum Jim and Tagish Charley, and one day all start together to place where gold is. Long, long time to get there. One day we came to Rabbit creek and George he lay down and sleep. While he sleep I fill pan with sand and put it beside him. He wake up and see pan and wash out dirt and in it is gold all same like three dollars. George glad. He find heap much gold and love Tagish Kate and buy me heap nice clothes. For five years he love Tagish Kate and take her in his arms and kiss her. He love papoose and buy heap much nice things. White chief George happy. Tagish Kate happy, papoose happy, all happy.

Then yellow hair she come to town. Tagish Kate no good after that, papoose no good after that. Tagish Kate want white man's divorce from white George. Yellow hair can have him. He no want me. Tagish Kate no want him. I give him love, he cheat me.

KAA GOOX (LATER KNOWN AS TAGISH CHARLEY AND THEN DAWSON CHARLEY) (1866–1908)

Dressed in white men's clothing with a gold-nugget collar pin, a watch chain with a gold-nugget fob, and a gaudy gold-nugget ring, Dawson Charley poses for a full-length-portrait in a studio in Seattle, Washington, at the turn of the nineteenth century.

YUKON ARCHIVES 2000/37, 2.
THEIR OWN YUKON PROJECT COLLECTION

THE GRAVE OF KATE CARMACK—ONE OF THE THREE ORIGINAL YUKON GOLD DISCOVERERS—IN THE CARCROSS CEMETERY

Káa Goox, later named Dawson Charley, died in 1908. His uncle Keish, given the English name "Skookum Jim" or James Mason, died in 1916, while his sister, Kate Carmack, the abandoned wife of George Carmack, died in 1920. George Carmack died in 1922 and was buried in the Evergreen Washelli Memorial Park in Seattle, Washington.

AUTHOR PHOTO

THE JAMES LEFFEL & COMPANY BOILER

This 7.5-kilowatt (10-horsepower) portable steam engine was built in Springfield, Ohio, and could easily have been used on Skookum Jim's Claim No. 1 above the Discovery Claim on Bonanza Creek. The boiler was first brought by sternwheeler to Dawson City and then dragged on steel skids by horses to the mining claims. These boilers were first built in 1890. The smokestack was hinged at the top of the first joint so that it could be laid down on top of the boiler during transport. The long lengths of hose filled with boiling water were lowered down the shafts to thaw the frozen ground so that the gravels could be hoisted to the surface. During the short, cold days of winter, the underground miners stayed reasonably warm, working with some source of light. The workers on the surface suffered most. The miners kept digging their shafts downward until bedrock, which contained the gold, was reached. This valuable gold-laden gravel was hoisted to the surface and carefully stockpiled for sluicing during the long days of summer.

AUTHOR PHOTO

TRIBUTE TO A MINER

In 2000, a monument was designed for the Klondyke Centennial Society by artist Halin de Repentigny. It now sits in front of the Elijah Smith Building in Whitehorse.

It reads: "Dedicated to the Klondike Gold Miners past, present and future in recognition of their contributions to Dawson City and the Klondike Region. In 1886, gold was discovered on Rabbit Creek by Skookum Jim, George Carmack and Dawson Charley, on the advice of fellow prospector Robert Henderson. This event sparked the Great Klondike Gold Rush of 1898, and Dawson City and the Yukon Territory were born."

AUTHOR PHOTO

THE LEWES RIVER MINING COMPANY DREDGE ON THE DISCOVERY CLAIM ON BONANZA CREEK, CIRCA 1903

The site had changed dramatically in the five years since George Carmack, Skookum Jim, and Dawson Charley had staked their original four discovery claims on Rabbit (later Bonanza) Creek on August 17, 1896. After four years of mining, the Carmack and First Nations partnership dissolved when George left Jim's sister. By the time this photo was taken, the gold finders had sold out their holdings and moved on to other ventures.

In this photo, the first dredge is slowly working its way through the valley in a pond of its own creation. The benchlands, which held ancient gold channels, were referred to as the White Channels. Oddly, the benchlands were not frozen and made the shaft-digging down to bedrock easier than in the valley floor. Eventually, huge hydraulic monitors were brought into the valley and tore up the side hills, causing them to wash down to the valley floor, where the gravels were put through the dredges and the endless quest for the yellow metal continued.

YUKON ARCHIVES PHOTO #86-87-113. EDMUND C. SENKLER FONDS

THE YUKON GOLD DIGGERS

Early days of placer gold mining in Yukon differed greatly from those in the milder climates of both California and BC. In the Far North, especially in the deep narrow valleys, the ground remained permanently frozen from surface to bedrock and had to be thawed in order to recover the gold.

In the early years of the gold rush, the frozen ground was thawed by fire. The miners would cut wood, usually spruce growing at lower elevations, and start a fire on the spot they had selected to sink a shaft. When they judged the fire had thawed a layer of ground, they let it die down and excavated the ashes and muck, then started a new fire. This would be repeated until bedrock was reached, sometimes to a depth of a thirty or more metres. The one advantage of the frozen ground was that the walls of shafts did not have to be shored up.

If only one miner was working, the removal of the muck was particularly tedious, even if a windlass had been erected for hoisting up the muck. Every time the miner had filled a bucket, he had to climb to the surface to hoist it up and then had to climb down to fill it again. When two persons were working together, one man would be on the surface at the windlass and the other in the shaft. The buckets to bring up first the muck and then the pay dirt were made of whipsawn lumber or split shakes, square and wider at the top, with a handle of thick rope. If commercial rope was not available, the men would braid rope from moose or caribou hide.

When several miners worked together, a barrel and winch were used at shafts that had been enlarged to a one-by-two-metre (three-by-six-foot) rectangle, and two men would operate the winch (one on each side) to bring up the heavier, larger buckets filled with pay dirt. Miners came up with the idea of using a boulder in one of the buckets to offset the weight of the buckets of pay dirt being hauled up. This system freed up one man and resulted in an easy task for the lone man at the top of the shaft on the windlass.

Drifts (horizontal tunnels) were often driven out from the shaft, much like the spokes of a wheel. This again involved thawing the ground with fire. The pay dirt was dumped on the surface during the winter months, and the miners did the panning during the summer.

This excruciating method of mining was somewhat alleviated when machinery arrived in the Klondike. This began with wood-fired boilers with iron pipes (wrapped in hair or woollen fabric against

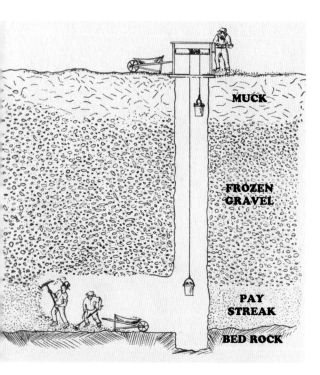

This drawing shows the removal of pay dirt in frozen ground by windlass and bucket. A second bucket was used as a counter balance similar to an elevator or dumbwaiter. Here all the muck and gravel has been removed from the shaft entrance by a wheelbarrow. The shaft appears to be between ten and twelve metres (thirty-five and forty feet), but it was not uncommon for shafts to go down sixty metres (two hundred feet) or more to bedrock.

YUKON ARCHIVES PHOTO #82-403-F27-13

the frost), which would bring steam to the underground areas to be thawed. The boiler operation and thawing were carried out during the night, and during the day the miners resumed their work.

The 1902 *Dawson City Golden Cleanup Edition* described an elevator-type shaft that was used in the goldfields. In winter 1900–1, William Northrup, a New Yorker, began the operation on American Gulch and Oro Fino Hill. The mine was operated through a shaft that went twenty-seven metres (ninety feet) deep. The shaft was divided into two compartments, each having a separate elevator capable of carrying two wheelbarrows loaded with pay dirt to the surface. As one elevator ascended, the other descended, and the lift was made in fifteen seconds. The mine was equipped with a twenty-six-kilowatt (thirty-five-horsepower) boiler of the locomotive type and a double cylinder reversible hoisting engine. The mine's record for hoisting was 1,325 wheelbarrow-loads of pay dirt in a ten-hour shift. From the mouth of the shaft, the wheelbarrows were easily wheeled over bunkers that fed the pay dirt directly into sluice boxes. The water for the sluicing was obtained from Bonanza Creek, where a pumping plant had been installed.

STEAM THAWING MACHINE SPLATTERED WITH RAVEN DROPPINGS AND RESTING ATOP A ROCK PILE ALONG THE KLONDIKE HIGHWAY AT BEAR CREEK ROAD NEAR DAWSON CITY

Like so much of the heavy equipment brought into Yukon in the search for gold, the boilers were often shipped by rail, then steamboat, and finally hauled on the last leg of their journey by several teams of horses. The wood- or coal-fed boilers were used to produce steam for the thawing of the permafrost to get down to the bedrock. The practice was to thaw the hard-frozen ground with steam lines coming down from the boiler. The resulting muck, containing the gold, was then hauled in a bucket to the surface with a man on a windlass. The men in the shaft used mallets to gently pound the six-point rubber hoses from the steampipes into the cement-like pay dirt. The boilers were hauled by horses from one shaft to another on wooden or steel skids.

JOHN A. GOULD, *FROZEN COLD*, 2001

MINING CLAIM NO. 2 ABOVE BONANZA CREEK, YUKON TERRITORY, CIRCA 1898

A tent town for miners sprang up on Bonanza Creek. Initially, miners lived in large tents with a sheet-iron stove and a telescoped stovepipe. Lumber cut and used for sluices, cribbing, and fires for the shafts and stoves quickly depleted the side hills of trees. The mining activity totally devastated the salmon spawning beds in the creek.

No 2 ABOVE BONANZA

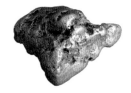

The above two nuggets, from the Barker claim, weighed 3.7 ounces (left) and 3.6 ounces (right).

Pay dirt was panned for testing and then placed in the tray at the head of this rocker, which was operated by the left hand. The tin dipper in the right hand was used to constantly supply water to the mixtures. Slats of wood served as riffles lower down to catch the coarse gold, and near the outlet was a tin sheet smeared with quicksilver that attracted and held the very fine gold.

DAWSON CITY MUSEUM

The above nugget, from the Black Hills claim, weighed 1.1 ounces.

A nugget from the Kirkland claim.

KLONDIKE NUGGET AND IVORY SHOP, DAWSON CITY

"Buckets were made of whipsawn lumber, and if this was not available, of split shakes, which were square but wider at the top than the bottom. A heavy rope was used for the bucket handle and windlass cable. In outlaying places where rope could not be bought, caribou or moose hide was braided into a rope and used."—Walter R. Hamilton, *The Yukon Story*. This windlass bucket was found in the restored cabin of author Jack London.

Belinda Mulrooney, holding a Stetson, stands in front of her roadhouse with other Yukon characters, circa 1897.

UNIVERSITY OF WASHINGTON DIGITAL COLLECTIONS HEG794. PHOTO BY ERIC A. HEGG

Located smack-dab in the middle of the Yukon gold rush at the confluence of the Eldorado and Bonanza Creeks, Grand Forks had the one thing Dawson City lacked—location, location, location, as they say in the real-estate business.

Entrepreneur Belinda Mulrooney operated the first road-house in Grand Forks a full year before the first hordes of gold seekers began to pour into the area and transform the face of the Yukon Valley. Almost as if by magic, in 1898 buildings began to be built down the valley of Bonanza Creek, while above on the nearby hillsides, inventive miners were scratching their way down through the moss and the frozen muck and gravel to reach the pay dirt on the bedrock. Cheechako Hill, French Hill, Gold Hill and others all yielded much more gold than the valley

LOOKING UP ELDORADO

E.A.Hegg

below. Mulrooney built a new roadhouse, called the Grand Forks Hotel, to provide drinking, eating, and sleeping needs for the weary miners.

By 1903, Grand Forks was incorporated, with a population of over three thousand. The town's location resulted in its demise, when the large dredges began taking large concessions in the Yukon Valley. By 1921, the dredges had reached the outskirts of Grand Forks, and since there was gold to be recovered from beneath the buildings, the residents had to move. The buildings were torn down and the ground turned upside down. Today, nothing remains of Grand Forks.

THE MANY ESTABLISHMENTS AT GRAND FORKS, LOCATED AT THE CONFLUENCE OF BONANZA AND ELDORADO CREEKS, CATERING TO THE NEEDS OF THE MINERS SINKING SHAFTS ADJACENT TO THE NEARBY CREEK IN THE SPRING 1898

Of the many entrepreneurs who were not miners, Belinda Mulrooney was quick to grasp the opportunities offered by the rich gold-mining district. She had already made profitable investments in Dawson City, and she found that her Grand Forks Hotel (seen here in the middle of the left-hand page) was but a stepping stone to buying up claims on these rich creeks. By the time this photo was taken, Mulrooney was listed as a mine owner in the Eldorado-Bonanza Quartz and Placer Mining Company, with a paid-up capital of $1.5 million.

Grand Forks lay on Claim No. 6, below the Discovery Claim and directly across from where Eldorado Creek entered into Bonanza Creek. Some of the miners living in tents on the hillside on the left-hand side of the photo have planted gardens with tall barricades to keep out animals. The long hours of daylight in summer ensured that the plants grew quickly.

UNIVERSITY OF WASHINGTON DIGITAL COLLECTIONS, HEG060.
PHOTO BY ERIC A. HEGG

KEITH and WILSON

MINE ON FRENCH HILL

231.Q
W&S   FRENCH HILL

THE KEITH AND WILSON MINE ON FRENCH HILL, YUKON TERRITORY, 1898

Gold was sometimes found on hillsides where creeks had once flowed. The man on the right stands at the windlass, ready to crank up buckets of pay dirt to be shovelled into the rocker being worked by the man on the left. Since there is only one bucket being lowered and raised—and one length of rope—the shaft is likely quite shallow. For the deeper, larger, more rectangular shafts, two buckets are used. The one farthest from the man on the crank is filled with a small boulder to offset the bucket with the pay dirt—much like the counterweight in an elevator or dumbwaiter. The elevator was so efficient that the trip from bedrock to surface could be achieved in just ninety seconds.

Trees on both sides of French Gulch have been stripped bare to be used as cribbing for the shafts, fuel for the stoves in the tents, brush to be positioned in the shaft to help thaw the permafrost down to the bedrock—and as fuel for the boilers used for thawing. Bundles of brush can be seen stockpiled on the opposite hillside—the largest neatly framed by the windlass. The tents in which the men live are just over the knoll and in the lower right-hand side of the photo. A white horse with a saddle is visible on the opposite hillside, ready to transport brush to the claims on the valley floor. It appears that the trees have been cut down all the way up to the Dome.

UNIVERSITY OF WASHINGTON DIGITAL COLLECTION #HEG495.
PHOTO BY ERIC A. HEGG

SLUCEING ON GOLD HILL

SLUICING ON GOLD HILL, WITH GRAND FORKS VISIBLE IN THE VALLEY BELOW, CIRCA SUMMER 1899

The men are seen shovelling pay dirt into the sluice boxes. Now that the warm weather has set in and the ground is thawing, they work hard, as they depend on the melted snow from the mountainside for water to sluice. In the background, Bonanza Creek is seen at the bottom of the mountain.

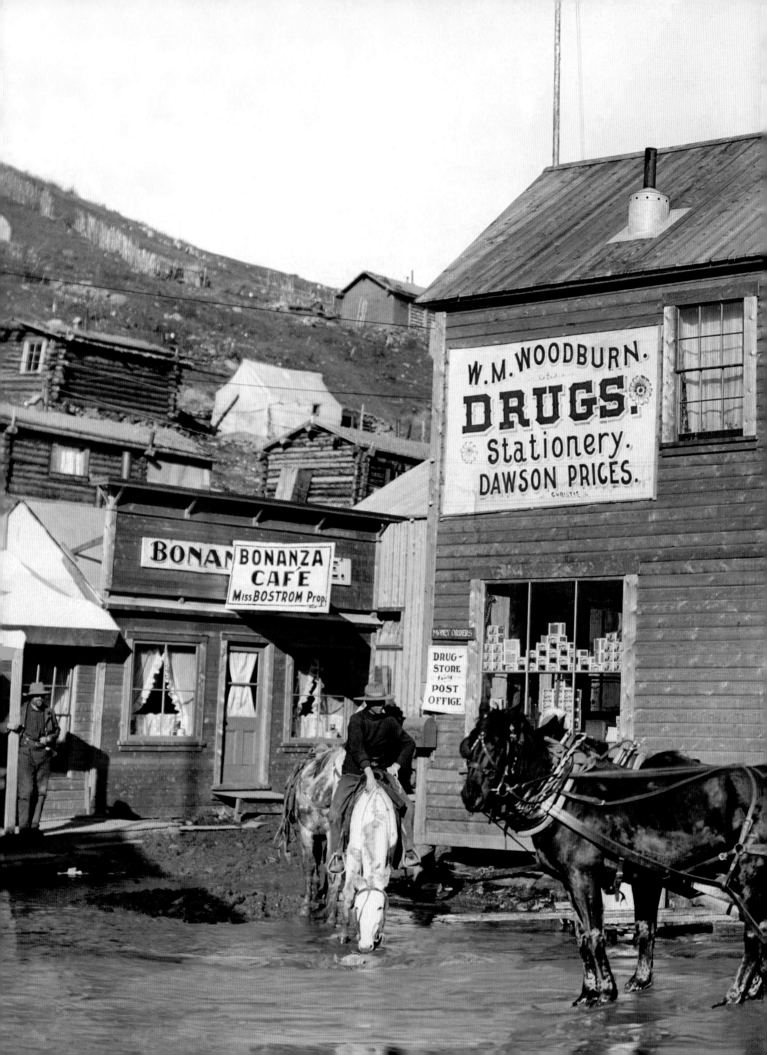

Bogged down in a deep rut, a teamster positions himself to help the driver and two horses pull a freight wagon during a flash flood in front of the Walter M. Woodburn Drugstore at Grand Forks in 1901.

Year-round Sluicing for Gold

231.C
H&S   FRENCH HILL

The challenges of getting the gold from the ground were never-ending, and the miners worked through the freezing cold spells of winter as well as in the summer months, with the hordes of mosquitoes. Winter or summer, the goldfields were a beehive of activity.

Three gravity trams extended from the level of these tunnels a distance of about ninety-two metres (three hundred feet) down to the level of the sluice boxes, near the foot of the hill. Over a thousand metres (five thousand feet) of steel tracks were laid in the tunnels and cross-cuts, and the immense cars of dirt brought down from the tunnels went hurrying down the mountainside to be dumped into immense hoppers, from where it was fed directly into the sluice boxes. No steam power was needed for propulsion anywhere in the mine, since all the work was accomplished by gravity and zip lines. The owners of mines on the hillsides often had to buy dumping grounds for their tailings and debris.

Hydraulic mining used a powerful stream of water from a monitor, also known as a giant, directed at gold-bearing gravel or sand. The combined forces of high-pressure water and air bubbles that formed in the waterspout caused gravel to dislodge. Larger boulders were removed by human labour when possible. The water and loose sediment mixture was diverted into sluice boxes in order to separate the gold from the sediment. "Hydraulicking" could, and often did, completely ruin the landscape. This hydraulic monitor was used for placer gold mining in the Klondike region after 1900.

Miners work at excavating a shaft to reach the pay dirt at bedrock. The muck was piled around the shaft, while the pay dirt was taken away in a wheelbarrow for sluicing in the spring.

YUKON ARCHIVES 89-29-8

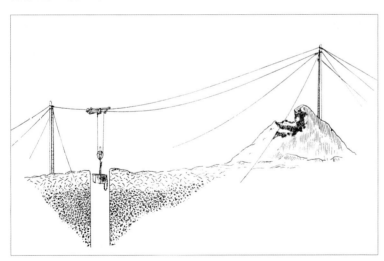

Drawing showing the removal of overburden (muck and dirt) in frozen ground with a self-dumper. A steam-powered hoist carried the self-dumper up a shaft or out of a drift operation. These devices often created enormous conical piles of overburden before the gold-bearing pay dirt on the bedrock was reached. The pay dirt was hoisted to the surface and placed in separate piles for spring sluicing.

YUKON ARCHIVES 82-403-F27-14, MISCELLANEOUS II PHOTOGRAPH COLLECTION

A cold gold miner works at the windlass at –40°C in the Yukon's valley floor during the winter of 1897–98.

UNIVERSITY OF WASHINGTON DIGITAL COLLECTION #MEE100
WALTER E. MEED COLLECTION

NO. 18 ON BONANZA CREEK

Some miners took the option of bringing their pay dirt down the hill to a place where water was more readily available. A wooden drum at the top of the mountain was part of a "gravity tram" mechanism that lowered a cable car with pay dirt to the valley floor, where it was stockpiled for sluicing during the summer months. The gold-bearing gravel, once sluiced, was moved into dump piles by a man with a horse and scraper. This type of mining was prevalent at Cheechako Hill, near the Discovery Claim.

UNDERGROUND 27 ELDORADO

These twelve miners, together with two young boys, pose by candlelight in an underground horizontal drift at the height of the Yukon gold rush. Number 27 Eldorado was owned by Alexander McDonald, one of the most prosperous miners in Yukon, who owned outright or had interests in Numbers 14, 19, 22, 30, 34, 35, and 36 on Eldorado Creek. One of McDonald's first claims on Eldorado Creek yielded over three hundred panned ounces a day.

The shaft to bedrock didn't have to be cribbed because the frozen sides stayed as hard as granite year round. The miners worked by candlelight with steel hoses that brought down heated water from above to thaw the permafrost. In winter, chunks of pay dirt were placed in buckets and hauled by a windlass to the surface, where they were stockpiled for sluicing during the long days of summer. Permafrost, seen here on the ceiling, kept the workplace like the inside of an ice locker.

Boys were brought into the mine shafts in order to work the tiny crevices, chasing after the nuggets. Like the men, the boys had to work in the cold and dark, and in stale air.

UNIVERSITY OF WASHINGTON DIGITAL COLLECTIONS, HEG091. PHOTO BY ERIC A. HEGG

ON THE FOURTH TIER ON GOLD HILL, OPPOSITE NO. 5 BONANZA, YUKON TERRITORY, CIRCA 1898

These six miners, aided by candlelight, use steam points and pickaxes to thaw the frozen ground in a deep underground horizontal drift at the height of the Yukon gold rush. A box for hauling the dirt to the surface and a rope ladder are visible directly behind the man with the gold pan. The man in the centre foreground proudly displays a couple of choice nuggets in his pan.

SPORTS DAY CELEBRATIONS AT GRAND FORKS ON DOMINION DAY, 1902

Men participate in throwing a heavy spherical object—the shot—as far as possible. While the town appears to be devoid of women, the North-West Mounted Police have made their presence known. One stands to the right of the thrower, arms folded and holding a riding crop, while a second stands at the landing spot for the shot. The British Union Jack is atop many buildings.

THE YUKON ORDER OF PIONEERS

The Yukon Order of Pioneers was a fraternal order formed on December 1, 1894, in the town of Forty Mile on the Yukon River. There had been several gatherings that year before this date, including one in April, one in June, and one in July. By December, the Pioneers had drawn up a constitution and bylaws. The group elected as president Leroy Napoleon ("Jack") McQuesten (often referred to as the "Father of the Yukon," or "Yukon Jack"). By this time, gold had been discovered on such streams as Birch Creek and the Minook River, a tributary of the Yukon River in Alaska. In February 1895, the Pioneers applied to form a charter to form a subordinate lodge at Circle City, a new town that had sprung up near the mouth of Birch Creek. This charter was issued on February 14, 1895.

Once gold was discovered on Bonanza Creek in August 1896, most of the miners from the goldfields of Alaska moved to the new town of Dawson City, at the junction of the Klondike and Yukon Rivers.

On July 24, 1897, a group of members of the Yukon Order of Pioneers got together in Dawson and formed a new lodge. They called it the Klondike Lodge and decided upon the word "Klondike" as the password. Thomas W. O'Brien, a businessman at Forty Mile, Circle City, and later Dawson City, was its first president. During following three years, two other lodges formed in Dawson.

By 1913, quite a few past presidents of the lodges were living in Dawson City. They decided that it was time to form an official Grand Lodge. Shortly afterward, Dawson City lodge acted as Grand Lodge, with Tom O'Brien elected as its first grand president. Later a lodge was formed at Mayo as No. 3, then another at Whitehorse as No. 4. In 1922, Lodge No. 5 was formed in Vancouver.

When gold was discovered on beaches in Nome, Alaska, many of the original pioneers went there and formed a Y.O.O.P. Lodge. In 1906, the Nome Lodge wanted a change in the constitution to allow anyone in Alaska by a specified date to be allowed membership, but Grand Lodge rejected the proposal. The Alaskans returned their charge and formed "Igloo No. 1" of the Alaska Pioneers. Fairbanks also had a Y.O.O.P. Lodge; then in 1910 they too requested a change in the constitution, which was refused. They returned their charter and formed Igloo No. 4 of the Alaska Pioneers.

The several lodges of the Yukon Order of Pioneers gradually died out until only Dawson City was left. The Dawson City Lodge kept the Yukon Order of Pioneers alive over the years. In 1966, a

THE PLAQUE AT THE ENTRANCE TO THE Y.O.O.P DAWSON CITY OFFICE

The plaque reads: "To the pioneers who blazed the trails to the Klondike that led to the greatest gold stampede the world has known. May the souls of the members who have passed into the great beyond rest in peaceful sleep and for the members to follow ever be faithful to our motto, 'Do unto others as you would be done by.'" —President Jack Meloy

lodge was formed in Whitehorse with No. 2 designate. These are now the only two lodges of the Yukon Order of Pioneers.

Many of the earliest Y.O.O.P. members are buried in the 8th Avenue Cemetery in Dawson City. The first burial was Frederick Washington Harte on November 7, 1897 (the second president of Grand Lodge, in 1886); the last burial was Walter H. Bigg, on August 13, 1934. In 1935, the pioneers acquired property on one of the hills for a new cemetery above Dawson City.

Mostly silver in colour, these pipe surrounds signify the location of Yukon Order of Pioneers graves in the Eighth Avenue Cemetery in Dawson City. The words on most of the wooden grave markers above the graves are no longer legible. The large cemetery contains Catholic, Protestant, and Jewish graves, as well as those of several fraternal orders that thrived in Yukon at the turn of the century.

DAWSON CITY FROM THE BASE OF THE MOOSEHIDE SLIDE, CIRCA 1910

Essentially wilderness in 1896, by 1898 Dawson was the largest city in Canada west of Winnipeg and only slightly smaller than Seattle or Portland. In this 1910 photograph, Dawson City was no longer the tent town of a decade earlier. Yukon's capital had taken on a more permanent appearance. At the start of the gold rush, Joseph Ladue had staked a claim of 65 hectares (160 acres) of boggy flats at the mouth of the Klondike to establish a townsite that he intended to name in his own honour. Instead, he was persuaded to name the place Dawson City in honour of George Mercer Dawson, an early surveyor into the Yukon. Several sternwheelers are tied up along Front Street. There are several log booms tied up at water's edge in readiness to be turned into lumber at Ladue's sawmill. Real estate, lumber, and gold made Ladue a very rich man, as some of his lots on Front Street sold for as much as $8,000. Ladue died in 1901 and was never able to enjoy much of his new found wealth.

Klondike Mines Railway

Among those who applied to develop a railroad, Ontario-born Thomas O'Brien, president of the Klondike Brewing and Malting Company, was successful. The Klondike Mines Railway was granted a charter in 1899, but it would take until 1906 to complete the line. O'Brien and his investors had dreamed of a railroad that would not only carry supplies to and from the goldfields but also be a passenger train, and they originally envisaged connecting their line to faraway Edmonton. The KMR's 50 kilometres (30 miles) of 1-metre (3-foot) narrow-gauge track were laid from Dawson City to Sulphur City near the 914-metre- (3,000-foot-) high Dome, the highest point in the centre of the goldfields.

By 1906, the rush that had begun as an ad hoc stampede was becoming a new kind of operation. Good wagon roads to the goldfields had already been developed, and stage lines operated into the larger camps.

The labour-intensive hand mining had given way to dredges that would forever change the landscape of the Klondike. With these dredges and heavy equipment came men who, like O'Brien, were visionaries.

The change in mining methods resulted in decreasing demand for manpower, and when gold was discovered in Nome, Alaska, many Dawson City inhabitants left, either on their way to Nome or, disappointed at not having made their fortune in the Yukon, returning south.

The KMR continued to operate, moving cordwood for thawing the earth, but soon the mining companies had stocked up all the cordwood they would need, and by 1913, the KMR wrapped up its operations. The Klondike Mines Railway never achieved the success O'Brien had dreamed of, but it did carve out a place in Yukon history.

KLONDIKE MINES RAILWAY LOCOMOTIVE #1
Manufactured by the Brooks Locomotive Works of Dunkirk, New York, the Klondike Mines Railway Locomotive No. 1 has been refurbished and stands on display at the Dawson City Museum.

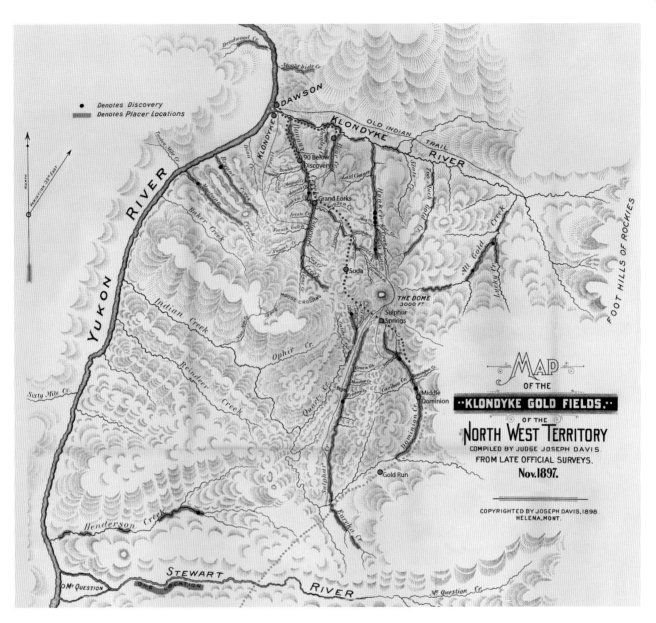

THE KLONDIKE GOLDFIELDS

This map was compiled by Joseph Davis, a judge from Helena, Montana. The black dot on Gold Bottom Creek—a tributary of Hunker Creek—marks the spot where Robert Henderson, a Canadian from Nova Scotia, made a gold discovery.

The black dot on Bonanza Creek at the confluence of Skookum Creek marks the spot where George Washington Carmack and his Native brothers-in-law Skookum Jim (James Mason) and Tagish Charley (Dawson Charley) made the gold discovery that started the Yukon Gold Rush.

The blue dots show the route of the fifty-kilometre (thirty-one-mile) Klondike Mines Railway that connected to 90 Below Discovery, Grand Forks, Soda, and Sulphur Springs. An ambitious and expensive project, its builders had hoped to connect with the

Vancouver, Westminster and Yukon Railway (green dots). As a result, the towns of Middle Dominion and Gold Run never came to exist.

This map has been altered from the original, and the route of the Klondike Mines Railway has been added, the blue line showing completed lines and the green lines showing proposed lines. The railway was built to transport machinery into the gold camps and also to extend the line to connect with the CPR line at Edmonton so that tourists could travel to see the mines. Like so many ambitious schemes around the turn of the century, the plan never materialized.

YUKON LEGENDS KLONDIKE JOE AND "SWIFTWATER BILL" GATES

JOE BOYLE AND SWIFTWATER BILL DURING THEIR TREK OUT OF THE YUKON, 1897

Joe was thirty, Bill twenty-eight.

YUKON ARCHIVES 89-29-8

Joseph Whiteside Boyle, who eventually became known as "Klondike Joe," was born in Toronto in 1867 and moved to Woodstock with his family in 1872. At seventeen, Joe ran away to sea on the Nova Scotia barque *Wallace*. He first gained recognition for rescuing a sailor from a shark by dispatching the huge fish with a knife. Another time, during a typhoon, Joe led the crew of the ship *Susan* for several days by manning the pumps so that both the ship and the men survived the ordeal. Young Joe gained a reputation as a take-charge person, and by the time he gave up his seafaring at age twenty, he was called Captain Boyle.

Back on dry land and married, Joe successfully started up a feed-and-grain business for livestock, but this occupation did not fit his adventuresome spirit. It was during this period that Joe fathered a son and daughter. Joe soon found excitement in the boxing ring and as a promoter chose for his ace fighter Frank Slavin, the thirty-five-year-old former champion from Australia. The pair toured Ontario and Quebec, staging fights before deciding to tour England. It was while in London that the two sparred before Edward, the Prince of Wales.

Joe and Frank were on a boxing tour on the Northwest Coast when the electrifying news of gold discoveries began to trickle in at San Francisco and Victoria. The two boxers staged fights to earn money to pay for passage to the Yukon. They made their way to Dyea, the trailhead for the Chilkoot route, and with a party of a dozen men, started out for Bennett Lake. Boyle was the natural leader who, upon realizing that the other men were not as physically fit as Slavin and himself, rallied the men onward. Boyle had packed a twenty-four-foot-long collapsible boat over the pass, and it was used to transport the men down the Yukon River to Dawson City.

It was on this trip that "Chilkoot" Charlie, a Native packer, joined the group and stayed on as Joe's guide and friend for a number of years.

While in Dawson City, Joe introduced himself to William Ogilvie, who had recently resurveyed the initial 170 claims on Bonanza Creek. The first gold discoverers had staked out their own claims and frequently staked out-of-proportion claims that overlapped one another. Ogilvie ultimately brought order out of the chaos.

William "Swiftwater" Charles Frederick Julius Anlauf Gates was born in Red Wing, Minnesota, on July 1, 1869. When Gates was thirteen, he moved with his family to Washington Territory. At twenty-one, he was prospecting for gold in Idaho Springs, Colorado. Later, while working for another grubstake at a copper mine in Michigan, he heard of a small gold strike at Forty Mile in the Yukon. He immediately booked passage for Juneau, Alaska, and in 1896 found employment in Circle City as a dishwasher in a roadhouse. Apparently, Gates earned his moniker for having walked around the rough waters of White Horse Rapids.

While tending tables at the roadhouse in Circle City, Swiftwater overheard some men talking about George Carmack's recent gold discovery on Rabbit Creek. Not alerting anyone, Swiftwater struck out alone, in a small boat, toward the stake in the wee hours of the morning. He found most of the nearby ground already staked, but Claim No. 13 Eldorado, though staked, had not been worked. The original owners had feared that bad luck accompanied the number thirteen. Swiftwater partnered with six other prospectors, including Joe Boyle, and was able to take a lay, or lease, on the unworked ground. After digging six shafts to bedrock and each time coming up with blanks (no pay dirt), the rest of the group except for Boyle became dispirited and abandoned the ground. Swiftwater and Joe worked on a final shaft themselves, thawing the ground by burning brush. Once it had melted, one of them climbed down into the shaft and filled the buckets, while the other hauled the buckets up on the windlass. It was backbreaking work, but at bedrock on the seventh hole, they hit unbelievably good ground. They kept quiet, played the discovery down, and bought the claim. They then took out a fortune estimated at somewhere between $300,000 and $400,000, after expenses.

Boyle and his party had a terrible time getting out to the provincial capital of Victoria. The men survived the cold by bedding down on fir branches and sleeping with their dogs for warmth. A dispatch from Victoria in 1897 announced the arrival of the richest party yet out of the Yukon district:

It is captained by Joe Boyle, the youngest son of Charley Boyle of Woodstock, Ontario, the trainer of Seagram's racing stable. Boyle had struck it rich. He is a partner in four of the richest claims on earth. Of the wealth the party of twenty-five brought back, a low estimate is $30,000 in dust and one million and a half in drafts and green backs.

Joe and his group proceeded from Victoria to Seattle with Joe's guide Chilkoot Charlie. The *Woodstock Sentinel Review* reported the following:

In appreciation of his leadership in getting the party safely through, despite almost insurmountable difficulties, the men gave Joe a dinner in one of the leading hotels in Seattle and presented him with a magnificent gold watch. Charlie was present, and an object of much interest. Joe went to some trouble to instruct Charlie in the use of silverware and dishes. Charlie proved an apt pupil and his table manners were soon the equal of his culturally advantaged peers.

When Boyle returned from Dawson in December 1897 [to Woodstock], he brought with him, besides a number of Malamute dogs, a Yukon Indian named Charlie, who was very fond of Boyle and called him Captain. Joe brought Charlie and the team of huskies to Woodstock. But when he went subsequently travelled to Toronto, Ottawa, Montreal, and New York to make business arrangements for his return to the Yukon, and when his business was delayed for many weeks beyond the time for his return, Charlie became restless and lonesome. "Me must see Captain," he said to Mrs. Boyle, Joe's mother, to whom Charlie became greatly attached and affectionately called "Mammy." Charlie hung about "The Firs," the home of Joe's parents, for a couple of weeks and then struck out for home at Carmack's Post and—to the great relief of Joe—made the trip.

CLAIM NO. 13 ON ELDORADO CREEK, ORIGINALLY OWNED BY SWIFTWATER BILL GATES

A huge snake-like flume, much of it on stilts, crisscrosses back and forth across Eldorado Creek, feeding water to the richest gold claims in the world. Swiftwater Bill Gates's Claim No. 13 Eldorado was a little over a kilometre from where Eldorado Creek emptied into Bonanza Creek. By the time this photo was taken, probably in 1898, every piece of available land had been staked 152 metres (500 feet) on both sides of Bonanza and Eldorado Creeks. Most of the trees in the valleys and on the hillsides had been chopped down for building of cabins and flumes—the much-needed structures that carried water to the piles of pay dirt for sluicing. Any leftover smaller logs were used for firewood to thaw the permafrost down to the pay dirt on the bedrock. Many of the claims above No. 13 Eldorado proved to be unbelievably rich and made all its owners millionaires. Although many of the miners still lived in tents, the more established mine owners by this time were living in cabins complete with stoves and glass windows. On Eldorado Creek, shafts rarely went down more than 4.5 to 6 metres (15 to 20 feet) before reaching bedrock and gold. On some of the other creeks, the shafts went down more than 30 metres (100 feet) to reach bedrock.

ELDORADO, LOOKING UP FROM Nº 13

Hegg & Co. PH
DAWSON, Y.T.

13

In her manuscript *Joe Boyle: Superhero of the Klondike Goldfields,* Jane Gaffin suggests that Swiftwater grubstaked miners for a percentage of the found gold and bought out properties that were believed to be duds but later turned out to be little bonanzas. She also states that Joe worked for Bill on a percentage basis, managing his mines and looking after his business affairs.

Swiftwater's ability to blow through money, and his love for women, the younger the better, became legendary. Soon after he became wealthy, he fell for a certain Gussie Lamour, previously an entertainer from Circle City. Gussie loved eggs, and one time Bill saw her having a breakfast of bacon and eggs in the company of another suitor in a prominent Dawson City restaurant. In a rage, Swiftwater bought up every egg in the town, and this act bestowed upon him the title "The Knight of the Golden Omelette."

Swiftwater later paid Gussie $30,000 in gold dust for the promise of her hand in marriage. She took the gold, but reneged on the marriage because she was already married and had a three-year-old child. Out of spite, Swiftwater married Gussie's younger sister Grace and bought her a $15,000 mansion in Oakland, California; however, they soon divorced.

THE OPERA HOUSE IN DAWSON AFTER THE FIRE OF APRIL 21, 1899

Swiftwater Bill Gates and Jack Smith's best-known palace of pleasure—the Monte Carlo—is open and ready for business in this photo. Catering to thirsty and sex-starved prospectors, the original Monte Carlo was unglamorous. The Hoffman, adjacent to the opera house, very likely escaped the fire because of the sprinkler system on the roof's peak.

IN DAWSON APRIL 26 '99
FIER.

One of the first investments Swiftwater made with his newfound money was partnering with John Smith of Circle City to build a "Palace of Sport" in Dawson City they called the Monte Carlo. Smith sent Swiftwater to Seattle to purchase accessories such as three-metre-high mirrors, velvet carpets, oil paintings, and $10,000 worth of fixtures. Swiftwater spent much of the money in Seattle wining and dining women before eventually returning to Dawson City with a dozen women to work in their high-end saloon in addition to the other supplies.

While the saloon prospered, Swiftwater basked in affluence. He always lusted for notoriety, and when he wasn't gambling, he was good-naturedly buying drinks for the patrons of his establishment.

The *Dawson City News* dated April 1, 1898, states that Swiftwater Bill Gates was the president of the Alaska Transportation Trading and Mining Company, with a capital of $2 million. Greedy capitalists down south saw in Bill a "good thing" with something to give away, with the result that "the sobriquet millionaire sold many of these gullible investors mines somewhere [Claim No.] 350 above Discovery on Nowhere Creek."

Returning to Seattle, Swiftwater had a friend introduce him to Mrs. Iola Beebe, who was planning to open a hotel in Dawson City. Swiftwater was more interested in Iola's two daughters, Blanche and Bera, than in the businesswoman's hotel venture. Although he was thirty-five at the time, Swiftwater ran off with and married fourteen-year-old Bera and returned to his claims.

His mother-in-law followed. Bera soon became pregnant and gave birth to a son in the dead of winter while they were living in a small cabin on Quartz Creek.

Swiftwater Bill Gates poses at his cabin on Quartz Creek with his mother-in-law, Iola Beebe (the red blouse), and his young wife, her daughter Bera. The people on the extreme left and extreme right of the photograph are unidentified.

COURTESY PAOLA GREER

LEFT—THE PARTIALLY RESTORED DREDGE NO. 4 RESTS NEAR THE DISCOVERY CLAIM ON BONANZA CREEK

This dredge was owned by Joe Boyle and was the largest in Yukon. It was three-quarters the length of a football field, eight storeys tall, and did the work of a thousand men. The dredge's trommel (gigantic sluice) was 2.4 metres (8 feet) in diameter and 15 metres (50 feet) long. The dredge eventually toppled over and sank.

BELOW—THE AFTERMATH OF YUKON'S MONSTER DREDGES

With the Klondike River rerouted to allow the dredges to churn up any gold that might have been deposited on the bedrock underneath its original channel, the devastation left by the dredges is complete. The Klondike Highway, to the right of the photograph, passes through the middle of the goldfields.

Taken from a crocus bluff, looking toward where the Klondike empties into the Yukon River. The southwest view shows the workings of Dredge No. 3, with Klondike City across the Klondike River. The Ogilvie bridge, just out of the photo on the right-hand side, connected Klondike City with Dawson City.

Joe Boyle introduced dredging into Yukon. Gold profits soared with the arrival of large-scale corporate mining, and for decades, from as early as 1906, the grinding and screeching of the dredges echoed throughout the Klondike. Working day and night, these "Monsters of the Creeks" churned through river valleys, separating gold from gravel and leaving behind eighteen-to-twenty-four-metre-wide (twenty-four-to-eighty-foot-wide) swaths of crescent-shaped tailing piles. A large hydroelectric plant supplied power to the dredges, while a small army of workers prepared the ground ahead of them, stripping away muck and thawing permafrost.

After the moss and muck were removed, hundreds of steampipes with points were driven into the ground to thaw the frozen gravel to bedrock.

MUSEUM OF HISTORY & INDUSTRY SHS7258. PHOTO BY JEREMIAH DOODY

A short time later, a second son was born. Swiftwater Bill later married his niece Kitty Brandon, his sister's daughter, while still married to Bera, which made him a bigamist (not to mention incestuous). In her 1908 book, *The True Life Story of Swiftwater Bill Gates*, Mrs. Iola Beebe describes Swiftwater Bill as a chauvinistic and selfish scoundrel.

While Swiftwater remained in the Yukon, Joe Boyle went to Ottawa to persuade the Dominion Government to grant the pair a concession on a sixteen-hectare (forty-acre) parcel of land on the Klondike River to override the claims already staked for a nominal fee. Dawson City lawyer C.M. Woodworth charged that the authorities in Ottawa were either fools or scoundrels on the take for making such a deal. Apparently, Harold Buchanan McGivern, an Ottawa lawyer-politician and friend of the Boyle family, was greatly influential in introducing Joe to Minister of the Interior and Indian Affairs Clifford Sifton. Boyle eventually obtained the dredging rights to almost eleven kilometres (seven miles) of the Klondike River valley that was fed by the richest creeks.

In an event that will always live in hockey trivia, Joe Boyle managed and bankrolled the Yukon Nuggets hockey team. The players set out on December 18, 1904, on an epic month-long voyage by dogsled from Dawson to Whitehorse, then by narrow-gauge rail from Whitehorse to Skagway, then by ship from Skagway to Vancouver, and finally by train from Vancouver to Ottawa—just in time to challenge the Ottawa Silver Seven for the 1905 Stanley Cup on January 13 in the best-of-three series. With Governor General Earl Grey in the packed Dey's Rink, Boyle's team lost the first game 9–2, and then lost the second game 23–2, with future Hall of Famer Frank McGee netting a record fourteen goals for the winners. Albert Forrest, the Yukon Nuggets goalie, was the youngest goalie in NHL history. It was the most lopsided defeat in the history of the Stanley Cup. The Yukon Nuggets and Boyle had no illusions of winning the cup; they just wanted a chance to play. The team then played a series of exhibition games in other cities before dismantling.

Boyle went to London, England, where he obtained enough money from investors to buy and ship to Dawson City the largest and most expensive hydraulic plants in the goldfields. By this time, he had amassed an immense tract of ground that was at least five kilometres (three miles) long and in some places three kilometres (two miles) wide and had previously consisted of some very rich claims. Boyle convinced Minister Sifton that huge monitors and electrically powered dredges were required to retrieve the gold from the creeks' bedrock. Thus, Joe brought dredging to Yukon.

Placer dredging had been developed in New Zealand and refined in California before being first introduced into the Yukon in 1898. The Canadian Klondike Mining Company, controlled by Boyle, was first on the creeks. They were followed by the Yukon Gold Mining Company, controlled by Guggenheim interests, a short time later.

The opportunities of gold bonanzas brought the moneyed financiers of both the US and Britain to the Yukon. The biggest players were the Rothschilds and the Guggenheims (Guggieville near Dawson City is named for this family). The Guggenheim family's dredges worked ground closest to Dawson City. Boyle worked both with and against the rich conglomerates, and the court cases between Boyle and these two families became legendary over the years. Boyle had a knack for tying up the rich and famous in legal mining disputes for years, but in the end always came out the winner. He also wound up owning the Canadian Klondike Mining operation, which included a large concession on Quartz Creek. By the start of the First World War, a dozen dredges worked in the Klondike.

By this time, Swiftwater Bill and Joe Boyle had parted company. Swiftwater had sold his Claim No. 13 Eldorado in 1896, and Joe had reason to get out of Dawson—his dredges were not producing as before, and the very day his battalion left for Vancouver, his monstrous Dredge No. 4 toppled over and sank. He left the whole mess in the hands of his son Joe Jr.

THE DAWSON CITY NUGGETS (ALSO KNOWN AS THE KLONDIKES) HOCKEY TEAM AT THE DEY'S RINK IN OTTAWA. THEY PLAYED AGAINST THE OTTAWA SENATORS, JANUARY 24, 1905.

Back row, left to right: Hector Smith, George Kennedy, Lorne Hanna, Jim Johnston, and Norm Watt.

Front row, left to right: Albert Forrest, Captain (later Colonel) Joe Boyle, and Dr. Randy McLellan.

Missing: Manager Welby Young and substitutes David Fairbairn and A. Martin.

YUKON ARCHIVES # PHOTO #88-25-1 PAUL FORREST FONDS

JOSEPH WHITESIDE BOYLE (1867-1923)
The photo is signed in the lower left-hand corner as follows: "Yours truly J.M. Boyle Jassy 4/6/18/10." Queen Marie of Romania made Boyle the Duke of Jassy.

Joe Boyle was too old to enlist when the First World War broke out in 1914. Although he knew nothing about military strategy, he quickly realized that modern weapons would dominate the battlefields. He offered a fully equipped machine-gun company of fifty Yukon miners to Minister of Militia and Defence Sir Sam Hughes, and the minister accepted. The company first trained in Dawson under the North-West Mounted Police and the Dawson Rifle Association, but later travelled to Vancouver to learn further warfare tactics. In September 1916, as a result of his donation of the machine-gun company, Joe Boyle was commissioned an Honorary Lieutenant Colonel of the Canadian Militia and allowed to wear a colonel's uniform, which he embellished with maple-leaf collar badges and buttons of Yukon gold. In 1917, at age fifty, Boyle left Yukon for good and went to Europe to participate in the war against Germany.

He had many adventures, and there were even rumours that Boyle, never divorced from his second wife, had a secret love affair with Queen Marie of Romania, the granddaughter of Queen Victoria. For his war services, Boyle was awarded the Distinguished Service Order (England); the Croix de Guerre (France); the Order of the Star of Romania; the Order of the Crown of Romania; the Order of Regina Maria (Romania); the Order of St. Vladimir (Russia); the Order of St. Anne (Russia); and the Order of St. Stanislaus (Poland). He received no immediate recognition from his home country of Canada.

Boyle died in 1923 at the age of fifty-six and was buried at Hampton Hill, just outside of London. In 1983, sixty years later, his coffin was dug up and his remains were repatriated back to Woodstock, Ontario, and buried in the Presbyterian Cemetery on the west side of Vansittart Avenue between Devonshire Avenue and Vincent Street. A huge six-metre (twenty-foot) cairn was erected over his grave. By this time, the Canadian government had bestowed upon Boyle the Distinguished Service Order. A plaque in the cemetery reads:

> *A legendary adventurer known as "Klondike Joe," Boyle was born in Toronto and came to Woodstock with his family in 1872. He worked at various jobs before attaining great success as a prospector and entrepreneur in the Yukon. At the outbreak of the First World War, Boyle raised, financed and equipped a fifty-man machine gun contingent. Determined to help the war effort further, he headed an allied mission to*

Russia in 1917 to help reorganize the railway system. His adventures soon took him to Romania where he became a confidant of the Royal Family. He was charged with obtaining famine relief for the Romanian people and with negotiating a peace treaty with Russia. Much honoured for his effort, Boyle died in England.

After squandering a fortune, Swiftwater left the Yukon and joined the rush for Nome, Alaska, where fortune smiled once more. He struck it rich and lost another fortune before turning his back on the Seward Peninsula and striking out for the Tanana diggings of the interior. Somehow, Swiftwater got a lay on what soon became the richest gold-producing creek in the district. Cleary, the camp that grew around his claims boomed, becoming the second-biggest town in the area, after Fairbanks. Originally it was known at Gates City. Cleary Town burned to the ground in 1907, but by then Swiftwater had already gone south, where he became involved in several promotional schemes in California. Swiftwater left Yukon for good in 1906.

By 1910, Swiftwater had sailed to Peru, where five years later, he married again, this time to a beautiful Peruvian woman who bore him six children. Not much is known about the years he spent in Peru. It seems he actually matured after his rambunctious youth, although the gambling bug stayed with him and he often squandered his fortunes away—not that they were as great as when he was in the Klondike or Alaska. Apparently, he found his niche in Peru and never left. Still searching for gold, he had an entire ship disassembled and packed over the Andes Mountains, where it was reassembled for exploration on the Amazon River.

When Clarence Woods, a tin-mining engineer from Bolivia who had also worked in Alaska, arrived in Caravaya country in 1928, Swiftwater had already been prospecting and mining there for several years. They became friends and partners in several enterprises, and during three months in 1931, they descended the Inambari River from La Oroya down into the Quispicanchi and Marcapata districts, where they explored many workable prospects. Swiftwater later recounted that they made this trip down the Inambari in a twelve-metre (forty-foot) canoe, with twenty Peruvian Natives paddling, and they met a "titanic" boa (likely an anaconda) that was longer than the boat. Swiftwater hit the snake with a pike pole and wanted to stop to kill it, but the Native men were so terrified that they paddled furiously several kilometres beyond the agreed-upon camping place—despite the fact that a few minutes before encountering the huge snake, they had almost mutinied due to exhaustion.

In 1937, Swiftwater was accidentally shot and killed one Sunday morning while sitting on the steps of a hut on a beach on the Tunquimayo River in the Andes Mountains in Peru. He was sixty-six. "Gringo Gates" was buried on site, and his body was probably washed down river as the result of miners panning for gold in the area in the early 1940s.

THE LION OF THE NORTH

Superintendent Samuel Benfield Steele was the man in charge of the North-West Mounted Police in Dawson City at the height of the Yukon Gold Rush.

This was the same Sam Steele who a few years earlier had investigated the murder of two miners at Wild Horse Creek (later Galbraith's Landing). When Steele left, Galbraith's Landing again underwent a name change—it was renamed Fort Steele.

The discovery of gold in the Canadian Yukon in 1898 created a stampede of would-be miners headed for what they thought and hoped would bring them instant riches. This sudden rush of people, who came from all over the world but in particular from around San Francisco, presented serious problems for the Canadian government. The most direct route to the goldfields was via Skagway, a wild American community at the base of the White Pass, and Dyea, also in Alaska, located sixteen kilometres (ten miles) from the base of the Chilkoot Pass. Canadian customs posts were established at the head of the two passes and at Lake Bennett. It fell to Steele and his colleague Superintendent Bowen Perry to set up command posts at the top of the two passes, claim the territory beyond as Canadian, and advise all who wanted to proceed farther that they would have to obey Canadian laws. This was an arduous and almost impossible task, but the two men, backed by a force of almost three hundred constables, accomplished it in excellent style.

The miners entering Canada by way of the Chilkoot or White Pass were referred to as Klondike Argonauts. Steele admired their grit and determination to reach their goal, which was still many kilometres away, at Dawson City. The Argonauts for their part respected the Mountie who laid down the law with no compromise.

Many of the new arrivals never made it to the goldfields. Some perished en route, some simply gave up and headed back to civilization, and some quickly realized that all of the gold-bearing property had been staked, so there was little or no chance of cashing in on the gold bonanza, but they could earn very good money by backpacking on the Chilkoot Trail. This became lucrative when Steele made it a condition of entry into Canada that everyone would have to have sufficient materials and supplies to sustain them until they reached their targeted goal of Dawson City—a total of about 635 kilograms (1,400 pounds) of supplies. Only when the goods were on hand at the summit would passage be granted into Canada. Steele set up headquarters for the NWMP at Bennett Lake but spent the majority of his time at the post situated at the summit of the Chilkoot Pass, where he would meet the men wanting to enter the Yukon and detail the rules that had to be obeyed and followed by everyone entering Canada.

After the initial rush settled down, Steele moved to Dawson City. He and his men were kept busy administering the law, providing mail service, looking after sick and injured individuals, collecting duties and fines, as well as doing everything possible to look after the well-being of the thousands of people now residing in Dawson City. For the work he accomplished, Steele was promoted and given full command of the NWMP in Yukon. He returned to Fort MacLeod and his wife and family after two years of service in the Yukon.

In 1900, Steele had an opportunity to demonstrate his organizational talent again when he was asked by Lord Strathcona to set up a light horse cavalry, based on the style and operation of the NWMP, for the Boer War in South Africa. Many of the Argonauts, mounted policemen, and backpackers he had befriended in the Yukon answered his call for volunteers for this new regiment, and within days 537 of them enlisted. This voyage with the horses to South Africa was difficult, but the Lord Strathcona Horse Cavalry did make a significant contribution to the war. When the war ended, Steele had become a national hero, was decorated by King Edward VII, and was made a Commander of the Bath and a member of the Victorian Order.

Samuel Benfield Steele died in England on January 30, 1919, of influenza. His body was taken to Winnipeg for a funeral with all honours. As the funeral procession passed, thousands of Winnipeg citizens lined the streets to pay their respect to a great Canadian.

SAMUEL BENFIELD STEELE (1848-1919)

A Canadian hero, leader of men, superintendent of the Mounted Police, Commander of the Lord Strathcona Horse Cavalry in South Africa, and a man who had faced and survived some of the most dangerous and difficult events in the history of Canada's police and military forces.

ALASKA STATE LIBRARY 277-001-181. PHOTO BY PER EDWARD LARSS AND JOSEPH E.N. DUCLOS

LARSS DUCLOS
PHOTOS
DAWSON, Y.T.

CHIEF ISAAC

by Allison Krissie Anderson, great-granddaughter of Jonathan Woods (Chief Isaac's brother) of the Moosehide Indian Village, and interpreter at the Cultural Centre

CHIEF ISAAC (CIRCA 1847–1932) AND HIS SON IN 1899

Clad in a traditional caribou parka with mittens held in place with moosehide sinew, the chief's bewildered-looking four-year-old son stares into the lens of the photographer's camera. Chief Isaac has adopted the white man's clothing of hat, sweater, vest, coat, and trousers. He even wears a gold fob chain, while a large gold nugget graces his sweater. The chief wears his traditional moosehide mitts.

ALASKA STATE LIBRARY. WICKERSHAM STATE HISTORIC SITES
PHOTOGRAPH COLLECTION P277-001-065.
PHOTO BY P.W. LARSS AND JOSEPH E.N. DUCLOS

An impressive orator, Chief Isaac often spoke at Dawson City celebrations such as Discovery Day and Victoria Day, as well as at the festivities of his own people. While Isaac welcomed the newcomers, he never failed to remind them that they prospered at the expense of the original inhabitants by driving away their game and taking over their land. Although they paid little heed to his message, Dawson City residents respected Chief Isaac and even made him an honorary member of the Yukon Order of Pioneers.

Isaac was born on the Alaska side of the US–Canadian border and spent his young manhood in the Forty Mile area until he married his wife Eliza and joined the people at the mouth of the Klondike River. The couple had thirteen children, four of whom survived to adulthood. The most influential leader of the Tr'ondek Hwech'in (formerly the Dawson City Indian Band), Chief Isaac led the Han-speaking people from some time before the Yukon gold rush until his death in 1932. In many ways, he was a bridge between the old ways and the new, mediating between his people and the newcomers. He arranged with government and church officials to move the Tr'ondek Hwech'in to Moosehide after they were displaced from Tr'ochek. He didn't want his people to become too civilized and learn bad habits from the white people. As a result, he convinced the government to move his people five kilometres downriver to Moosehide.

In about 1892, Chief Isaac met Bishop William Bompas and was baptised. While the Anglican Church claimed Isaac as a Christian, he followed a middle path between the gospel and the ways of his ancestors. He attended church conferences and participated in services. He was also honoured as a keeper of the First Nation traditions and was often asked to lead in potlatches in other communities such as Fort Selkirk, Forty Mile, and Eagle.

In 1902, Chief Isaac travelled to the land of the newcomers on a visit to San Francisco, Seattle, and other coastal cities. He was interested in all that he saw and glad to meet old Yukon friends. Nonetheless, he told a Seattle reporter, "Yes, I have seen so many strange and great things that I am tired and want to return to my people."

Water played an important role in placer mining, and the summer of 1905 was so dry that Controller of the Currency for the Yukon

John Lithgow, proposed to the miners that Charles Hatfield, a rain maker from California, be given a $10,000 contract to come to the Klondike. It turned out that Hatfield was too busy in California to come north, but he agreed to come the following year for $10,000—$5,000 to be put up by the government and $5,000 by the miners. Hatfield arrived on June 6, 1906, with an assistant and his brother, and the trio set up on the King Solomon Dome at the headwaters of Hunker, Quartz, Sulphur, Dominion, and Bonanza Creeks.

There was very little rain, and the miners wanted a meeting to cancel Hatfield's contract. With the contract cancelled, the rain maker loaded all his equipment into a buggy and was en route to Dawson City when the skies opened with a downpour. Hatfield left Dawson City having only been allowed expenses from the contract and was never heard from again. According to Chief Isaac, he had four of his medicine men making "big medicine" so that Hatfield would make no rain. As a result, the First Nation medicine men took full credit for the heavy rains.

The Han-speaking people lived along the Yukon River in eastern Alaska and western Yukon Territory, with one of their largest camps being at the junction of the Klondike and Yukon Rivers. It was near here that George Carmack, Skookum Jim, and Dawson Charley made the first big gold strike, and within two years some thirty thousand gold seekers had poured into Han territory. The newcomers' hunting and timber cutting left the Native population in near poverty. Chief Isaac was so worried about the future of his people that he sent some of their most sacred tribal possessions and songs to the Han elders in Alaska for safekeeping.

On December 15, 1911, Chief Isaac was quoted in the *Dawson City News*:

> *All Yukon belong to my papas. All Klondike belong my people. Country now all mine. Long time all mine. Hills all mine; caribou all mine; moose all mine; rabbits all mine; gold all mine. White man come and take all my gold. Take millions, take more hundreds fifty millions, and blow 'em in Seattle. Now Moosehide Injun want Christmas. Game is gone. White man kills all moose and caribou near Dawson. Injun everywhere have own hunting grounds. Moosehides hunt up Klondike, up Sixty Mile, up Twenty Mile, but game all gone. White man kill all.*

Chief Isaac died of influenza at age seventy-three. During his lifetime, he experienced unbelievable changes and worked hard to ensure his people's survival. The strength, wisdom, and spirit of Chief Isaac continue to inspire the Tr'ondek Hwech'in.

Chief Isaac's favourite chair was made from a misshapen birch tree that had been sawn in half. The rest of the chair was made from branches and boards carefully positioned into place.

TR'ONDEK HWECH'IN CULTURAL CENTRE

The chief holds a bow with a string guard and wears a decorated hide quiver while standing in front of his tent near the Yukon River's edge, on the Dawson City side of the Klondike River. The NWMP barrack appears in the top right background.

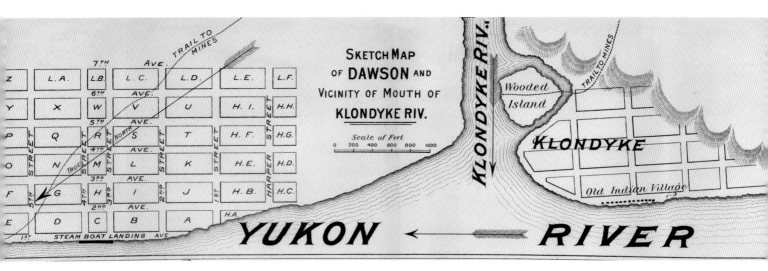

THE MOUTH OF THE KLONDIKE RIVER EMPTYING INTO THE YUKON RIVER

Joseph Francis Ladue staked a claim to 65 hectares (160 acres) of boggy flats at the confluence of the Klondike and Yukon Rivers that he named Dawson City after the renowned geologist and scientist George Mercer Dawson. Across the Klondike River from Dawson City, a second, smaller town sprung up that was named Klondike City. Much of this location was built on the unoccupied Moosehide First Nation village. After conferring with the clergy and police, Chief Isaac moved the Moosehide First Nation people five kilometres (three miles downriver) once Dawson City began having white married couples with young children. The prostitutes from Dawson City's 2nd Avenue were run out of town and across a bridge that spanned the Klondike River and forced to live in Klondike City—with the result that it was casually referred to as Lousetown. This altered map of Dawson City and Klondike City was compiled by Joseph Davis.

KLONDIKE KATE

The woman who was eventually dubbed the "Queen of the Klondike," "Flame of the Yukon," "Belle of the North," and "Klondike Kate" in Dawson City was born Kathleen Eloisa Rockwell in in 1876 in Junction City, Oregon, and grew up in Spokane, Washington. Her stepfather had stature in the community, and the family lived in a large mansion until economic failures caused tensions in the home. Kate grew up a bit of a tomboy and often played with boys rather than girls. To deal with her rebellious nature, her parents sent her to boarding schools and convents, but she either ran away or was expelled. In the 1890s, after her mother had divorced her husband, mother and daughter moved to New York, where Kate made an unsuccessful attempt as an entertainer.

Kate joined a travelling song-and-dance theatre that went to Yukon in 1900. First working as a tap dancer in Skagway and later Whitehorse, she found her stride in Dawson City as a member of the Savoy Theatrical Company. Kate subtracted five years from her age and as a "teenage performer" was much loved by the miners. Although far from the best singer or dancer in Dawson City, Kate was a tireless and shameless self-promoter. On Christmas Eve 1900, miners gave Kate a tin can for a crown with the edges cut into sharp points upon which were affixed lighted candles. The patrons of the saloon dubbed her the "Queen of the Klondike" at that all-night party, and she clung to the name for the rest of her life. It was reported that Kate made $200 a week for her "flame dance," but on the floor dances, she often cleared $500 a night as a percentage of champagne sales. Her legs were frequently bruised from being hit with gold nuggets thrown by the miners. She occupied the plush "Star's Room," which was trimmed in red and gold, upstairs over the theatre.

Kate had an intense love affair with Alexander "Pericles" Pantages, a struggling waiter and bartender, who was born on the Greek Island of Andros in 1867. Pantages's first job in Dawson City was peddling coal oil from a hand-drawn sleigh. Before long, he persuaded Kate to join forces with him and open a saloon and brothel in Dawson City. Their venture was a huge success until the Mounties busted Kate for operating a bawdy house and she was sentenced to one month of hard labour.

It was while Kate was cooling her heels in jail that she decided to take revenge on Katherine Maud Ryan, the first female special constable with the North-West Mounted Police and the original

OPPOSITE—KATHLEEN ELOISA ROCKWELL, "KLONDIKE KATE" (1876-1957)

PERICLES (ALEXANDER) PANTAGES (1867–1936), CIRCA 1910

Klondike Kate's former partner went to the "Outside" and opened a theatre he named the Crystal in Seattle. He later opened a string of five hundred theatres across North America, becoming known as the famous "Theatre King." Pantages eventually sold out his theatre chain to Radio-Keith-Orpheum for $24 million. The new owner was Joseph P. Kennedy, father of President John F. Kennedy.

"Klondike Kate." In 1897, Ryan, a nurse from Johnville, New Brunswick, who was born in 1869, had moved to the Yukon and gotten a job with the police as a woman guard. This imposing woman, almost six feet tall, had returned home in 1901 and was amazed by the stories told about her work in the Yukon. She had been dubbed "Klondike Kate" of Yukon, and everything said or written about her was positive. Kate Rockwell, upon being released from jail, began promoting herself as the "real" Klondike Kate, performing at the Grand Palace. In so doing, she completely and irrevocably ruined the reputation of Kate Ryan.

The Grand Palace, according to Ella Lung Martinsen's book *Trail to North Star Gold*, was the original Savoy Theatre, first owned by Abram Hensen Meadows ("Arizona Charlie"). It was in the Grand Palace that Klondike Kate soon became famous. Arizona Charlie had just built this new plush theatre, and it was here that Klondike Kate did the exciting "cake-walk," wearing a crown of lighted candles and performed the breathtaking "flame act." She would come out onto the stage, wearing an elaborate dress covered in red sequins and also an enormous cape. She would remove the cape to reveal a cane to which was attached several yards of red chiffon. She'd then leap and twirl with the chiffon until she resembled a great ball of fire. She danced with spectacular fury to fast-moving music, swirling the filmy gauze up and down and across the stage, illuminated under very fiery, flame-coloured spotlights (coal-oil carbon). It was here that Kate reached the peak of her career and became known as the "Queen of the Klondike."

Before leaving the goldfields, the industrious Kate and Alex bought the Orpheum Theatre with her savings, and Kate billed herself as the star attraction. The Orpheum's receipts were initially $8,000 a day, but as the boom in the Yukon petered out, they dropped down to a point where the two were barely able to cover expenses. The couple closed shop, headed south, and brought back clean stage entertainment. The project didn't work, so in 1902 they sold out and headed for the "Outside" with, according to Kate, $150,000.

Over the following years, Kate performed on various stages from San Francisco to New York, giving the money she earned to Pantages, who had begun to buy theatres. But in the end the two fell out, and although Kate tried to recoup some of the money, she was left with very little. She returned to the North and played in a few vaudeville troupes, but her magic was gone. She danced in some of the saloons, but because of weight gain, she no longer turned the eyes of the patrons in her direction. She bought a hotel in Fairbanks, Alaska, but this building burned down and she lost everything.

In 1910, at age thirty-seven, Kate married for the first time to Floyd Warner, a cowboy, of Bend, Oregon, but the marriage failed. In 1933, she married John Matson, a Swedish miner from her Klondike days. She was fifty-seven and he was sixty-nine. The wedding took place in Vancouver. It was a strange marriage; she lived in Bend, while he lived in Yukon. They communicated by way of his love letters to her and her poems to him. Matson opened a bank account in her name before returning back to Yukon to his gold claim and trapline. She came up to see him several times, and during these visits they stayed in separate hotels in Dawson City. She would walk by the Orpheum Theater, which was boarded up and rundown, with nothing but silence within its leaning walls. Cruel old-timers of Dawson City shook their heads and muttered, "There's that bitch again, back for more of Matson's gold." The marriage lasted until Matson's death in 1946 at the age of eighty-two. Kate received a short last letter from the "Silent Swede" that simply read, "My dearest wife, I am so tired after this trip."

In Bend, Kate had opened a restaurant on one of the main streets and was known affectionately by the locals as Aunt Kate. She often shared her money with the needy and volunteered her time to take care of those affected by the flu epidemic. Still the tireless self-promoter, she was always ready to chat with anyone who would listen and give away portraits of herself from when she was a dancer in Dawson City. These portraits were always signed Klondike Kate or Kate Rockwell.

In 1942, Kate went to Hollywood to discuss making a movie about the Yukon Gold Rush that resulted in the movie Klondike Kate, which came out a year later and starred Ann Savage.

At seventy-one, Kate married for a third time, this time to William Van Duren. In May 1948, Mr. and Mrs. Van Duren visited Vancouver on an extended honeymoon, and Kate agreed to an interview with Major James Skitt Matthews, the city's archivist. Kate Rockwell Warner Matson Van Duren died in 1957 in Sweet Home, Oregon, at eighty years old. As she had requested, her ashes were scattered over the high desert of Oregon.

Kate Ryan, the original "Klondike Kate," never married. She died in Vancouver in 1932.

Klondike Kate's metal mesh evening bag.

MACBRIDE MUSEUM, WHITEHORSE

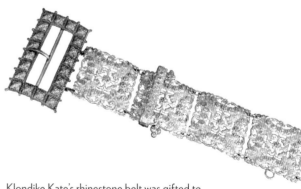

Klondike Kate's rhinestone belt was gifted to jewellery store owner George Murdock on Kate's last visit to the Yukon in the late 1940s or early 1950s.

MURDOCK'S GIFTS GOLD JEWELLERY, WHITEHORSE

ACKNOWLEDGEMENTS

Producing a book is never a solitary task, and I want to acknowledge the many people who gave me their support. I started work on the book in the 1970s, so some of the people who helped me are no longer alive.

In 1975, en route to Barkerville, the one-time gold capital of the world, I stopped at the Clinton Museum and left this treasure house with the understanding that I would pay its curator a longer visit on my way home. As it turned out, I found Barkerville so intriguing that I overstayed my allotted time, which resulted in a non-stop drive homeward that had me passing through Clinton in the middle of the night. Other commitments took priority in my life, and thirteen years passed before I was able to resume work on the project. I then realized the value of the interviews from that first trip.

The people who gave me time and information were Avis L. Choate, curator of the Clinton Museum; Branwen C. Patenaude of Quesnel; Renée Chipman, curator of the Quesnel Museum; John Dunwoody "Woody" Jackson and Dorothy Jackson of Clinton; Lorne Purdy of the 83 Mile House; Brian Young and Barbara McLennan of the BC Archives; Gordon Yusko, Fort Langley National Historic Site; Glenn Wong and Larry Pawlowicz, both of the Barkerville National Historic Site; brothers Reginald J. Rankin and Gerald M.J.T. Rankin, both of Soda Creek; and J. Alexander "Sandy" Stevenson and Roberta E.L. Myers of Sardis and Chilliwack.

This project has been a continuing work in progress since I retired in 2004. I would like to thank those who have assisted me over the past ten years: Michel Picard at the Canadian Museum of Nature in Hull, Quebec; Gary Mitchell, Don Bourdon, Kathryn Bridge, Kelly Nolin, and Derek Swallow at the BC Archives; Leslie Mobbs, Heather Gordon, Carol Haber, Megan Schlase, Nancy Mulligan, Jeannie Hounslow, Melanie Hardbattle, Glen Dingwall, and Chak Yung at the Vancouver City Archives; Rudolf Traichel, Katherine Kalsbeek, and Ken Hildebrand at UBC Rare Books and Special Collections; Andrew Martin, Melina Bowden, Kim McCarthy, Michelle Greig, and Alison Rintoul at the Vancouver Public Library; Trevor McKeown at the Grand Masonic Lodge of BC and Yukon; Elisabeth Duckworth at the Kamloops Museum; Ron Candy at the Vernon Museum; Joyce Austin and Andy Cant at the Rossland Museum and Archives; Kathy Paros at the Ashcroft Museum; Jerry Wilkin and Jennifer Douglass at the Hedley Museum; Peter Ord and Randall S. Manuel at the Penticton Museum; Bruce Blair, Kim Love, and Sari Burgoyne at Natural Resources Canada, Ottawa; Calvin Woelke at the Land Title and Survey Authority, Victoria; Jacqui Underwood (Native Daughters of British Columbia Post #1) at the Old Hastings Store Museum, Vancouver. I must also thank Sharon Keen, Elmer Schules, and Werner Kashel.

My wife, Tina, and I made our first trip to Whitehorse and Dawson City in 2013 and enjoyed the help of Patricia Cunning, manager of the McBride Museum, Whitehorse; Casey Mclaughlin at the Transportation Museum; Superintendent David Robatensky of the Klondike National Historic Sites; Glenda Bolt, manager and curator at the Tagé Cho Hudän Interpretive Centre, Dawson City; Sylvia Burkhard, proprietor at Claim 33; Dawne Mitchell at the Jack London Museum; Donna Darbyshire and Susan Twist at the Yukon Archives, Whitehorse; Christopher Collin, tour guide at Husky Bus, Dawson City; Laura Mann, curator at the Dawson City Museum; Nancy Taylor Stonington, artist; and Michael S. Gates, Yukon writer.

Some of the smaller museums allowed me to make high-resolution scans of many original photographs that until now have never been published.

I am equally grateful to all the people who contributed text to this book: Allison Krissie Anderson, Fred Braches, Stan Copp, Gino Del-Ciotto, Jennifer Douglass, David Gregory, Derek Hayes, Marilyn L. Morris, Arthur Raymond "Bud" Ryckman, and Grant Zazula.

I want to especially thank the Honourable Iona Campagnolo, the Lieutenant-Governor of British Columbia from 2001 until 2007, and still the Honorary Patron of Barkerville, for writing the foreword.

Three people whose support and guidance ensured this book would become a reality are Helmi Braches, my editor, Fred Braches, my mentor, and designer Johannes Schut. Fred's generous advice and Helmi's careful edits and suggestions have been invaluable—however, I am responsible for any errors in the book. I spent many hours working with Johannes on the book, moving the photos and text around and making decisions on the book's layout.

I am deeply grateful to Rodger Touchie of Heritage House Publishing for taking on the book with a hands-on approach and thus making a dream come true for me, and for carefully going over the text once more. I also thank copyeditor Karla Decker and Lara Kordic, senior editor at Heritage House, for applying the finishing touches.

Lastly, I thank my beloved wife and soulmate, Tina, for her unwavering and loving support while this project was on my mind and on my desk. I dedicate this book to her.

BIBLIOGRAPHY AND FURTHER READING

BOOKS

Antonson, Rick, Mary Trainer, Brian Antonson. *Slumach's Gold: In Search of a Legend.* Surrey, BC: Heritage House, 2007.

Atwood, Mae. *Border Gold.* Grand Forks, BC: The Orris Press, 1981.

Barlee, N.L. *Gold Creeks and Ghost Towns.* Surrey, BC: Hancock House, 1984.

——. *Lost Mines and Historic Treasures of British Columbia.* Surrey, BC: Hancock House, 1989.

——. *The Guide to Gold Panning in British Columbia Gold Regions, Methods of Mining and Other Data.* Canada West Publications, 1980.

Barnes, Harry. "The Nickel Plate: 1898–1932." *BC Historical Quarterly,* Vol. XIV, June 1950.

Beebe, Iola. *The True Life Story of Swiftwater Bill Gates.* Seattle: Lumbermans Printing Company, 1915.

Beeson, Edith. *Dunlevey: From the Diaries of Alex P. McInnes,* Lillooet, BC: Lillooet Publishing, 1971.

Berton, Pierre. *The Klondike Fever: The Life and Death of the Last Great Gold Rush.* New York: Carroll & Graf Publishers, 2004.

——. *The Klondike Quest: A Photographic Essay 1897–1899.* Erin, ON: Boston Mills Press, 1983.

Cox, Doug. *Mines of the Eagle Country: Nickel Plate & Mascot.* Penticton, BC: The Skookum Press, 1997.

Dalzell, Kathleen E. *The Queen Charlotte Islands Volume 1: 1774–1966.* Queen Charlotte City, BC: Bill Ellis, Publisher, 1981.

Downie, William. *Hunting for Gold.* San Francisco: California Publishing Co., 1893.

Downs, Art. *Pioneer Days in British Columbia.* Surrey, BC: Heritage House, 1975.

Gould, John A. *Frozen Gold: A Treatise on Early Klondike Mining Technology, Methods and History.* Whitehorse, YT: Pictorial Histories Publishing Co., 2001.

Hamilton, Walter. *The Yukon Story.* Vancouver: Mitchell Press, 1964.

Harris, Lorraine. *Barkerville: The Town that Gold Built.* Surrey, BC: Hancock House, 1983.

Johnson, James Albert. *George Carmack: Man of Mystery Who Set Off the Klondike Gold Rush.* Kenmore, WA: Epicenter Press, 2001.

Johnson, R. Byron. *Very Far West Indeed.* London: S. Low, Martson, Low & Searle, 1872.

Jones, Lawrence F. and George Lonn. *Historical Highlights Canadian Mining 1603–1972.* Toronto: Pitt Publishing, 1973.

Lonn, George. *The Mine Finders.* Toronto: Pitt Publishing, 1966.

Ludditt, Fred W. *Barkerville Days.* Vancouver, BC: Mitchell Press, 1969.

Martinsen, Ella Lung. *Trail to North Star Gold.* Portland, OR: Binford and Mort, 1974.

Patenaude, Branwen. *Trails to Gold: Roadhouses of the Cariboo.* Surrey, BC: Heritage House, 1996.

——. *Golden Nuggets: Roadhouse Portraits along the Cariboo's Gold-Rush Trail.* Surrey, BC: Heritage House, 1998.

Paterson, T.W. *British Columbia: The Pioneer Years.* Langley, BC: Stagecoach Publishing, 1977.

Ramsey, Bruce. *Ghost Towns of British Columbia.* Vancouver, BC: Mitchell Press, 1971.

——. *Barkerville: A Guide to the Fabulous Cariboo Gold Camp.* Vancouver, BC: Mitchell Press, 1974.

Taylor, G.W. *Mining in BC: The History of Mining in British Columbia.* Saanichton, BC: Hancock House, 1978.

Topping, E.S. *Chronicles of the Yellowstone.* Hudson, WI: Ross & Haines, 1968.

Wallace, Robert. *The Miners (Old West Time-Life Series).* Alexandria, VA: Time-Life Books, 1976.

Wright, Richard Thomas. *Discover Barkerville: A Gold Rush Adventure.* Vancouver, BC: Maclean Hunter, 1984.

WEBSITES

Colonial Despatches: The Colonial Despatches of Vancouver Island and British Columbia, 1846-1871: bcgenesis.uvic.ca/search.htm.

Gaffin, Jane: "Joe Boyle: Superhero of the Klondike Goldfields." Unpublished manuscript from the Yukon Archives.

diarmani.com/Articles/Gaffin/Joe%20Boyle%20--%20SuperHero%20of%20the%20Klondike%20Goldfields.htm.

MAGAZINES, JOURNALS, AND NEWSPAPERS

Daily San Francisco News
Dawson City Golden Cleanup Edition
Dawson City News
The Examiner
Harper's Weekly
Klondike News
Victoria Colonist
Victoria Gazette
Woodstock Sentinel Review

Use of italic script indicates reference to caption.

Abbott and Jordan Company, 41
Adler, Samuel, 36
Aldridge, Walter Hull, 160
Alexandra Suspension Bridge, *125*
American miners: arrival of, 19, 29; and Haida, 14–15
Anaheim, Dehtus, 21–22
Anderson, Alexander Caulfield, 25
Antler Creek gold rush, 38–39, 41, *44*, 66–67
Argonauts. *see* miners
artists: John Innes, *43*, *69*; Rex Woods, *139*; William G.R. Hind, 88
Arundel, Constantine, 173, 175, 177, 181
Ashcroft Trail, *120*
Atwood, Harry, 169
Aurora Claim, 108, *111*

Baker, Peter, 22, 23
Ballou, William T., 118, 119
Barker, Elizabeth (Collyer), 74, 77
Barker, William "Billy," 48, 74, *76*, 77
Barker Company, 74, *76*
Barkerville, 74–77, 85, 86; area map, *97*; fire of, 100–109; Masonic Lodge, 108, *111*
Barlee, N.L. (Bill), 16, 184
Barnard, Francis Jones, 119, 122
Barnard's Express, 68, 122, *123*
Barry, William Prosper, 36
Beatty, Henry, 78
Beebe, Bera (Gates), 236, 240
Beebe, Iola, 236, 240
Beedy, Josiah Crosby, 36, 119
Begbie, Matthew Baillie, 28, 74
Bell, James, 56
Black Jack and Burns Company, 48, 50
Blanshard, Richard, 10–11
Boer War volunteers, 244
Bonanza Creek, 190, 191; 205–217, *221*; mining methods, *198*, 201–204, 218–223, *229*, 230, 232, *237*

Boothroyd, William and George, 118
Bordeau, Oliver, 152
Boston Bar, 112, *120*
Bourgeois, George "Bushway," 153, 155
Boyle, Joseph "Klondike Joe," 230–243
Bralorne Mines, 170–171
Brew, Chartres, 118–119
bridge construction, 115, 119, *125*, *135*, 169
Bridge River area, 169–172
British Columbia: boundary, 15, 29; colony, 17; gold field maps, 30, *56*, *60*; mining regulations, 19, 29, 66
Brown, Michael Costin, 39–40
Brown, Robert C., 87
Burns, Michael, 39–40

Cadwallader Creek, 169–170
Cahill, George, 176, 182
Calaveras Company, *73*
Calbreath, John Colin, 28, 112–113, 115, 119, 124
Caledonia Company, *55*
camels, 28
Cameron, Allan, *83*, 84
Cameron, Christina Emma (Woods), 84, 85
Cameron, John A. "Cariboo," 48, 77–86, *83*; transport of wife's casket, 80–81, 83, 84
Cameron, Margaret Sophia (Groves), 77, 79, 80, 85
Cameron, Roderick, 83, 84
Cameron Company, 38, 80, *81*, 83–84
Campbell, Alexander, 108
Campbell, Edward, 22, 23, 56
Canadian Klondike Mining Company, 240
Canadian Pacific Railway (CPR), 160
Carcross (Caribou Crossing), 186–188, 192, 193, *196*
Cariboo Wagon Road: construction, 112–119, 125–131, 134–139; maps of, 30; roadhouses, 23; transportation, 119–123, 142–151

Carmack, George Washington, 188–196
Carmack, Graphie, 191, 192, 193
Carmack, Kate (Shaaw Tláa), 188, 189, 191–196
Carmack, Marguerite (Laimee), 191–192, 193
Cawston, Richard (Dick), 172–173
cemeteries, *76*, 77, 85, 86, *129*, 193, 225
Chance, Johnny, 166–167
Charley, Tagish "Dawson," 188, 189, 192, 193, *195*
Charlie, "Chilkoot," 230, 231
Cheadle, Walter Butler, 83
Cheechako Hill, 221
Chilcotin: gathering, 21–22; smallpox, 88
Chilkoot Pass, 230, 244
Chinese, 29, 93, 119
Chuchuwayha First Nation, 176
Clinton, 36, 115, *143*, *144*
Collins, Murtz J., 39–40
Collyer, Elizabeth (Barker), 74, 77
Company of Welsh Adventures, *56*, 94–99
Connolly, William, 25
Cook, Mortimer, 36, 112
copper mining, 155–156, 160
Cornish Claim, 48, *70*
Cornish water wheel, 52
Costello, James, 39–40
costs: mail, 119; provisions, 40, 78; travel, 36, 87
Coulthard, John Oswald "Ozzie," 172–173
Crane, Samuel, 78, 79
Crow, Ira, 20, 22
Cunningham, William Wallace, 40, 56, 67

Dally, Frederick, 100–101, 109, *125*
Daly, Marcus, 155, 160, 173, 174, 176, 178
Dawson City, *226*, 228, 234; cemetery, 225; site, 191, 224, *249*; theatre, 250–251

Dawson City Nuggets hockey team, 240, *241*

Deroche, Joseph, *130*

Dewdney, Edgar, 37

Dietz, Wilhelm "Dutch Bill," 39–40, *43*, 48

Diller, Isaiah Frederick, 48, 50

Douglas, James: about, 25, *29*; and Fraser River gold, 18–19; and Haida gold, 15, 17; and road construction, 24–36, 114, 119; and Rock Creek, 29

Douglas Trail, 25, 28

Downey, George, 41

Dufferin Coach, 162

Dunlevey, Peter Curran, 20–23, *149*

Edenshaw, Albert Edward, 11, 13, 15

Eldorado Creek, 205, *207*, 222, 231, *232*, 240

Elwyn, Thomas, 66, *67, 69*, 74, 79

Emptage, William Henry, 14

Engineers' Road, 37

SS *Enterprise*, 118, 119, *147*

Evans, John, *56*, 94–97

firearms, 36

First Nations: Chief Isaac, 246–249; fish camp, *122, 124*; gathering of, 20, 21; and gold discovery, 10, 18, 188; grave site, *129*; Haida, 10, 11–15; as labourers, 113; mixed marriages, 191–196; moving of reserve, 176; Nincumshin, *140*; oral history of Spaniards, 164–165; smallpox, 81, 88, 115

Fort Alexandria, 22, 36, 118

Fort Kamloops, 18, 24

Fort Simpson, *11*

Fort Victoria. *see* Victoria

Fort Yale, 20, *24*, 36, 68, 117

Fraser River: canyon, 87–88, 112, *122, 125, 126*; ferry, 28, 36; gold rush, 18, 19, 169; trails, 36

freemasons, 108, *111*

French Hill, *213*

Gates, Bera (Beebe), 236, 240

Gates, Grace (Lamour), 234

Gates, Kitty (Brandon), 240

Gates, Swiftwater Bill, 230–243

Georgiana, 14–15

Gibson, Peter, 83

Glendinning, Charles and Richard, 78, 79–80

Gold Bottom Creek, 189, 190, 191, *229*

gold commissioners, 19, 29, 66

Gold Harbour, 13, 14

Gold Hill, *215, 223*

Grand Forks, Yukon, 205–217, *223*

Granite Creek gold rush, 166–167

Grant, John Marshall, 112

Grouse Creek, *60*

Groves, Margaret Sophia (Cameron), 77, 79, 80, *85*

Haida, 10, 11–15

Haida Gwaii. *see* Queen Charlotte Islands

Hankin, Charles C., 80

Hatfield, Charles, 247

Hedley (town), 172, 181–182, 184

Hedley Gold Mine (Nickel Plate Mine), 172–180, 182–183

Heinze, Fritz Augustus, 155–156, 160

Helgesen, Hans Lars, 22, 23

Henderson, Robert, 188, 189–191

Hill, James J., 173–174, 177

Hind, William G.R., 88, *92, 93*

hockey club, 240, *241*

Hood, William, 115

horses and mules, 21, 28, 77, 122, *130, 150*

Houston, James, 18, 19, 23

Howay, Frederick William, 186

Hudson's Bay Company (HBC), 18, 21, 24, 25

Hume, John, 56

Innes, John, *43, 69, 91*

Isaac, Chief, 246–249

Jackass Mountain, 130

Jones, Gomer Philip "GP," 177, 178

Joyner, Lucy (Rodgers), 174, 180

Káa Goox. *see* Charley, Tagish "Dawson"

Keith and Wilson Mine, *213*

Keithley, William Ross, 38–39, 41, 236

Keithley Creek, 38, 39

Kinder, Fred, 169

Klondike City, *249*

Klondike gold rush: access to, 244; aftermath, *237*; discoverers, 186–199, *229*; map, *229*

Klondike Joe, 230–243

Klondike Kate, 250–253

Klondike Mines Railway, 228–229

Lac la Hache, gathering, 20–21

Ladue, Joseph F., 188, 191, *226, 249*

Laimee, Marguerite (Carmack), 191–192, 193

Lamour, Grace (Gates), 234

Lamour, Gussie, 234

Last Chance Company, *73*

Laumeister, William, 28

Le Roi claim, 153–155, 156, 160–161

Lewes River Mining Company, *198*

Lewis, Thomas B., 112, 113, 114

Lightfall, W. Henry, 56

Lightning Creek, 56, 94–97

Lillooet, 25, 169

Lolo, St. Paul, 20, 21, 22

Lowhee Creek, 40–41, *64, 73*

Lytton, 36, 112, 113, *129, 132*

MacDonald, Allan, 38, 78

MacDonald, Ranald "Black," 38–39, 41, 43

MacKintosh, Charles, 160

Manifee, Thomas, 20, 118

Mark, William, 41

Marshall, Thomas, 36

Mascot Fraction, 176, 182–184

Mason, James. *see* Skookum Jim (Kèish)

Matson, John, 253

Mayne, Charles, 30

McDonald, Alexander, *222*

McLean, Donald, 18

McLean, John, 21, 23

McLeese, Robert, 23, *149*

McMartin, Duncan, 22, 23

McMicking, Thomas and Robert, 87

McQuesten, Leroy Napoleon "Jack," 224
Meadows, Abram Hensen "Arizona Charlie," 251
Metz, John "Kansas," 39–40
Milton, William Fitzwilliam, 83
miners: inexperienced, 36; and road construction, 25, 113–114; sports day, *156*, 168, *223*; underground, *163*, 222, *223*
mining: fees, 15, 29; gold claims, 39, *181*; ore smelter, 155–156; use of children, 222
mining equipment: assayer's furnace, 177; buckets, *75*, *204*; candle, *78*; Cornish water wheel, 52; dredges, *196*, *237*; ingot mold, *174*; ore car, *153*; rocker, 54, *55*, 180, 204; stamp mill, *173*, *179*; steam boiler, *197*, 200–201; tools, *64*, *93*, 168, 177, 178
mining methods: dredging, *238*, 240; in frozen ground, *197*, 200–201, 222, *223*; gold pan, 16; gravity trams, *184*, 218, 221; hydraulic, 52, *70*, 218, 240; shaft construction, 48, 50, 75, 94–95, 219; windlass and bucket, *75*, 200, *204*, *213*; zip line, *207*, 218
Minto Camp, 171–172
Mitchell, William, 14, 15
Moberly, Walter, 112, 113, 114, 115, 119
Monte Carlo, Dawson City, *234*, 236
Montgomery, Samuel, *83*
Moody, Richard Clement, 28, 112
Moore, John, 21
Moosehide First Nation, 246–249
Moris, Joseph, 152–153, 155
Morris, John "Grizzly," 28
Muench, Edward Julius, *120*
Mulrooney, Belinda, 205, 207, *208*
Munroe, Malcolm, 119

Nelson, 172
Nickel Plate Mine, 172–180, 182–183
Nickel Plate Mountain, 172–173, 176, 182, 183
Nind, Philip Henry, 66
Nome, Alaska, 228, 243
North-West Mounted Police, *223*, 244–245, 250–251
Nutt, Jonathan, 108

O'Brien, Thomas W., 224, 228
Ogilvie, William M., 188, 189, 230
Oppenheimer, Charles, 112, 113, 114–115
Oppenheimer, David, 113, *115*
Oppenheimer store, 68
O'Reilly, Peter, 29, 66
Oro Plata claim, *181*
Overlanders, 87–92
oxen, *120*, *130*, *143*

packers, 21, 28, 40, 43
Palmer, Henry Spencer, 30, 66
Pantages, Alexander "Pericles," 250, 251
Parsons, Otis, 28, 36
Patterson, Asa H. and Thomas P., 40–41
Peyton, Isaac, 154, 160
Phinney, Bill, *55*
photography, 100
Pioneer Gold Mines, 169–170
platinum ore, 167
Port Douglas, 36, 81, 112
Port Simpson, *11*
Princeton, 172
provisions: cattle, 67; cost of, 40, 78; food, 23, 95

Queen Charlotte Islands, 10–17
Quesnel Mouth, 22, 23, 87, 88
Quesnel River, 36, *150*
Quesnel Forks, 28, 36

Rabbit Creek. *see* Bonanza Creek
railway lines, 153, 156, 160, 177, 228–229
Reid, Bill, *11*
Reid, James, 23
Richfield, 66–73
Rivers, Richard, 78, 79
roadhouses, 23, 28, 36, 112, 118, *128*
roads. *see* trails and roads
Rock Creek, 29, 37
Rockwell, Kathleen "Klondike Kate," 250–253
Rodgers, Lucy (Joyner), 174, 180
Rodgers, Myron Knox, 173–180

Rose, John A., 38–39, 41, 43
Rossland, 152–161
Royal Engineers: Cariboo Wagon Road, 112–151; construction work, *139*; Engineers' Road, 37; first projects, 28, 36; maps of, 30
Ryan, Katherine Maud, 250–251, 253

Salter, George, *128*
Schubert, August, 87
Schubert, Catherine O'Hare, 87
scurvy, 95
Sellars, James, 20, 22, 23
Shaughnessy, Thomas, 160, 161
Sheepshead Company, 75
Skookum Jim (Kèish), 188, 189–191, 192, 193, *194*
Slavin, Frank, 230
smallpox, 81, 88, 115
smelter, 155–156
Smith, Joseph Lorenzo, 36
Smith, Robert T., 119
Soda Creek, 20, 23, 118, *147–149*
Spanish Mound, 164–165
Spence, Thomas, 112, 115, *134*
Spences Bridge, 115, *134*
stage coach lines, 122, *123*, 183
Stanley, 56, 97
Stanley Cup, 56, 240
Steele, Samuel Benfield, 244–245
Steele and Company, 67
Stevenson, Robert, 77–78, 79, 80, *83*, 84, 85
stopping houses, 23, 28, 36, 112, 118, *128*
Stout, Ned, 74
Susan Sturgis, 14, 15

Taylor, Austin Cottrell, 170–171
telegraph, *120*, *136*
Thompson, Joshua, 108
Thompson, Ross, 155
Thompson River, *134*, *136*
Tilton, Hanson, 40–41
Tingley, Stephen, 122, *123*
Tláa, Shaaw "Kate," 188, 189, 191–196
Tomaah and family, 20, 22
tools. *see* mining equipment
Topping, Eugene Sayre, 153–154, 155, 156

Trail (town site), 155

trails and roads. *see also* Cariboo Wagon Road; Ashcroft Trail, *120*; Chilkoot Pass, 244; Douglas Trail, 24–25, 36; Engineers' Road, 30; Fraser River route, 36, 112

transportation: Dufferin Coach, 162; and economic development, 112; freight wagons, 120, *123, 136, 143*; of gold, 67–68, *69*, 122, 124; of mail, 118–119; pack animals, 21, 28, 77; paddle-wheel steamers, 23, 28, *114*, 119; by rafts, 88; road steam engines, 119–120; stage coach lines, 122, *123*, 183; toll booths, *144*

Trutch, Joseph William, 112, 115, *125, 126*

Una (HBC vessel), 14, 15

United States: expansionism, 15; investors, 155, 160–161

Upper Similkameen Indian Band, 184

Van Winkle Creek, 56

Victoria, 25; Adelphi Hotel, 40; arrival of gold seekers, 19–20; Mrs. Cameron's burial, 83; Ross Bay Cemetery, *76*, 77; Royal Hotel, 77

War Eagle claim, 153, 155, *163*

Watson, Robert, 36, 112, *144*

Wattie, James and William, 86

Way, Franklin, 36

Weaver, George W., 38–39, 41, 43

Whitehorse, monument, *197*

Williams, Shuswap, 22, 36

Williams Creek: area map, 48; Davis Claim, *52*; gold rush, 39–40, 41; gold strikes, 66–67; towns, 48, 66

Williams Lake, 36

Willoughby, Richard, 40–41

Wilson, John, 78–79, *86*

women: business owners, 205, 207, *208*; dancers, 250–253; in mining towns, *64*, 74, 77, 234, *249*; Native, 191–196; as police, 250–251; and travel, 87

Woods, Christina Emma (Cameron), 84, 85

Woods, Duncan, 176, 181–183

Woods, Rex, *139*

Woolaston, Francis, 173, 175, 177, 181

Work, John, 11, 13–14, 15

Wright, Gustavus Blin (Gus), 28, 112, 115, 118, 119, *144*

Wright, J. Whitaker, 160, 162

Yale, 20, *24*, 36, 68, 117

Yukon Order of Pioneers (Y.O.O.P.), 7, 193, 224–225, 246

ABOUT THE AUTHOR

Donald E. Waite is a former RCMP officer, an established historian, an accomplished bird photographer, and the author of numerous books. Born in Renfrew, Ontario, Waite joined the RCMP at age nineteen and trained in the Identification Section, which sparked his interest in photography. In 1971, after seven years of service, Waite left the force and opened a camera store and portrait studio in Maple Ridge, BC. It was here that he first became interested in local history, and over the next several years wrote numerous books, including historical portraits of the Fraser Valley and the Cariboo. In 1975, Waite began taking photographs of birds in flight, and in 1984 he co-authored (with Isidor Jeklin) *The Art of Photographing North American Birds*. Today, his bird photography can be found on globalbirdphotos.com. In 1993, Waite began specializing in oblique or slanting aerial photography. He established globalairphotos.com, a business his son currently owns. Now retired, Waite continues to pursue bird photography, sources out historical photographs, and writes. He and his wife, Tina, have five children, fourteen grandchildren, and one great-grandchild.